★ THE ★
SEASIDE
READER

⭐ THE ⭐

SEASIDE

READER

EDITED BY DERY BENNETT

LYONS & BURFORD, PUBLISHERS

For Alan K. Stitt, who loved the seaside
and wanted all of us to respect it

Design by Catherine Lau Hunt

Printed in the United States of America

10 9 8 7 6 5 4 3 2 1

Library of Congress Cataloging-in-Publication Data

The Seaside reader / edited by D. W. Bennett.
    p.   cm.
  ISBN 1-55821-197-7
    1. Seashore ecology—United States.   2. Natural history—United
States. 3. Coasts—United States. I. Bennett. D. W.
  QH104.S43 1992   92-21430
  508.314'6'0973-dc20   CIP

Contents

Going Underwater

Author, Author (An Interlude)

Fishing For Fun And Profit

Introduction

THE COAST, where the land meets the sea, is, at once, the most productive part of the ocean and the place where more and more Americans want to live. Come to think of it, the coastal sea — the seaside — is the extent of most people's view of the ocean. A person can see out about five miles.

Most of what is contained in this collection describes those five miles of ocean water close to land. You will find very little emoting about such things as a boundless sea, the wonder of the ocean wilderness, or the spirits of the deep. Rather, here are encounters with living creatures, notes about small bodies of water, descriptions of tidal rivers and coastal ponds.

Also here are comments on the impacts that humankind is having on marine life and its coastal habitat. It is estimated that about three-quarters of all U.S. residents live within fifty miles of a coast (if one includes Great Lakes states as coastal, as the Federal Coastal-Zone Management Act does). At the same time, seven out of ten fish that are caught for food or fun depend on a coastal habitat at some time during their life cycles. So do all the clams and oysters, many of the shorebirds and waterfowl, plus most of the lobsters, shrimp, and crabs. A gathering of seaside writing can hardly exist if it doesn't pay some attention to those numbers.

This collection, of course, bears a close resemblance to what I like to read, what I wish I had been able to write, and what I urge upon others when they make the mistake of asking for a shoreside reading recommendation. In fact, I recommend some books to spite publishers who have let them lapse from print, hoping that readers will borrow the book from the library, read and enjoy it, and take the time to berate the publisher for letting the book drop out of sight.

Some of these books are from my youth. Others are recent arrivals, and several were called to my attention by other more discerning readers. Several books just failed to make the list, but beg for mention here. One is Witmer Stone's classic *Bird Studies of Old Cape May*, written half a century ago. Among other things, it records the annual fall carnival when citizens gathered at the southern tip of New Jersey to gun down migrating hawks. He describes cars parked along the Cape May Point turnpike: "The bombardment begins as soon as it is light enough to see and we find in the assemblage Italians, negroes, boys and 'sportsmen,' the last group ranging from baymen and farmers to businessmen and men of leisure, participating in the sport."

Later he writes: "In 1932, Robert Allen estimated that of the gunners who took part in the hawk shooting 40% were natives who used the birds for food; 55% were Italian who made similar use of them; while 5% were sportsmen who killed the birds for sport and as good practice for wing shooting."

What are we to make of all this? How did Allen tell a native from an Italian? And did he miss the negroes that Stone saw or just lump them in with "natives?" One can almost see Stone, dressed in proper tweeds, heavy field glasses at his neck, leatherbound notebook in hand, shocked by the hawk slaughter but still able to count ("...hmm, there's an Italian, a negro, another Italian, a bayman (muddy boots), two boys, and a sportsman.")

Another book that I loved as a kid was *The Call of The Surf*, by Van Campen Heilner and Frank Stick. My personal copy is inscribed "To Dr. C. C. Slaughter. Christmas 1900 from A.L.M." The authors get right into it: "Game and fish are fast disappearing as our remoter sections become settled, as lakes and bayous are drained, and I have been assured that the time is not far distant when we will have degenerated into a race of stoop-shouldered, anaemic creatures fit only for such mild re-creative pastimes as bridge whist contests and pink teas."

But before that happens, the authors go on to describe surf fishing in all its guts and glory, landing lots of big fish of various species. But what caught my eye while rereading it for possible inclusion here was the chapter on beach camping, which reads in part as follows: "Primitive instinct, or pioneer spirit, which-ever it may be, is not entirely a male characteristic, not by any means. As a matter of fact, a woman, if she be of normal strength, and normal in her ideas and ideals, is every bit as good a companion in camp as the average male...most men... are apt to be more exacting in their demands than are their sisters and wives. I speak now of those who dwell in large com-munities...in rural and backwoods districts this condition does not exist."

By now the author (this happens to be Stick speaking) is up to his neck in ichthyological sociology. He may feel that he's losing his predominantly male audience, so he backs away from the verbal mess he has got into: "I do not wish to imply that in-dividually men are not better campers than women, for such is not the case. The male is the natural hunter and fisherman, the provider, and if his environments and his training have given him experience in the life of the open, or without great experi-ence, if his desires and his impulses are toward the out-of-doors, then he is the one to tie to. He is a sportsman."

I don't recall what impact this had on me at fourteen. I sup-pose I quickly turned back to the parts about catching fish. Nor will we ever know what Dr. C.C. Slaughter thought of this line of reasoning. At any rate, neither Stone nor Heilner/Stick make the final cut.

Other books, while eminently worthy reading, fall outside the realm: Robert Boyle's work on the Hudson River, Bruce Stutz's on the Delaware, and Alexander Netboy's on the Columbia are three excellent river guides. Archie Carr wrote great stuff about beaches and turtles and about the Suwannee River. Eugenie

Clark helped bring sharks into focus with her writing. And it would have been enjoyable to leave chuckling with an Ed Zernism, but he is freshwater funny.

What follows is my personal selection of seaside books, ones that I have read more than once with pleasure. I have used the term "seaside" loosely. Some of the writing goes up rivers, others go out to sea a bit. Also, I have tended to focus on writing about sea creatures as a way of inviting the reader to dip into the shallow sea to learn and enjoy, for it is the creatures, I think, that make the seaside so special.

The plan here is to entice you with small selections from chosen authors. Maybe then you will go to your shelves or to the library to draw out whole volumes for more thorough reading.

A number of people were especially helpful with the editing/choice process. The collection was Peter Burford's good suggestion. Larry Ogren, George Reiger, and Frank Steimle brought noble works to my attention. Hannah (Words) Johnson helped in many ways, not the least of which was keeping the manuscript from being erased by the wrong processor command. And loyal American Littoral Society members have continued to support coastal caring — seaside sensibility. They deserve much of the credit for funding the cause and keeping the faith.

Beaches and How They Got There

We start this seaside wander with writings about beaches, mostly of sand, moving and shifting, reacting to wind and wave, inherently unstable platforms upon which mankind has erected structures. Such treatment of the shore doesn't always work out.

THE BEACH AND NIGHT ON THE GREAT BEACH
by Henry Beston

From his book, The Outermost House. *Beston was born in Quincy, Massachusetts, in 1888. He served in U.S. Navy submarines during World War I, and then fled civilization, first to Cape Cod and later to the Maine coast. He served on the staff of the Atlantic Monthly and wrote books about his Maine days.*

The Outermost House is about a year Beston spent in a small cabin on the Cape Cod shore, writing down the day's events in longhand at the kitchen table. In 1964, the house on the dunes was proclaimed a National Landmark, with a plaque bearing the names of Endicott Peabody, Governor of Massachusetts, and Stuart L. Udall, U.S. Secretary of the Interior. The house was destroyed during a violent storm in the fall of 1978. Maybe Beston, a believer in the power of the surf compared to the works of man, would have appreciated the fate of his structure.

⚓

THE CLIFF I WRITE OF and the bordering beach face the Atlantic on the forearm of the Cape. This outer earth is now scarce more than a great dyke or wall some twenty-five miles long and only three and four miles wide. At Provincetown it rises from the sea, beginning there in a desert of dunes and sand plains of the ocean's making. These sands curve inland toward the continent, bending toward Plymouth even as a hand may be bent down at the wrist, and Provincetown harbor lies in the curve of palm and fingers. At Truro, the wrist of the Cape — the forearm simile being both exact and inescapable — the land curve falls from the east and west down through an arc to the north and south, and the earth cliff begins and rises rather suddenly to its greatest elevation. South by east from the Highland Light to Eastham and Nauset Coast Guard Station, the rampart fronts the sea, its sky line being now a progress of long undulations, now a level as military as a battlement, hollows and mounded hills here and there revealing the barren moorland character of the country just above. At Nauset, the cliff ends, the sea invades the narrowing land, and one enters the kingdom of the dunes.

The cliff ends, and a wall of ocean dunes carries on the beach. Five miles long, this wall ends at a channel over whose entrance shoals the ocean sweeps daily into a great inlet or lagoon back of the dunes, an inlet spaced with the floors of tidal islands and traced with winding creeks — the inlet of Eastham and Orleans. Very hig tides, covering the islands, sometimes turn this space into bay. Westward over the channels and the marshland one looks to the uplands of the Cape, here scarce a good two miles wide. At Eastham, the land is an open, rolling moor. West over this lies Cape Cod Bay. A powerful tribe of Indians, the Nausets, once inhabited this earth between the seas.

Outermost cliff and solitary dune, the plain of ocean and the far, bright rims of the world, meadow land and marsh and ancient moor: this is Eastham; this the outer Cape. Sun and moon rise here from the sea, the arched sky has an ocean vastness, the clouds are now of ocean, now of earth. Having known and loved this land for many years, it came about that I found myself free to visit there, and so I built myself a house upon the beach.

My house stood by itself atop a dune, a little less than halfway south on Eastham bar. I drew the homemade plans for it myself and it was built for me by a neighbor and his carpenters. When I began to build, I had no notion whatever of using the house as a dwelling place. I simply wanted a place to come to in the summer, one cosy enough to be visited in winter could I manage to get down. I called it the Fo'castle. It consisted of two rooms, a bedroom and a kitchen–living room, and its dimensions over all were but twenty by sixteen. A brick fireplace with its back to the wall between rooms heated the larger space and took the chill off the bedroom, and I used a two-burner oil stove when cooking.

My neighbor built well. The house, even as I hoped, proved compact and strong, and it was easy to run and easy to heat. The larger room was sheathed and I painted the wainscoting and the window frames a kind of buff-fawn — a good fo'castle color. The house showed, perhaps, a somewhat amateur enthusiasm for windows. I had ten. In my larger room I had seven; a pair to the east opening on the sea, a pair to the west commanding the marshes, a pair to the south, and a small "look-see" in the door. Seven windows in one room perched on a hill of sand under an ocean sun — the words suggest cross lights and a glare; a fair misgiving, and one I countered by the use of wooden shutters originally meant for winter service but found necessary through the year. By arranging these I found I could have either the most sheltered and darkened of rooms or something rather like an inside out-of-doors. In my bedroom I had three windows — one east, one west, and one north to Nauset light.

To get drinking writer, I drove a well pipe directly down into the dune. Though the sea and the beach are alongside, and the marsh channels course daily to the west, there is fresh water here under the salty sand. This water varies in quality, some of it being brackish, some of it sweet and clear. To my great delight, I chanced upon a source which seems to me as good water as one may find here anywhere. Beneath the floor, the pipe descended into a bricked-up and covered pit housing a petcock through which I drained the water from the pump in freezing weather. (On bitter days I simply pumped a few pails full and stood them in the sink, and drained the pump immediately.) I had two oil lamps and various bottle candlesticks to read by, and a fireplace crammed maw-full of driftwood to keep me warm. I have no doubt that the fireplace heating arrangement sounds demented, but it worked, and my fire was more than a source of heat — it was an elemental presence, a household god, and a friend.

In my larger room I had a chest of drawers painted an honest carriage blue, a table, a wall bookcase, a couch, two chairs, and a rocker. My kitchen, built yacht fashion all in a line, stood at my southern wall. First came a dish and crockery cupboard, then a space for the oil stove — I kept this boxed in when not in use — then a shelf, a porcelain sink, and the corner pump. Blessed pump! It never failed me or indulged in nerves.

Using a knapsack, I carried my supplies on my own shoulders. There is no road through the dunes, and, even if there were, no one would have made deliveries. West of the dunes, it is true, there exists a kind of trail on which Fords may venture, but even the most experienced of the villagers are wary of it and tell of being mired there or stuck in the sand. Nevertheless, my lumber came by this trail, and now and then I could get my oil cans carried down by a neighbor who had a horse and cart. These helps, however, were but occasional, and I counted myself fortunate to have had them at all. My knapsack remained the only ever-ready wagon of the dunes. Twice a week, by arrangement, a friend met me at Nauset station with a car, took me shopping to Eastham or Orleans, and brought me back again to Nauset. And there I would pack my milk and eggs and butter and rolls — being very careful as to which was sitting on which — and strike off down the beach along the breakers.

The top of the mound I built on stands scarce twenty feet above high-water mark, and only thirty in from the great beach. The coast guards at Nauset, a scant two miles away, were my only neighbors. South lay the farther dunes and a few faraway and lonely gunning camps; the floor of marsh and tide parted me on the west from the village and its distant cottages; the ocean besieged my door. North, and north alone, had I touch with human things. On its solitary dune my house faced the four walls of the world.

My house completed, and tried and not found wanting by a

first Cape Cod year, I went there to spend a fortnight in September. The fortnight ending, I lingered on, and as the year lengthened into autumn, the beauty and mystery of this earth and outer sea so possessed and held me that I could not go. The world today is sick to its thin blood for lack of elemental things, for fire before the hands, for water welling from the earth, for air, for the dear earth itself underfoot. In my world of beach and dune these elemental presences lived and had their being, and under their arch there moved an incomparable pageant of nature and the year. The flux and reflux of ocean, the incomings of waves, the gatherings of birds, the pilgrimages of the peoples of the sea, winter and storm, the splendor of autumn and the holiness of spring—all these were part of the great beach. The longer I stayed, the more eager was I to know this coast and to share its mysterious and elemental life; I found myself free to do so, I had no fear of being alone, I had something of a field naturalist's inclination; presently I made up my mind to remain and try living for a year on Eastham Beach.

Our fantastic civilization has fallen out of touch with many aspects of nature, and with none more completely than with night. Primitive folk, gathered at a cave mouth round a fire, do not fear night; they fear, rather, the energies and creatures to whom night gives power; we of the age of the machines, having delivered ourselves of nocturnal enemies, now have a dislike of night itself. With lights and ever more lights, we drive the holiness and beauty of night back to the forests and the sea; the little villages, the crossroads even, will have none of it. Are modern folk, perhaps, afraid of night? Do they fear that vast serenity, the mystery of infinite space, the austerity of stars? Having made themselves at home in a civilization obsessed with power, which explains its whole world in terms of energy, do they fear at night for their dull acquiescence and the pattern of their beliefs? Be the answer what it will, today's civilization is full of people who have not the slightest notion of the character or the poetry of night, who have never even seen night. Yet to live thus, to know only artificial night, is as absurd and evil as to know only artificial day.

Night is very beautiful on this great beach. It is the true other half of the day's tremendous wheel; no lights without meaning stab or trouble it; it is beauty, it is fulfilment, it is rest. Thin clouds float in these heavens, islands of obscurity in a splendor of space and stars: the Milky Way bridges earth and ocean; the beach resolves itself into a unity of form, its summer lagoons, its slopes and uplands merging; against the western sky and the falling bow of sun rise the silent and superb undulations of the dunes.

My nights are at their darkest when a dense fog streams in from the sea under a black, unbroken floor of cloud. Such nights are rare, but are most to be expected when fog gathers off the coast in early summer; this last Wednesday night was the darkest I have known. Between ten o'clock and two in the morning three vessels stranded on the outer beach — a fisherman, a four-masted schooner, and a beam trawler. The fisherman and the schooner have been towed off, but the trawler, they say, is still ashore.

I went down to the beach that night just after ten o'clock. So utterly black, pitch dark it was, and so thick with moisture and trailing showers, that there was no sign whatever of the beam of Nauset; the sea was only a sound, and when I reached the edge of the surf the dunes themselves had disappeared behind. I stood as isolate in that immensity of rain and night as I might have stood in interplanetary space. The sea was troubled and noisy, and when I opened the darkness with an outlined cone of light from my electric torch I saw that the waves were washing up green coils of sea grass, all coldly wet and bright in the motionless and unnatural radiance. Far off a single ship was groaning its way along the shoals. The fog was compact of the finest moisture; passing by, it spun itself into my lens of light like a kind of strange, aerial, and liquid silk. Effin Chalke, the new coast guard, passed me going north, and told me that he had had news at the halfway house of the schooner at Cahoon's.

It was dark, pitch dark to my eye, yet complete darkness, I imagine, is exceedingly rare, perhaps unknown in outer nature. The nearest natural approximation to it is probably the gloom of forest country buried in night and cloud. Dark as the night was here, there was still light on the surface of the planet. Standing on the shelving beach, with the surf breaking at my feet, I could see the endless wild uprush, slide, and withdrawal of the sea's white rim of foam. The men at Nauset tell me that on such nights they follow along this vague crawl of whiteness, trusting to habit and a sixth sense to warn them of their approach to the halfway house.

Animals descend by starlight to the beach. North, beyond the dunes, muskrats forsake the cliff and nose about in the driftwood and weed, leaving.intricate trails and figure eights to be obliterated by the day; the lesser folk — the mice, the occasional small sand-colored toads, the burrowing moles — keep to the upper beach and leave their tiny footprints under the overhanging wall. In autumn, skunks, beset by a shrinking larder, go beach combing early in the night. The animal is by preference a clean feeder and turns up his nose at rankness. I almost stepped on a big fellow one night as I was walking north to meet the first man south from Nauset. There was a scamper, and the creature ran up the beach from under my feet; alarmed he certainly was, yet was he contained and continent. Deer are frequently seen, especially north of the light. I find their tracks upon the summer dunes.

Years ago, while camping on this beach north of Nauset, I went for a stroll along the top of the cliff at break of dawn. Though the path followed close enough along the edge, the beach below was often hidden, and I looked directly from the height to the flush of sunrise at sea. Presently the path, turning, approached the brink of the earth precipice, and on the beach below, in the cool, wet rosiness of dawn, I saw three deer playing. They frolicked, rose on their hind legs, scampered off, and returned again, and were merry. Just before sunrise they trotted off north together down the beach toward a hollow in the cliff and the path that climbs it.

Occasionally a sea creature visits the shore at night. Lone coast guardsman, trudging the sand at some deserted hour, have been startled by seals. One man fell flat on a creature's back, and it drew away from under him, flippering toward the sea, with a sound "halfway between a squeal and a bark."

I myself once had rather a start. It was long after sundown, the light dying and uncertain, and I was walking home on the top level of the beach and close along the slope descending to the ebbing tide. A little more than halfway to the Fo'castle a huge unexpected something suddenly writhed horribly in the darkness under my bare foot. I had stepped on a skate left stranded by some recent crest of surf, and my weight had momentarily annoyed it back to life.

Facing north, the beam of Nauset becomes part of the dune night. As I walk toward it, I see the lantern, now as a star of light which waxes and wanes three mathematic times, now as a lovely pale flare of light behind the rounded summits of the dunes. The changes in the atmosphere change the color of the beam; it is now whitish, now flame golden, now golden red; it changes its form as well, from a star to a blare of light, from a blare of light to a cone of radiance sweeping a circumference of fog. To the west of Nauset I often see the apocalyptic flash of the great light at the Highland reflected on the clouds or even on the moisture in the starlit air, and, seeing it, I often think of the pleasant hours I have spent there when George and Mary Smith were at the light and I had the good fortune to visit as their guest. Instead of going to sleep in the room under the eaves, I would lie awake, looking out of a window to the great spokes of light revolving as solemnly as a part of the universe.

All night long the lights of coastwise vessels pass at sea, green lights going south, red lights moving north. Fishing schooners and flounder draggers anchor two or three miles out, and keep a bright riding light burning on the mast. I see them come to anchor at sundown, but I rarely see them go, for they are off at dawn. When busy at night, these fishermen illumine their decks with a scatter of oil flares. From shore, the ships might be thought afire. I have watched the scene through a night glass. I could see no smoke, only the waving flares, the reddish radiance on sail and rigging, an edge of reflection overside, and the enormous night and sea beyond.

One July night, as I returned at three o'clock from an expedition north, the whole night, in one strange, burning instant, turned into a phantom day. I stopped and, questioning, stared about. An enormous meteor, the largest I have ever seen, was consuming itself in an effulgence of light west of the zenith. Beach and dune and ocean appeared out of nothing, shadowless and motionless, a landscape whose every tremor and vibration were stilled, a landscape in a dream.

The beach at night has a voice all its own, a sound in fullest harmony with its spirit and mood — with its little, dry noise of sand forever moving, with its solemn, overspilling, rhythmic seas, with its eternity of stars that somtimes seem to hang down like lamps from the high heavens — and that sound the piping of a bird. As I walk the beach in early summer my solitary coming disturbs it on its nest, and it flies away, troubled, invisible, piping its sweet, plaintive cry. The bird I write of is the piping plover, *Charadrius melodus*, sometimes called the beach plover or the mourning bird. Its note is a whistled syllable, the loveliest musical note, I think, sounded by any North Atlantic bird.

Now that summer is here I often cook myself a camp supper on the beach. Beyond the crackling, salt-yellow driftwood flame, over the pyramid of barrel staves, broken boards, and old sticks all atwist with climbing fire, the unseen ocean thunders and booms, the breaker sounding hollow as it falls. The wall of the sand cliff behind, with its rim of grass and withering roots, its sandy crumblings and erosions, stands gilded with flame;

wind cries over it; a covey of sandpipers pass between the ocean and the fire. There are stars, and to the south Scorpio hangs curving down the sky with ringed Saturn shining in his claw.

THE BEACHES ARE MADE OF CONTINENTS
by Wallace Kaufman and Orrin H. Pilkey

From their book The Beaches Are Moving *(*The Drowning of America's Shoreline*). Kaufman builds houses; Pilkey teaches geology at Duke University. Together they put together this call to arms: sea level is rising, we're building too close to the ocean, let's think about better ways to inhabit the coastline.*

Pilkey has gone on to edit a series of books about how to design with and cooperate with nature along the shoreside. The books are titled "Living with the Texas Shore," "Living with the North Carolina Shore," and so forth. Periodically, Pilkey makes forays into foreign territory (i.e., other states), preaching his gospel of geologic common sense. It drives coastal engineers and land boomers nuts.

⚓

ALTHOUGH THE SUNBATHER lying sleepy and vulnerable on the warm sand seldom knows it, he is lying on one of the most ingenious defensive structures in the world. In nature's endless interplay of force and material, the beach is a buffer zone, shock absorber, and biological way station between the sea and the land. All this is made of wastes, materials cast off by the continent, and in some cases by the life under the sea itself. In nature, of course, waste is mainly a matter of definition and point of view. The wastes that form the beaches are not only vital in the coastal environment but are the first line of defense for the mainland from whence they issued.

Since the ancient separation of the land from the water, exposed rocks have been splitting and crumbling, forming smaller and smaller pieces and finally cobbles, pebbles, sand, and mud. Some of this debris becomes a vital part of life-giving soil. Sooner or later most of it reaches the edge of the continent.

At this moment, high in the Cascade Mountains of Washington, a mountainside lies far beneath a thick sheet of ice, a glacier moving with infinite slowness. In the arid Badlands of South Dakota groundhogs excavate their burrows in weathered soil. These animals, as averse to extra work as humans, always push the excavated material down-hill. High in Minnesota a cold clear ribbon of water, the beginning of the Mississippi River, slips over rock and curves against low soil banks. In Alaska's Tongass Forest a spruce loses its rocky footing and falls across the stream, loosening a few pebbles from the earth. So for many millions of years in the most remote parts of the continents, the materials of the beach have begun their journey toward the sea.

The sand, silt, debris, and flotsam which form the beaches of America come also from the Appalachian Mountains, the Grand Canyon, the glacial bluffs of New England, the bays and estuaries of New Jersey, the coral reefs of Florida, and the dark continental shelves beneath the Gulf of Mexico and the Atlantic and Pacific oceans.

The story of beach materials is even more complex than this, and many of us understand it no better than the king who lost the recipe for his favorite muffins understood baking. He commanded his wise men to analyze the last muffin and say of what it was made. They brought back their findings: The muffins were made out of crumbs.

To say that beaches are made of sand does not tell us how to make a beach. The recipes for beach material are often simple, but there is no national cuisine. Each beach has its own special materials, its own provincial recipe. Nature relentlessly reminds us of this even in relatively quiet inland waters.

In 1955 the U.S. Army Corps of Engineers came to rescue the eroding beaches of the Presque Isle peninsula in Lake Erie. From the quiet harbor behind the curving peninsula huge pumps poured 150,000 cubic yards of sand a year onto the lakeshore beaches. For a while bathers enjoyed broad, soft shores, but the sand soon began to vanish. Four years later the beaches weve still losing 25,000 cubic yards a year. In the 1960s the corps returned and pumped in 688,000 cubic yards of sand, enough to fill several football stadiums to the top of the stands. Again the sand disappeared.

The part of the recipe overlooked was grain size. The sand the corps had been pumping out of the harbor had smaller grains than the natural beach. A beach of small, closely packed grains is not as porous as a coarser beach and does not absorb as large a part of incoming waves. The combination of stronger backwash and lighter grains quickly washed out the public investment in saving the beach. The money is gone with the waves, but the beach was finally saved when the corps changed tactics and pumped up 1.2 million cubic yards of coarse sand.

Not only does beach material vary in size from microscopic grains to boulders, but the recipe varies with the season. Each beach gets the materials it needs to survive under a given set of conditions. An expert studying the materials of the beach on any given day can tell us something about the mood of the sea which transported the material. The beach preserves itself against seasonal changes in the sea much as humans preserve themselves by dressing according to the weather. During storms, and in fall and winter when waves roll in faster and higher, more and more fine sand is captured and held by the surf. It only comes to rest offshore in deeper water. Tle larger, heavier sand grains and pebbles remain on the beach. The coarser materials of the winter or storm beach, both above and below high water, act like a battlefield full of pitfalls over which an onrushing army advances and retreats, losing some of its force with each motion. The coarse sands are in fact a kind of natural armor, But fine or coarse, the secret of success is adaptation and flexibility. Beaches of sand or gravel can absorb blows that tear apart concrete walls in a few seasons.

Even driftwood can be a valuable beach material. The beaches of Grand Isle, Louisiana, are forever covered with bits and pieces of tree limbs from inland forests and flotsam from the Gulf. In the 1930s bathers convinced local officials to clean up the beach. No sooner was it clean than it began to disappear.

Day by day it grew smaller, and during storms erosion would reshape the entire length of the beach. Prior to 1933 and the anti-driftwood campaign, erosion had been slow. The driftwood detested by bathers was not just debris, it was part of the beach itself, and when it went trouble followed. Though driftwood moves with the tides, it also seems to be effective in breaking waves and trapping sand — a kind of natural seawall and sieve, and no less a part of the beach than sand.

As singular as beaches are, their life depends on the sea in front of them and the landscape for miles behind them, sometimes for thousands of miles behind. Nothing could impress upon us more clearly the complex interaction of beach and continent than a tour of the coast from Maine to Alaska. On such a tour we would see more kinds of beaches than most men dream of, some of them stranger than most dreams.

THE SANDY BEACHES

The Gold Coast of Fitzgerald's *Great Gatsby* is the hilly north shore of Long Island with its high bluffs, stony beaches, and intimate coves and harbors. The mansions of the rich in many places still look north across the flooded glacial river valley of Long Island Sound toward New England. When a native of the north shore first travels south across the eighteen-mile width of Long Island to the ocean, he is stunned by the great dunes and in front of them the broad, bright beaches stretching in a straight line as far as he can see. The green waves roll in cleaner and saltier than the water that eddies in and out of Long Island Sound. The beach is smooth and hard and makes the north shore's most carefully groomed public beaches seem like gravel dumps. Though part of the same island, the open-ocean beach seems an entirely different world, and indeed it is.

In the eighteen miles from the north to the south shore of Long Island, you pass from the glacial coast to the beginning of the relatively straight, low coast whose sandy beaches stretch, with small exceptions, all the way from Long Island to Texas and beyond into Mexico. This is also the barrier-island coast, buffered by narrow islands, each with its own character and citizenry of plants and animals, yet each island vitally dependent on its neighbors. Nowhere in the world is there a barrier-island coast either as long or as varied as North America's. To understand this vast whole we must begin with its smallest pieces — grains of sand.

The East Coast from New York to Florida is one of the nation's most heavily traveled landscapes. Its farms and cities are so much a part of our history that hardly anyone realizes that most of the land east of Philadelphia, Washington, Richmond, Raleigh, and Augusta was once not landscape but seascape. This is also true for all of Florida, Mississippi, Louisiana, and great parts of Alabama and southeastern Texas. As sea level rose and fell in counterpoint to several million years of ice ages, the shoreline crossed back and forth across the rock and earth washed from the inland hills. Like a slow broom, its strokes smoothed and leveled the great apron of sediment that stretches from Piedmont fall line to oceanic abyss. The only lands flatter than the eastern coastal plain are the salt flats of Nevada and Utah and parts of the Great Plains. These are former bottoms of inland seas. Vast numbers of humans now grow tobacco and soybeans in the sandy soils, and mine the phosphates and limestone left by ancient sea animals. Secure in our travel, trade, and urban cares, we are as little aware of the land's former life as is an empire of ants secure in the warm hollow of an old oak.

The broom that sweeps and levels the coastal apron is a narrow one, an area of high wave energy known as the shoreface, which extends from the coastal dunes seaward for some three to six miles and sometimes reaches a depth of sixty feet. This constant sweeping has kept sand in motion, building both beaches and underwater bars. As a result, the sand deposits on the continental shelf are relatively thin, often less than ten feet deep, and outcrops of rock and old coral reefs are common.

Behind the beaches the smoothness of the coastal plain is interrupted only by rivers and by streaks of low ridges running parallel to the coast but well inland. These ridges are part of an ancient seascape, the remains of old beaches and barrier islands formed between glaciers and left to be colonized by terrestrial plants and animals when sea level dropped. As the shoreline followed the sea, rivers cut through the coastal plain and carried sand for new beaches. These rivers are still delivering the old materials to the modern coast, but not to the beaches and shoreface. The Delaware, Susquehanna, Savannah, Cape Fear, Altamaha, and other rivers yield their materials slowly, and their sluggish currents do not have the great delivery power of western rivers, plunging out of the mountains close to the Pacific. Most of the sediment that rides these eastern rivers settles into the estuaries and lagoons behind the barrier islands. One day, as sea level rises, this sand may again form beaches. Meanwhile, the beaches are sustained from the more distant past.

A walk on a mid-Atlantic beach is a walk on sand more ancient than the bluffs of New England. These beaches are sustained by reservoirs few people ever see. Most of the sand from the ancient rivers lies offshore in a thin layer on the continental shelf. How does this sand return to the continent? Even at the edge of the continental shelf, at depths of three hundred feet and more, wave action nudges a few grains of sand toward land. The closer they get to the shoreface, the stronger the nudges become until the sand enters the surf. But even the sands from the dark ocean floor once lay far inland. We can prove the inland origin of beaches by analyzing the mineral content of their sand. Light-colored particles of sand are usually quartz and feldspar, minerals so common they might have come from hundreds of sources. The less common dark grains, however, are usually unstable heavy minerals from the original source. Heavy minerals on Atlantic beaches tell us their sands originated not in the nearby coastal plain but in the far inland Piedmont, that rolling landscape of worn-down mountains that rises above the famous "fall line," whose falling rivers attracted colonial mills and industry.

While the heavy minerals give us the specific origins of sand, the general appearance is dominated by quartz and feldspar, making a thousand miles of sandy beaches look all the same. The explanation is fairly simple. With the exception of these two minerals, all others are present only in minor quantities. Quartz and feldspar are chemically stable and physically hard. After millennia of weathering and journeying, only these two remain out of a great variety of rocks. Quartz and feldspar are so hard that tumbling by rivers and tossing by waves do little even to round the sharp grains.

From this longest sandy coastline in the world, the nation demands almost a billion tons of sand a year for highways, homes, offices, pipes, bridges, and ballparks. Sand has become a scarce resource, but not because we can't find it. We simply have run out of deposits that can be mined without digging unfillable holes in valuable real estate. Nevertheless, stripping sand from the Virgin Islands has left those resorts with beaches that are shadows of their natural state. The sand on Puerto Rico's white beaches is being trucked off in sight of signs saying: DON'T REMOVE SAND FROM BEACHES. Where sand mining does not conflict with property values, it threatens the natural environment. Many bays and estuaries, including Jamaica Bay, which was dredged to build Kennedy Airport, have been devastated in the quest for the sand lying in their quiet waters. As our appreciation of wetlands grows, developers look beneath deeper waters.

The U.S. Army Corps of Engineers estimates the offshore East Coast sand supplies at some 450 billion tons, and one recent corps study estimates 270 billion tons of this sand lies the inner continental shelf off New York City. Construction interests have begun to eye these deposits for both onshore construction and for the building of deep-water ports and offshore nuclear power plants. The corps also suggests these deposits might be pumped up onto eroding beaches. The quantity of sand mined may not be as important as the holes it leaves in the seafloor. Because of the costs, "offshore mining" will be close to being onshore. Its holes will change the direction and intensity of waves approaching the beaches. Recent history records one Connecticut beach whose valuable sand disappeared from "natural causes" after dredges mined sand offshore.

While an ancient landscape provided the sand for today's beaches, ancient animals also paid their dues to nature's systems, which demands that all parts give as well as take. As shell collectors know, the farther south we go, the easier it is to find beaches strewn with conches, clams, mussels, and scallops. To the "shellers" dismay, the shells are usually broken. This is also part of the process by which nature maintains the beaches. North of Virginia the shell, or calcium carbonate, part of sand is usually 1 percent or less. Where warm southern waters come shoreward off North Carolina, the portion ranges from 5 percent to 25 percent. And further south, marine life is so abundant that bone and shell fragments are dominant sources of beach material. Not only shellfish but corals, fish, and even microscopic plankton contribute by their death to the East Coast's most famous beaches and most valuable real estate south of the Mason-Dixon Line. In Miami tourists play on a beach that is 50 percent dead animals. In extreme southern Florida, in the Keys, and in Puerto Rico the beaches are often 100 percent calcium carbonate. The startling white of those beaches shines from the bleached remains of organisms washed up from nearby reefs. Were the seas not so productive of animal life, those shorelines most likely would be far inland of where they are today, and southern Florida might not exist at all.

The animal origin of the white southern beaches does not make their sands a renewable resource, not in the time scheme of human development. An observant sheller walking the ocean beach should know that the contributing animals are not all modern. Live shells like coquina appear in the surf, but what accounts for oyster shells on the beach when oysters live only in quiet estuaries and bays? Quantity rules out the remnants of old oyster roasts. Besides, the oysters are mixed with lagoon clams and salt-marsh snails. Clearly when sea level was lower, the bays and estuaries were in front of today's beaches. Not only do we find ocean beaches made of shells of quiet-water species, but of species that have not lived in a given area for thousands of years. The shell content of beaches is largely fossil shell. Three samples of Miami Beach sand, radiocarbon-dated by Dr. Gene Rusnak of the U.S. Geological Survey, showed an average age of some thirteen thousand years, with some material over thirty thousand years old. While development hastens shoreline erosion, its related pollution may be endangering the reefs and animals that should become tomorrow's beaches.

IMPULSIVELY GENERATED WAVES
by Willard Bascom

From his book Waves and Beaches. *This has to be a candidate for the most accurately titled book. Not only that, it draws an important connection — beaches are formed by and depend on waves.*

Bascom grew up in New York but moved to the West Coast, where he worked as an oceanographic engineer. The book is full of good explanations of why beaches take on different looks and what waves do to beaches. This excerpt is scientific but also just plain fun, because it talks about huge waves, the fifty-footers of our dreams and nightmares.

WHEN A FORCE IS SUDDENLY APPLIED TO A WATER SUR-FACE, waves are generated. The impulse of a pebble tossed into a puddle sends out a train of waves in concentric circles. In the ocean an earthquake, a volcanic eruption, a landslide or a nuclear explosion may produce the same effect on a much larger scale. The train of waves leaving such an event often contains a huge amount of energy and moves at high speed. As a result the waves may be tremendously destructive when they encounter a populated shore.

The general public has long referred to these waves as tidal waves, much to the annoyance of American oceanographers who are acutely aware that there is no connection with the tides. In an effort to straighten out the matter they adopted the Japanese word tsunami, which now is in general use. Later they discovered that tsunami merely means tidal wave in Japanese, but at least the annoyance has been shifted overseas.

SEISMIC SEA WAVES

A somewhat more descriptive term that applies to waves caused by earthquakes is seismic sea waves.

There are several mechanisms by means of which earthquakes can generate seismic sea waves. One such is a simple fault in which tension in the submarine crustal rock is relieved by the abrupt rupturing of the rock along an inclined plane. When such a fault occurs, a large mass of rock drops rapidly and the support is removed from a column of water that extends to the surface. The water surface oscillates up and down as it seeks to return to mean sea level, and a series of waves is sent out. If the rock fails in compression, the mass of rock on one side rides up over that on the other, and a column of water is lifted, but the result is the same: a tsunami.

A second mechanism is a landslide, which is set in motion by an earthquake. If the slide begins above water, abruptly dumping a mass of rock into the sea, waves are made by the same action as the plunger in the wave channel. An example of such an event will presently be cited. If the slide occurs well below the surface, it creates waves.

The waves so created are very long and very low. Their period is of the order of a thousand seconds; their wave lengths may be as much as one hundred and fifty miles; their height, only a foot or two in deep water. The slope of the wave front is imperceptible and ships at sea are unaware of their passage.

Because the wave lengths are so long, tsunamis move as shallow-water waves, even in the deepest ocean. As such, their velocity is controlled by the depth.

$$C = \sqrt{gd}$$

Thus, if $g = 32$ and $d = 15,000$ feet (average depth of the Pacific basin), the velocity of a wave in the deep Pacific is 692 feet per second or 472 miles an hour. Fortunately the Pacific is large enough so that waves moving at even that speed take considerable time to cross it, and a seismic sea wave warning system has been established to warn coastal inhabitants of approaching tsunamis.

The events so far mentioned usually take place out of sight of man, where they can do little harm. It is when these waves approach a coastline that they are at their spectacular worst. There the influence of the bottom topography and the configuration of the coastline transforms the low waves of deep water into rampaging monsters.

The first tsunami of which there is a record wiped out Amnisos, Crete, about 1400 B.C. A thousand years later, according to Pausanias, an ancient Greek, "the town of Helice perished under the waters of the Gulf of Corinth where the population was drowned to a man." In that millennium perhaps ten tsunamis were recorded. Now two or three a year cause local catastrophes. Certainly there is no change in the activity of undersea earthquakes; the reason for the apparent increase is mainly that the world's population has grown so that people and wealth are now spread along once deserted shores. Since this trend is certain to continue, the danger to mankind from great sea waves is increasing.

A list of two hundred and seventy seismic sea waves from antiquity to 1940 was compiled by N. H. Heck of the U.S. Coast and Geodetic Survey. In reading them one easily envisions great walls of water suddenly towering above frantic crowds; harbors being swept clear of ships; soaked and terrorized survivors of the first wave racing the next wave to high ground. Table I contains some choice samples.

TABLE I
SOME GREAT SEISMIC SEA WAVES

SEPTEMBER 14, 1509	TURKEY. Sea came over the walls of Constantinople and Galata following earthquake.
DECEMBER 16, 1575	CHILE. Intense wave in the inner port of Valdivia. Two Spanish galleons wrecked.

MARCH 25, 1751 — CHILE. City of Concepción was extensively damaged for the fourth time in a century by earthquakes. Sea withdrew and returned at great height several times. Disastrous effects at Juan Fernández Island.

NOVEMBER 1, 1755 — PORTUGAL. Great Lisbon earthquake. Waves fifteen to forty feet high along Spanish and Portuguese coasts. Very high at Cádiz, where eighteen waves rolled in.

DECEMBER 29, 1820 — CELEBES, Makassar. A wall of water sixty to eighty feet high swept over the port of Boelekomba. Great damage at Nipa-Nipa and Serang-Serang. A similar great wave at Bima, Sumbawa, carried ships over houses.

AUGUST 13, 1868 — SOUTH PERU (now north Chile). USS *Wateree* carried a quarter mile inshore by a wave with a maximum height of seventy feet. Receding wave uncovered Bay of Iquique to a depth of twenty-four feet and then returned with a forty-foot wave, covering the city of Iquique.

JUNE 15, 1896 — NORTHEAST JAPAN. Sea waves nearly one hundred feet high at head of bay; elsewhere, ten to eighty feet. 27,000 lives lost along 320 kilometers of coast; 10,000 houses swept away.

MARCH 16, 1926 — PALMERSTON ISLAND, Cook Group. Island submerged and natives lost their means of sustenance.

NOVEMBER 21, 1927 — CHILE, Aysén River region. Sea invaded land along twenty-five miles of coast. Boat *Mannesix* with crew flung into treetops of forest.

NOVEMBER 18, 1929 — NEWFOUNDLAND, Burin Peninsula. A tidal wave from the Grand Banks earthquake swept up several narrow inlets to a height of fifty feet, destroying villages and causing heavy loss.

On reading Heck's notes my first reaction was that their very terseness tended to make them more exciting than reality by stimulating the reader's imagination. However, upon examining the more extended accounts from which he took his data, I concluded that it would take a rare imagination to equal the actual circumstances. For example:

The USS *Wateree*, a Civil War side-wheeler gunboat, was stationed at Arica, Peru, in August 1868, when the tidal wave referred to by Heck occurred. According to a witness, it was "carried by an exceptionally heavy wave completely over the town, scraping the tops of the highest buildings and was safely deposited on some sandy wasteland about a mile inland. Thanks to her flat bottom she fetched up on an even keel and although it was impossible to get the ship back into her accustomed element she was in no danger structurally. The ship was therefore left in full commission for several months until sold. Service routine continued but with certain readjustments. Sanitary facilities were erected ashore and a vegetable garden was started. The most unusual modification was the substitution of burros for boats. If the captain wanted to go 'ashore,' the bosun's mate would pipe and call, 'Away brig.' Thereupon the coxswain would run out on a boom, slide down a pennant to a burro, cast off and come alongside to the ladder which had been lengthened to reach the ground. The captain would mount and ride off into the dunes."

The author well remembers how his own interest in tsunamis was generated. On April, 1, 1946, our field party returned to the Berkeley campus of the University of California after five months of daily observation of the waves and beaches of the north Pacific coast and was greeted by: "Did you see the big wave?" It sounded much like an April Fool's Day joke, but, sadly, it was not. There had been a landslide in the Aleutian Trench early that morning and its waves were wreaking havoc around the Pacific basin. After the bad luck of missing the actual arrival of the waves by a day we set about collecting whatever data we could.

The next few days were spent questioning people who had seen the wave, surveying high-water marks and photographing wrecked houses and stranded boats. Some of the stories were amusing and each contained some useful fact that could be applied to the understanding of seismic sea waves. For example, we found that the first arriving crest is often so small it is unnoticed, but it is soon followed by a major recession of the water.

This happened at Half Moon Bay, where a surveying party was mapping the shoreline at the site of a proposed breakwater. The rodman's instructions were to hold the rod at the water's edge. As the water retreated with the first trough, he followed instructions. Just as the engineer on the transit was beginning to wonder how he could be reading five feet below sea level on the rod, the direction of the water movement changed; rodman and rod inadvertently surfboarded in on the first large crest.

Areas of bottom or rocks never before seen may be exposed. Tle first trough suddenly stranded the Half Moon Bay fishing fleet on a sandy bottom in an anchorage where it normally floated at the lowest range of the tide. But not for long. Before another ten minutes had passed the boats had refloated, dragged their anchors several hundred yards, and were stranded again — this time on a paved road thirteen feet above the original water level.

The arrival of the trough of one of these great waves should serve as a warning, but instead it attracts the curious, who often follow the receding water out to pick up flopping fish and look at the newly exposed bottom instead of running for high ground. When the next crest arrives it may come fast — in some cases it is a huge breaking wave — and the curious pay for their folly. This drop in water level over a period of several minutes without change in the appearance of the usual waves is something like the rapid ebbing of the tide. In a similar way the incoming crests may be seen only as a rapid rise in the general level of the water without any observable wave front. Doubtless this tidelike action, which occurs in twelve minutes instead of twelve hours, is partly responsible for the usual misnomer "tidal wave."

On the same occasion in the cove at Pacific Grove, California, a man was dozing on a bench fifteen feet above the normal water level. He awakened when one dangling hand was wet by the gently rising water and sat bolt upright on the still-dry bench to watch the surrounding water slowly recede again. At the same instant, in nearby Monterey harbor, marine biologist Rolf Bolin noticed unusual currents around his skiff but no important rise or fall of water level.

These incidents raised an interesting question. Why should there be this major difference in the height of the wave at two points only a mile apart? Part of the answer seems to be that Pacific Grove faced away from the wave, Monterey faced into it.

Later, over a period of years, I traveled to many Pacific shores asking about the effects of that tsunami. Remarkably often points facing into the waves and bays facing away from them were hardest hit. For example, Taiohai village at the head of a narrow south-facing bay in the Marquesas Islands four thousand miles from the earthquake epicenter was demolished. Hilo, Hawaii, only half as far from the disturbance and whose offshore topography seems precisely suited to funnel tsunamis toward the town, fared worse. There the captain of a ship standing off the port watched with astonishment as the city was destroyed by waves that passed unnoticed under the ship. Another ship, the *Brigham Victory*, was unloading lumber at Hilo when the tsunami struck. The ship survived with considerable damage but the pier and its buildings were destroyed. One hundred and seventy-three persons died and $25 million in property damage was done by the waves at Hilo that morning.

But the truly great waves of April 1 struck at Scotch Cap, Alaska, only a few hundred miles from the tsunami's source, where five men were on duty in a lighthouse that marked Unimak Pass. The lighthouse building was a substantial two-story reinforced concrete structure with its foundation thirty-two feet above mean sea level. None of the men survived to tell the story but a breaking wave over one hundred feet high must have demolished the building at about 2:40 A.M. The next day Coast Guard aircraft, investigating the loss of radio contact, were astonished to discover only a trace of the lighthouse foundation. Nearby a small block of concrete one hundred and three feet above the water had been wiped clean of the radio tower it once supported.

TSUNAMI WARNING SYSTEMS

Largely as a result of the Hilo disaster a seismic sea wave warning system has been developed by the U.S. Coast and Geodetic Survey. It works like this. Ten seismograph stations around the Pacific rim from the Philippines to Alaska and from Peru to Japan are equipped with automatic alarm systems and visible recorders. When the tremors from a large earthquake are received, the alarm sounds, alerting the local observers, who transmit the recorded data to a central station in Honolulu. If analysis there of the arrival times of the first earthquake shock at the various stations shows that the quake is located under the ocean, a radio message containing estimated times of arrival of a possible tsunami is sent to tide-measuring stations nearest the quake's epicenter. Each station is asked to report back whether or not such waves actually arrive. If unusual wave activity is reported, a warning is issued to local authorities (civil defense and police) in coastal areas that may be affected. At present no attempt is made to estimate the height of the waves to be expected, but that may be possible after further research is done.

Walter Munk was an early consultant in the development of tsunami warning devices and on passing through Hilo in 1950 could not resist the chance to ask about the workings of the embryonic system. He found the instrument was mounted at the outer end of the Hilo pier and was designed to detect waves in the one thousand second band midway between the longer period tides and the shorter period swell. The arrival of a tsunami at this finely tuned instrument would actuate an alarm bell in the police station some distance inland and the city could be warned in time to flee to higher ground.

However, the police chief, with a fine distrust of such gadgets, passed the word that no warning would be given until he telephoned a man at the end of the pier who would visually inspect the standard tide gauge and confirm the existence of unusual waves. Aside from the obvious delay involved under the best of circumstances, this procedure seemed to place undue emphasis on the necessity for tsunamis to arrive during working hours. Even then, if the phone on the pier was not answered, a question would remain as to whether the pier, gauge, and telephone had been swept away or whether the observer was busy elsewhere. But the plan did eliminate false alarms.

After a more recent trip, several tsunamis later, Professor Munk reports an increased mutual respect between the ocean and the chief.

The need of Pacific-rim cities for a wave warning system was clear enough and over a period of years a combination of false alarms and small tsunamis made it possible to "work the bugs out of the system." When needed for one of the greatest tsunamis of the past century, it was ready.

On May 22, 1960, a violent earthquake (magnitude 8.5) shook the coast of Chile. A volcano erupted; there was widespread faulting, subsidence, and hundreds of landslides. In a local disaster area five hundred miles long, four thousand people died, half a million homes were damaged, and $400 million worth of property was destroyed. There was also a major subsidence on the great undersea fault that parallels the coast, and this generated a tsunami that was felt on all Pacific shores.

In Chile itself dozens of waterfront towns were devastated. Coastal cities in New Zealand, Australia, the Philippines, and Okinawa were flooded by several feet of water. On the U.S. coast, Los Angeles and San Diego harbors suffered a million dollars worth of damage to piers and small craft. In Japan, nine thousand miles from the origin, the waves were as much as fifteen feet high. There, 180 people died and the damage was estimated at $50 million,

But Hilo, Hawaii, again took the worst blow, and although the property damage was more serious than in 1946, this time the population was warned and there were few deaths. The sequence of events abstracted from the log of the U.S. Coast and Geodetic Survey's Honolulu observatory is an interesting record of the progress of the wave:

0938   Alarm sounded by distant earthquake.

0959   Requested data from other stations.

1014, 1120   Seismograph stations at Berkeley, Tucson, Fairbanks, Suva report in.

1059   Requested tide report from Balboa, Canal Zone.

1159   Issued bulletin (not warning) to Honolulu police and military:
This is a seismic sea wave advisory bulletin. A severe earthquake has occurred in Chile. It is possible a damaging sea wave has been generated. If so, it will reach Hawaii about midnight.

1204   Valparaiso reports tsunami on coast of Chile.

1340   Issued news bulletin reconfirming that a wave may be on the way.

1847   Issued official warning:
This is a seismic sea wave warning. The estimated time of arrival of the first wave at Hawaii is midnight. The danger may last several hours. The intensity of the wave cannot be predicted. [Arrival times estimated for Tahiti, Christmas Island, Samoa, Fiji, Canton, Johnson, Midway.]

1924   Balboa reports no wave; Christmas Island reports negative.

2223   Tahiti reports unusual wave activity [first actual tsunami report other than Chile].

2255, 0011   Samoa and La Jolla report tidal rise.
0035   Heard via broadcast band radio that unusual wave activities had begun in Hilo.
0611   All clear sounded by civil authorities.

The "unusual wave activities" that began almost exactly at midnight at Hilo included the arrival of a series of waves whose crests reached fifteen feet above the normal high-water mark. As these successive walls of water swept across the city, they carried before them virtually all the buildings on seven city blocks.

There is little practical action that can be taken to prevent property damage by such waves. Changing the underwater configuration or building a sufficiently large breakwater would be exceedingly expensive, but these possibilities are now being tested on models of the Hilo offshore area. Probably Hilo's best solution is to move to higher ground nearby and make the waterfront area into Tsunami Park. Doubtless this low area will be swept again and again by future waves.

The remarkable thing about the ocean is how calm and stable its surface is. Considering its breadth and depth, the changes in height caused by waves and tides are insignificant, except to those who live at the water's edge.

A fascinating example of a seismic sea wave generated by an above-water landslide is the Lituya Bay incident. Lituya Bay on the Alaska coast is an active earthquake region. Two glaciers flow into the upper end of the steep-sided bay; near its center is Cenotaph Island; a sandspit across the mouth keeps out the big waves from the Gulf of Alaska so that fishermen regard Anchorage Cove, just inside the entrance, as a safe haven.

On July 9, 1958, two fishing boats, the *Badger* and the *Sunmore*, were anchored just inside the spit when a major earthquake occurred. The shock started landslides which cleaned the soil and timber off the mountainsides at the upper end of the bay at eighteen hundred feet above sea level and at the same time caused great masses of ice to fall from the front of the glaciers into the water.

An eyewitness account by the skipper of the forty-foot *Badger* gives a vivid picture of the result. He felt the earthquake, and looking inland saw the first wave building at the head of the bay. As it passed Cenotaph Island he estimated its height at fifty feet (measurements made later indicated it probably was much higher). It swept through Anchorage Cove, carrying the *Badger* over the spit at an altitude of about a hundred feet and dropping it in the open sea. There the boat floundered, but the boatman was able to launch a skiff and he and his wife were picked up by another fishing boat. The fifty-five-foot *Sunmore* was not so fortunate; it was swept against a cliff and no trace of it or its crew was ever found.

This wave, although very high, was very localized. The somewhat unusual circumstance of its origin leads one to muse on the great waves that must have been generated in billions of years of geological time. One can visualize the walls of water that must have raced outward when whole mountains suddenly slid into the sea, or when a continental perimeter abruptly shifted, or when a great meteorite landed in the sea — a pebble in earth's puddle.

Watery Habitats

Sea water makes a good environment for living things of wondrous diversity. There are microscopic plankton, there are things that crawl, and things that crackle, there are soft things and there are fast things. They live in mud, in sand, they build coral houses, they are abroad at night. They are everywhere in the sea.

THE DOCK AT NIGHT
by Jack Rudloe

From his book The Living Dock at Panacea. *Rudloe is Brooklyn born and raised, but wanted a less-populated coastal edge and moved to the Florida panhandle, where he started up the Gulf Specimen Company, collecting for marine labs and teaching institutions. On the side, he has fought development of Florida's low-lying coastal stretches.*

⚓

NIGHT TIME IS WHEN THE LIGHT-SHY BRITTLESTARS COME WRITHING OUT OF THEIR HIDINGS and cover the sea bottoms, spreading their arms and waving them gently back and forth. Pink shrimp kick their legs and beat their pleopods and rise from the cushioning mud by the thousands to join the traffic of the night.

It is a restless period when animals are on the move. A sluggish batfish swims rapidly over the mud flat on its urgent business, the toadfish makes its high-pitched love call from its burrow, and silversides leave the marshes to swim in the open and feed upon the plankton blooms in the sea. The water is filled with fiery flashes of luminescence as tiny bits of plankton glow like blue fire when mullet or mackerel streak through the waters. During the summer the waters are hot and tepid and still by day, but they are alive and filled with creatures at night.

Anne and I were slowly carrying a large bulky wire trap down the dock. It didn't weigh much because it was made of hardware cloth and Styrofoam, but in the darkness its corners seemed to catch on every possible obstruction.

"You don't really think this thing's going to work, do you?" she asked, trying to dislodge it from under the railing.

"Why not? You can catch crabs and and lobsters in traps, and they're supposed to be more highly evolved than squid. Why not a squid trap?"

"Because squid are more intelligent than crabs. The brain of a cephalopod is more developed; they're not going to swim into this thing. If you ask me, it's a waste of time and money. How much did you have to pay Carlton Messer to build it?"

I hesitated, thought about lying, and then finally owned up to it: "About fifty dollars."

"Oh, good, we're already spent four hundred dollars on a light that doesn't work, and now we just paid another fifty for a trap that won't work either. We barely have money in the checking account to pay this month's utilities. Why don't we get out of the squid business before it puts us out of business?"

"It's worth a try, at least one more. If we can trap squid we may revolutionize the industry."

We arrived at the end of the dock and interrupted a great blue heron that had been sitting on the boat stall, spearing fish with its long bill. It rose into the air, giving an indignant squawk, and beat its wings into the darkness, hoarsely crying out its displeasure at human intruders. With the heron deposed from its perch, we began setting up the squid trap.

We lowered the bulky contraption into the water and switched on the light bulb that was suspended from the stationary dock by an electric cord, then maneuvered the large wire cage so that the glow of the light bulb would shine down squarely in the center of the trap and lashed the frame to the floating boat stall with ropes.

"Bad weather would tear it up this way," I explained, "but this is just a prototype. If it works, we'll build a good one."

When the trap was finally in place, the Styrofoam rim was bobbing just above the surface and the funnels were completely under the water. We made ourselves comfortable on one of the floating docks, preparing to watch the nightly show of life.

Sitting on the floating dock in the warm evening was pleasant. There was enough of a breeze that night to keep the gnats from eating us alive and there weren't any mosquitoes. Overhead the sky was beautiful, clear and filled with twinkling stars. We had the vastness of space above us, and the shallow sea below.

I had no sooner flicked on the light over the trap when a silverside, *Menidia*, swamp up to the trap, nudged the wire, and turned, leaving an empty watery void behind. I wasn't worried. It took time for creatures to come to the light. Soon the sea would be filled with life.

Downshore, against the black marshes, men and boys were carrying blazing gasoline lanterns, wading or poling small boats as they hunted for flounder. They followed the shoreline of the entire bay, illuminating the water in a most eerie fashion. Now and then we could see the silhouette of a body, or hear a distant voice calling or the knock of an oar against the side of a boat.

"They make the whole night seem enchanted," Anne said as the ghostly globes passed along the shore. "They really are beautiful."

There is more than beauty in floundering. It is a tradition that has grown over the years, a tradition of fishermen walking over miles and miles of tide flats in search of the elusive flatfish, which they catch with "gigs" or spears. It is one of the most primitive forms of fishing, perhaps dating back to man's first use of tools. Maybe floundering appeals to some atavistic memory in us that makes us feel the urge to stalk the flats as predator.

When the elliptical shape is outlined only slightly against the sandy bottom, food is in sight. A quick savage thrust of the spear, and the sand churns up from the frantic flouncing and beating of the fish. You can feel its fight, its strength and power, as the steel stake stabs through its flesh and the fish strives desperately to get away.

Unless you press your weight on the gig and pin the flounder solidly to the bottom, it may get away. But then you reach down, and your fingers feel its squirming, flat smooth body. You feel for its gills; your fingers touch its mouth, you feel the short sharp teeth and its gill rakers, and then you grab it, jerk it out of the water, flapping, and put it on your string.

At night as I walked out on the summer tide flats I often met other people floundering. Some did it for a livelihood, others for sport because it was a wonderful way to spend a night. In the little town of Panacea, where there is nothing much to do at night except watch the blue light of the television or hang around the convenience store, floundering is about the most popular recreation.

But our dock provided us with plenty of entertainment and over the years we had become more and more absorbed in the life around it. There were always things to see, whether it was pelagic creatures that drifted by the dock in the currents, such as jellyfish, or sea cucumbers that lived in the mud beneath the dock. There was life to explore on the pilings, life on the floating dock, and life even up above the dock: we could watch an osprey winging its way across the bay with a fish clenched in its talons. But at night the dock was most rewarding of all.

From the moment we flicked on the light, we heard mullet leaping and splashing in the water, and listened to the flurry of little fish and jumping shrimp. There were other sounds of night. From the water down below came the lonesome beeping call of the toadfish. Beneath the lights we watched the tide come in and go out and always there was something different. There might be a portunid crab swimming on the surface with one claw outstretched and the other folded against its shell while it paddled along with its rear swimming legs. Their aggressiveness was fantastic: they moved with confidence and power and energy, as if daring any fish to come bother them. The next night, or even a few hours later, there would be no portunid crabs to be found anywhere.

Or the night traffic might be full of anchovies and small eels and needlefish. And then a mad whirling dervish only a few millimeters in length would come spinning up to the surface. After watching it long enough, curiosity must be satisfied: swoop it up in your dip net and you'll be surprised to see that it's only a tiny white isopod. A parasitic isopod, it normally spends its life clinging to the scales or gills of a fish, but at night it can be found swimming freely, perhaps looking for a new host. It orients to the light and thereby finds new hosts that are also attracted to the light. The isopod has sharp little hooks that it embeds in your fingers, and it holds on for dear life until you pry it loose.

Then the dance of the sea cucumbers starts, and from down in the soft mud around the dock emerges *Leptosynapta crassipatina*. This glassy little sea cucumber is so slender, so delicate, and so agile as it bends and flexes in the vertical column of water that it is hard to believe it is even distantly related to the large lumpish holothurians that live in the mud bottom and move so sluggishly. *Leptosynapta* look like a worm in shape, but they are almost transparent, and somehow strangely beautiful as they sway and dance in the light. The current sweeps by and there may be hundreds of them, undulating, changing shapes, moving back and forth in the range of your eyes, and then they are gone. If you lay your dip net down before them, the water pressure forces it open and they will glide into the distended webbing. But when the net is lifted up, you may have to look very closely to spot them. In the water the wraith-like creatures are impressive and real, but when they are hauled out of their liquid domain they are nothing but a flaccid bit of jelly.

Some years *Leptosynapta* are so common that on any given summer night, hundreds of them can be seen looping around in the current. Other years they are scarce or completely non-existent. Perhaps they have some long-range cycle. To learn about it one would have to station oneself on the dock, year after year, recording all the various creatures that appear and disappear, and maybe after fifty years it might be possible to predict when *Leptosynapta* would have a "good year."

It seems that each year brings in an abundance of different animals that were either obscure or didn't exist the year before. One year the waters were filled with delicate pelagic nudibranchs, *Polycera hummi*, which float upside down on the surface film. I had never seen them before — they were so soft and small, and so blue in color — and I have never seen them since, although I learned that they were first reported in nearby Alligator Harbor twenty-five years earlier. There was the year of the transparent hydromedusae, *Aequorea*, and then there was the year of the acorn worms.

One summer season saw a population explosion of half beaks. They were everywhere, and even the most unobservant visitor to the dock was aware of them, with their long slender bodies and elongated needly lower jaw and cut-off upper jaw. This odd morphology enabled them to speed through water and feed upon plankton and small fish. That same season the water also swarmed with anchovies that glittered like diamonds as their scales caught and reflected the light.

But I think the most impressive year of all was the year of the Atlantic threadfins, *Polydactylus octonemus*. I can't recall ever having seen threadfins in the past — but maybe I had, as an obscure little brownish gray fish with whiskerlike barbells that came up in the shrimp nets.

Then one spring they came in, not by the hundreds but by the millions. They swarmed in a huge circle at night, in a frenzied swirling movement that looked like a living whirlpool, and they kept swimming and swimming and growing in numbers until the entire sea looked as if it were going to erupt like a volcano and spew out little fish all over the earth. Sitting there on the dock, I was enthralled by this sudden appearance of strange fish. I swooped my dip net among them and caught more than a hundred. I could have collected them by the thousands, had I wanted to.

They swirled so rapidly that I felt myself being hypnotized by them, caught up in their movements, drawn along into the sea of life. When I pressed the dip net through the school, they didn't dart off in a frenzy. The school merely parted and then rejoined; that is the way of a school, how it avoids predators. A school works by confusion, offering so much food at one time that a would-be attacker doesn't know which to strike first and lunges at every one and gets no one.

The threadfins bloomed, they took over; they dominated and far outnumbered every other creature in the bay. They were sucked into the intake of electrical-power generating systems and ended up in the pipes of the chemical companies down the coast, and for a while they were in every shrimp net. And then they were gone. They disappeared as suddenly and inexplicably as they had appeared, and not a single specimen has been seen since. If I didn't have a jar filled with preserved specimens to prove it, I might have thought the whole thing was a figment of my imagination. It was almost as if they had been created by spontaneous generation.

Anne was thoughtfully watching a sand eel undulating along in the water. For a moment it looked like a *Leptosynapta*, but it swam with fishlike determination right into the trap. But since it was so thin, it easily swam through the half-inch mesh wire on the other side and disappeared. Sometimes the bay was filled with leptocephalid eel larvae that were crystal clear, and only their shadows gave any hint of their presence. When we dipped them up and looked at them closely, the only visible part was a tiny pair of eyes.

There were other fish in the trap before long. Some larger minnows that swam in found themselves trapped and began banging into the steel wire. Some became gilled in the net, while others just swam around aimlessly looking for a way out. After the light had been on for an hour, there were tens of thousands of tiny larval fish inside the trap that had obviously swum through the wire mesh and were swimming around and around under the bulb in a dizzying circle.

They were swimming around horizontally, the way all fish swim, but in their midst were several small golden leather jackets standing vertically on their heads. The leather jacket appeared to be another small and insignificant fish of the night traffic but it had smooth golden skin and a mouthful of sharp teeth that resembled the jaws of a mackerel. Whenever we saw this fish at night it was standing on its head, suspended in the midst of a sweeping current. When I first saw one, I thought it was sick, but when I dipped it up and put it in a bucket, it righted itself and swam horizontally, but only for a moment.

I wondered about it for some time until I met an ichthyologist who was also puzzled by this strange behavior and wrote a paper about it. By watching this fish very carefully he learned that the leather jacket made its living in part by cleaning the parasites off other fish and this strange positioning served as a signal to others that cleaning service was available.

Larger fish, like the jacks and sheepshead and croakers, stood in line while the little golden leather jacket hovered about them, biting off their parasitic copepods and cleaning out funguses from their scales with its sharp little needly teeth. No fish was observed to strike at it, no fish even swam forward aggressively to investigate it. There was something different about the leather jacket; its shiny smooth coat, its bright eyes, its odd swimming behavior — all told the tale of the services that it provided in the marine community.

It was now eleven o'clock and there still was no sign of squid. But we sat there waiting patiently, just as we had night after night. Experience had taught us that just when we were about to call it a night and go home to bed, the waters would start teeming with squid. All during the summer we had been involved with them, dragging for squid with our shrimp nets, seining for them, and night lighting.

Squid have giant axons that delight neurophysiologists, who can easily insert electrodes into the nerve bodies and study the electrical impulses that are generated. Every year these scientists, their families, and graduate students move to Massachusetts to work at the Marine Biological Laboratory in Woods Hole. The laboratory charters a large vessel that goes out and drags for squid, keeps them in large vats of running sea water, and delivers them each day to the researchers.

Squid have always been considered difficult to keep alive for any length of time, and next to impossible to ship across the country. However, one customer from Canada had contracted us to provide him with routine shipments of living squid, and we rose to the challenge.

At first, we tried dragging for them in a small shrimp net that we pulled behind the tunnel boat in front of our dock and over the mud flats at the head of Dickerson Bay. Sometimes our nets passed through schools of squid that came into the shallows to feed on grass shrimp and minnows, and we filled our buckets with them. Other times, not even one squid could be found.

But it soon became obvious that trawling was not the best way to catch squid. Even though the little estuarine dwarf squid, *Lolliguncula brevis*, was considered one of the tougher species, they were often damaged or killed by the shrimp net. We did everything we could to keep them alive, hurriedly taking them out of the net, changing water every time they jetted out a cloud of ink, and packing them into individual plastic bags and charging them with oxygen right on the boat. But even then we lost squid. The pressure of the net swooping along the bottom and the compressions of fish, crabs, sponges, and other creatures were too much for them.

So we decided to try night lighting. Scientific literature is full of accounts of squid being attracted to light. When Anne had been diving offshore on the Florida Middlegrounds at night, on the university's oceanographic vessel, she described the beauty of hundreds of glittering squid with green eyes, hovering in the beam of her underwater light, beating their tail flukes and holding a tight formation. I had seen schools of squid attracted to the lights of our shrimp boat at night, far offshore.

Night lighting from the dock was easy enough. We hung a light bulb from a rope and suspended it above the water and waited to see what would happen. At first, nothing. A few fish appeared swimming in the current and a few isopods buzzed around. And then I began to think my eyes were playing tricks on me, because there were shadowy creatures out there that seemed to have no real substance. They were like spirits down there, shadows and wraiths. I was about to declare it part of my imagination, when I suddenly saw a pair of tiny pale green eyes flash among the shadows.

I swooped my dip net down with a hard splash and when I lifted it, I thought the net had caught nothing but a mass of clear ctenophore jellyfish that had been drifting by in the current. But at that same instant, I realized that no jellyfish behaved like that, spurting water, jumping, and squirting black ink. We had succeeded. We had captured over a dozen squid, ranging from one to three inches in length.

We hurried back to the lab and put them in one of our large concrete tanks, and watched them for hours. Almost immediately they grouped together in a tight school, all moving forward or backward at one time. It didn't take them long to get acclimated to the big tank. Since they weren't damaged in the least by collecting, we didn't have a single fatality.

If squid are to be kept alive they must be fed constantly. They will not touch dead food, and they are quite selective about their live food, but no squid can resist shrimp. I scooped up a net full of grass shrimp from the aquarium and dropped them in front of the squid. In a flash of a second, almost faster than the eye can see, the school advanced forward. One squid shot out its two longest tentacles and ensnared a shrimp. Then, turning it around, holding it firmly with its sucker discs while beating a holding pattern with its tail flukes, the squid chewed the shrimp up with its powerful parrotlike beak and swallowed it. We could actually see the bits and pieces of shrimp going down its translucent body.

Our client in Canada set up large aquariums to maintain his squid and to keep them fed. We seined the marshy creeks and ditches to provide him with ample grass shrimp. However, he found that keeping his charges fed proved to be a problem. The dwarf squid were insatiable; they practically ate their weight in shrimp each day.

Between night lighting for squid, and slogging through the marsh and seining the creeks to get grass shrimp by day, we were kept busy. Too busy, in fact, and that was why we were trying out the squid trap. I yawned loudly. We had spent the last three nights out on the dock, looking at the reflection of the light bulb, and we hadn't seen the first squid. We had stayed up as long as we could, but sooner or later we got tired and went home to bed, never knowing whether or not they showed up after we had left.

I watched a small flounder undulate its flattened body up from the depths and head toward the light. It brushed against the wire trap, turned, and swam off into the darkness. Ctenophore jellyfish, *Mnemiopsis macrydi*, being swept along in the current, also crashed into the wire, and illuminated the water with their brilliant blue bioluminescent flashes, and then were swept away. I was at my wits' end. We couldn't go on sitting on the dock night after night. My last attempt at improvising a quick and easy solution to catching squid had ended in an expensive failure.

About a month earlier, after having been sucked bloodless by mosquitoes and bitten to insanity by the annoying little sand gnats that swarmed in the air when the wind quit blowing and still not catching the first squid after two sleepless nights, it had occurred to me that there must be a better way. I was getting desperate. I was bumbling around in the mornings, too sleepy to do my work. Our customer, who was in the midst of his research, was desperate for more animals. I looked at the seventy-five-watt light bulb dangling from the dock over the water, and decided that if this little bit of light managed to sporadically catch squid, a great big floodlight should do an even better job. I would install a super light on the dock. Who knew, maybe it would attract all sorts of animals. There was only one way to find out. But the light I wanted — the type that illuminates football stadiums — was very expensive. I called our electrician, who estimated that it would run up into hundreds of dollars. Yet our customer was prepared to buy several thousand dollars' worth of squid. So I looked in our diminishing checking account, fretted, and decided to defer paying even the most essential bills so that we could go ahead with the lights. Always act positively.

The next day there was a big procession on my dock — men with spools of wire and a large pole and this huge light. It was 220 volts, with 1,250 watts of mercury-vapor light, guaranteed to light up the whole ocean. It should draw squid out of the Gulf of Mexico — who knew, maybe up from the Dry Tortugas! As they worked on tying it down and hooking up guy wires, they talked about its brightness. With a flick of a switch the blackest night could be turned into bright day. All day long I waited impatiently for nightfall. We were itching with anticipation.

At last darkness came, at the end of a very long day. Anne, Leon, Doug, Mary Ellen, Edward, and I walked down to the end of the dock to christen it. We looked up at the big metallic light shield that was reflecting the moonlight. The moment of truth was about to happen. With a flick of the switch the sun came on. The floating boat stalls were illuminated and the light burned down into the water. Fish began jumping and leaping out in the bay — veritable showers of them; and then there was silence and stillness.

We all waited, looking down into the water, but no fish showed up. For a moment we had seen fish around the dock, when the light came on so bright that it illuminated far down into the water. It gave more light than we had ever seen, even on the brightest, sunniest days. But then all the silvery bodies disappeared into the darkness. And there, beneath this bright burning globe that cost four hundred dollars, was a biological desert. There was empty water...not a living thing in it.

The fish didn't come up from the Dry Tortugas, and we didn't draw in whales and deep-sea squid from far out in the Gulf, and we certainly didn't draw in squid either. Everyone shook his head and I switched off the sun and darkness returned. Then fish started jumping and splashing all around, as if overjoyed to be rid of the unnatural brightness. Grimly I plugged in my little seventy-five-watt bulb, hung it over the water, and in a few minutes fish started to appear. Four hours later they were followed by a school of squid.

We dipped up all the squid we could, but luck wasn't running with us. The next morning we shipped them off, but instead of transferring in Atlanta they were shipped on to Chicago and delayed, and arrived stinking in Toronto.

Several days later I was sitting on the dock at three in the morning, trying to replace the order, and through my daze came an inspiration. Why not build a squid trap?

I had stayed up the rest of the night, sketching it out, designing it so the squid could swim through the four-foot-long flat funnels that would sit just below the surface. It would have to be big and deep, but it just might work.

It was now past midnight, and I was getting stiff sitting on the dock. The cool night air was seeping down into my bones and my skin felt cool and clammy. Inside the trap were thousands of tiny larval fish whirling in a mad dizzying circle, and small fish and blue crabs swam into the funnels, but still no squid. Perhaps this too was a failure, I thought. If it was, I didn't know what to do. I was on the verge of calling it off for the night, when Anne said suddenly, "Look...next to the piling...over there...squid, a bunch of them!"

Sure enough, just outside the illuminated water, I could see the flattened shadowy forms just below the surface. I could catch only the slightest glint of their green eyes. I couldn't tell how many there were, but there was certainly a school of squid about six feet away from the trap. They were hovering on the surface, beating their tail flukes and holding a tight formation as they watched the tiny minnows circling the center of the trap.

I reached for my dip net.

"Don't disturb them," Anne cautioned. "Let's just watch them for a while and see how they react to the trap."

"All right, but if they don't go into it pretty soon, I'm going to swoop them up," I said nervously. "We have to fill that order or we'll be in trouble.... Come on, squid, swim through the funnels. We have to pay for that dumb light!"

Then suddenly one of the squid raced forward and swam right through the funnel, and hovered there among the swirling fish. A second later I saw the shadowy forms of ten more squid bunched together in the very center of the trap.

"They'll swim out, I'll bet they will," said Anne. "No squid is going to be trapped like a mere blue crab."

But they didn't. They instantly realized that they were surrounded and they followed their normal instinct. They sounded to the bottom until they hit the wire floor. And there they stayed until we scooped them out with the dip net.

"Phooey," said Anne disgustedly. "I'm glad we figured out how to catch them. But who would have thought it. Squid sure went down in my estimation!"

I was afraid they might go into a frenzy and beat themselves against the wire and we would have damaged specimens that weren't fit to ship. But that wasn't the case.

Not a single squid managed to swim back out of the entrance funnels after they came in at night. However, we learned that if we didn't get them out of the trap immediately after the sun rose, they did manage to get their bearings and leave as a school. It was only the light burning down through the trap at night that kept them confined.

So we could now leave the light burning on the dock all night and catch squid while we slept. The only trouble was that during certain seasons there were no squid in the bays, and if the tides and the winds were wrong they were scarce, but both we and our squid customer had to accept that.

WINDS BLOWING SEAWARD
by Rachel L. Carson

From her book Under the Seawind. *Rachel Carson wrote four books, in order of publication:* Under the Seawind *(1941);* The Sea Around Us *(1951);* The Edge of the Sea *(1956); and* Silent Spring *(1962). Trained as a zoologist, she did a year of postgraduate work at Johns Hopkins University before joining the staff of the U.S. Fish and Wildlife Service. Under the Seawind was not a big seller (it came out just weeks before Pearl Harbor), but her next book,* The Sea Around Us, *did very well. Her last book,* Silent Spring, *covered an entirely different subject, and the insecticide business hasn't been the same since.*

THE NEXT MORNING the north wind was tearing the crests off the waves as they came over the inlet bar, so that each was trailing a heavy smoke of spray. Mullet were jumping in the channel, excited by the change in the wind. In the shallow river estuary and over the many shoals of the sound, the fish sensed the sudden chill that passed to the water from the air moving over it. The mullet began to seek the deeper waters which held the stored warmth of the sun. Now from all parts of the sound they were assembling in large schools that moved toward the channels of the sound. The channels led to the inlet, and the inlet was the gateway to the open sea.

The wind blew from the north. It blew down the river, and the fish moved before it to the estuary. It blew across the sound to the inlet, and the fish ran before it to the sea.

The ebbing tide carried the mullet through the deeper green glooms and over the white sandy bottom of the channel, scoured clean of living things by the strong currents that raced through it each day, twice running seaward, twice landward. Above them, as they moved, the surface of the water was broken into a thousand glittering facets that shone with the sun's gold. One after another the mullet rose to the shimmering ceiling of the sound. One after another they flexed their bodies in a quickening rhythm, gathering their strength and leaping into the air.

Going out with the tide the mullet passed a long, narrow sandspit called Herring Gull Shoal, where a wall of massive stone was built along the channel to prevent the washing in of the loose sand. Green, turgid fronds of seaweed were anchored by their holdfasts to the stones, which were crusted whitely with barnacles and oysters. From the shadow of one of the stones of the breakwater a pair of small, malignant eyes watched the mullet as they passed seaward. The eyes belonged to the fifteen-pound conger eel who lived among the rocks. The thick-bodied conger preyed on the schools of fish that roved down along the dark wall of the breakwater, hurling itself out of its gloomy cavern to seize them in its jaws.

In the upper layer of water, a dozen feet above the swimming mullet, schools of silversides quivered in formation, each fishlet a gleaming mote reflecting the sunlight. From time to time scores of them leaped out of the water, bursting through the surface film of the fish's world and falling back again like raindrops — first denting, then piercing the tough skin between air and water.

Past a dozen sandspits of the sound, each with its little colony of resting gulls, the tide took the mullet. On an old shell rock which the sea was in process of turning into an island by dropping silt and sand among the shells and by bringing, on its ebb tides, the seeds of marsh grasses to bind the soil, two gulls were hunting busily for sunray clams, which lay half buried in the wet sand. Finding them, the gulls chipped away at the heavy, vitreous shells, rayed with bands of fawn color and lilac. After much work with their strong bills the gulls were able to crack the shells and eat the soft clam bodies within.

On the mullet went, past the big inlet buoy that was leaning toward the sea with the press of the tide. Its iron bulk rose and fell with the water, even as the music of its iron throat changed pitch and tempo with the changing rhythms of the sea. The inlet buoy was a cosmos unto itself, rolling in the waters of the sound. Ebb tide and flood tide were of its own making, coming alternately as the buoy lifted to the passing of a wave and rolled in its trough.

The buoy had not been taken in for scraping and repainting since the previous spring, and it was thickly crusted with the shells of barnacles and mussels and with saclike sea squirts and the soft moss patches of the bryozoa. Deposits of sand and silt and green threads of algae had lodged in the many crevices between the shells and among the rootlike attachments of the dense mat of animals. Over and among this thick, living growth, slender-bodied animals called amphipods, in jointed armor, clambered in and out in endless search of food; starfish crept over the oysters and mussels and preyed upon them, gripping the shells with the sucking discs of their strong arms and forcing them open. Among the shells the flowerlets of the sea anemones opened and closed, spreading fleshy tentacles to seize food from the water. Most of the twenty or more kinds of sea animals that lived on the buoy had come to it months before, during the season when the waters of the sound and inlet swarmed with larvae. Many of these myriad beings, as transparent as glass and more fragile, were doomed to die in infancy unless they found a solid place of attachment. Those that chanced upon the great bulk of the buoy in the sound attached themselves by cementing fluids from their own bodies or by byssus thread or holdfast. There they would remain throughout life, a part of the swaying world, rolling in watery space.

Within the inlet the channel widened and the pale-green water grew murky with the wave scourings of loose sand. On the mullet went. The mutter and rumble of the surf grew. With their sensitive flanks the fish perceived the heavy jar and thud of sea vibrations. The changing pulse of the sea was caused by the long inlet bar, where the water foamed to a white froth as the waves spilled over it. Now the mullet passed out through the channel and felt the longer rhythms of the sea—the rise, the sudden lift and fall of waves come from the deep Atlantic. Just outside the first surf line the mullet leaped in these larger swells of ocean. One after another swam upward to the surface and jumped into the air, falling back with a white splash to resume its place in the moving school.

The lookout who stood on a high dune above the inlet saw the first of the mullet running out of the sound. With practiced eye, he estimated the size and speed of the school from the spurts of spray when the mullet jumped. Although three boats with their crews were waiting farther down the ocean beach, he gave no signal at the passing of the first mullet. The tide was still on the ebb; the pull of the water was seaward and the nets could not be drawn against it.

The dunes are a place of high winds and driven sand, of salt spray and sun. Now the wind is from the north. In the hollows of the dunes the beach grasses lean in the wind and with their pointed tips write endless circles in the sand. From the barrier beach the wind is picking up the loose sand and carrying it seaward in a haze of white. From a distance the air above the banks looks murky, as though a light mist is rising from the ground.

The fishermen on the banks do not see the sand haze; they feel its sting in eyes and face; they feel it as it sifts into their hair and through their clothing. They take out their handkerchiefs and tie them across their faces, and they pull long-visored caps low on their heads. A wind from the north means sand in your face and rough seas under your boat keel, but it means mullet, too.

The sun is hot as it beats down on the men standing on the beach. Some of the women and children are there, too, to help their men with the ropes. The children are bare-footed, wading in the pools left in the scoured-out depressions of the beach, ribbed with sand waves.

The tide has turned, and now one of the boats is shot out between the breakers to be ready for the fish when they come. It's not easy, launching a boat in this surf. The men leap to their places like parts of a machine. The boat rights itself, wallows into the green swells. Just outside the surf line the men wait at the oars. The captain stands in the bow, arms folded, leg muscles flexing to the rise and fall of the boat, his eyes on the water, looking toward the inlet.

Somewhere in that green water there are fish — hundreds of fish — thousands of fish. Soon they will come within reach of the nets. The north wind's blowing, and the mullet are running before it out of the sound, running down along the coast, as mullet have done for thousands upon thousands of years.

Half a dozen gulls are mewing above the water. That means the mullet are coming. The gulls don't want the mullet; they want the minnows that are milling about in alarm as the larger fish move through the shallows. The mullet are coming down just outside the breakers, traveling about as fast as a man could walk on the beach. The lookout has marked the school. He walks toward the boat, keeping opposite the fish, signaling their course to the crew by waving his arms.

The men brace their feet against the thwarts of the boat and strain to the oars, pulling the boat in a wide semicircle to the shore. The net of heavy twine spills silently and steadily into the water over the stern and cork floats bob in the water in the wake of the boat. Ropes from one end of the net are held by half a dozen men on shore.

There are mullet in the water all around the boat. They cut the surface with their back fins; they leap and fall. The men lean harder to the oars, pulling for the shore to close the net before the school can escape. Once in the last line of surf and in water not more than waist-deep, the men jump into the water. The boat is seized by willing hands and is dragged out on the beach.

The shallow water in which the mullet are swimming is a pale, translucent green, murky with the loose sand which the waves are stirring up. The mullet are excited by their return to the sea with its bitter salt waters. Under the powerful drive of instinct they move together in the first lap of a journey that will take them far from the coastal shallows, into the blue haze of the sea's beginnings.

A shadow looms in the green, sun-filled water in the path of the mullet. From a dim, gray curtain the shadow resolves itself into a web of slender, crisscross bars. The first of the mullet strike the net, back water with their fins, hesitate. Other fish are crowding up from behind, nosing at the net. As the first waves of panic pass from fish to fish they dash shoreward, seeking a way of escape. The ropes held by fishermen on the shore have been drawn in so that the netting wall extends into water too shallow for a fish to swim. They run seaward, but meet the circle of the net that is growing smaller, foot by foot, as the men on shore and in water up to their knees brace themselves in the sliding sand and pull on the ropes — pull against the weight of water — against the strength of the fish.

As the net is closed and gradually drawn in to shore, the press of fish in the seine becomes greater. Milling in frantic efforts to find a way of escape, the mullet drive with all their combined strength of thousands of pounds against the seaward arc of the net. Their weight and the outward thrust of their bodies lift the net clear of the bottom, and the mullet scrape bellies on the sand as they slip under the net and race into deep water. The fishermen, sensitive to every movement of the net, feel the lift and know they are losing fish. They strain the harder, till muscles crack and backs ache. Half a dozen men plunge out into water chin-deep, fighting the surf to tread the lead line and hold the net on the bottom. But the outer circle of cork floats is still half a dozen boat lengths away.

Of a sudden the whole school surges upward. In a turmoil of flying spray and splashing water mullet by the hundred leap over the cork line. They pelt against the fishermen, who turn their backs to the fish raining about them. The men strive desperately to lift the cork line above the water so that the fish will fall back into the circle when they strike the net.

Two piles of slack netting are growing on the beach, the heads of many small fishes no longer than a man's hand caught in the meshes. Now the ropes attached to the lead lines are drawn in faster and the net takes on the shape of a huge, elongated bag, bulging with fish. As the bag is drawn at last into the shallow fringe of the surf the air crackles with a sound like the clapping of hands as a thousand head of mullet, with all the fury of their last strength, flap on the wet sand.

The fishermen work quickly to take the mullet from the net and toss them into the waiting boats. By a dexterous shake of the net, they toss on the beach the small fish that are gilled in the seine. There are young sea trout and pompano, mullet of the last year's spawning, young ceros and sheepshead and sea bass.

Soon the bodies of the young fish — too small to sell, too small to eat — litter the beach above the water line, the life oozing from them for want of means to cross a few yards of dry sand and return to the sea. Some of the small bodies the sea would take away later; others it would lay up carefully beyond reach of the tides among the litter of sticks and seaweeds, of shells and sea-oats stubbles. Thus the sea unfailingly provides for the hunters of the tide lines.

After the fishermen had made two more hauls and then, as the tide neared the full, had gone away with laden boats, a flock of gulls came in from the outer shoals, white against the graying sea, and feasted on the fish. As the gulls bickered among themselves over the food, two smaller birds in sleek, black plumage walked warily among them, dragging fish up on the higher beach to devour them. They were fish crows, who took their living from the edge of the water, where they found dead crabs and shrimps and other sea refuse. After sundown the ghost crabs would come in legions out of their holes to swarm over the tide litter, clearing away the last traces of the fish. Already the sand hoppers had gathered and were busy at their work of reclaiming to life in their own beings the material of the fishes' bodies. For in the sea, nothing is lost. One dies, another lives, as the precious elements of life are passed on and on in endless chains.

All through the night, as the lights in the fishing village went out one by one and fishermen gathered around their stoves because of the chill north wind, mullet were passing unmolested through the inlet and running westward and southward along the coast, through black water on which the wave crests were like giant fish's wakes, silver in the light of the moon.

THE BOTTOM OF THE HARBOR
by Joseph Mitchell

From his book The Bottom of the Harbor. *Mitchell, a North Carolinian, wrote for* The New Yorker, *and he wrote extremely slowly; his entire output for the magazine consists of about thirty-five pieces, some collected in* McSorley's Wonderful Saloon. *The* Harbor *collection contains articles about a dragger captain from Stonington, Connnecticut, and the rats of the New York waterfront.*

What Mitchell wrote about New York Harbor fifty years ago mostly holds. The waters have improved some, but there are still putrid sections and seasons, the fish are still there, and people still hang around the waterfront to watch the harbor's magic. (Pantheon has just published a Mitchell anthology. Good Move.)

THE BULK OF THE WATER in New York Harbor is oily, dirty, and germy. Men on the mud suckers, the big harbor dredges, like to say that you could bottle it and sell it for poison. The bottom of the harbor is dirtier than the water. In most places, it is covered with a blanket of sludge that is composed of slit, sewage, industrial wastes, and clotted oil. The sludge is thickest in the slips along the Hudson, in the flats on the Jersey side of the Upper Bay, and in backwaters such as Newtown Creek, Wallabout Bay, and the Gowanus Canal. In such areas, where it isn't exposed to the full sweep of the tides, it accumulates rapidly. In Wallabout Bay, a nook in the East River that is part of the Brooklyn Navy Yard, it accumulates at the rate of a foot and a half a year. The sludge rots in warm weather and from it gas-filled bubbles as big as basketballs continually surge to the surface. Dredgemen call them "sludge bubbles." Occasionally, a bubble upsurges so furiously that it brings a mass of sludge along with it. In midsummer, here and there in the harbor, the rising and breaking of sludge bubbles makes the water seethe and spit. People sometimes stand on the coal and lumber quays that line the Gowanus Canal and stare at the black, bubbly water.

Nevertheless there is considerable marine life in the harbor water and on the harbor bottom. Under the paths of liners and tankers and ferries and tugs, fish school and oysters spawn and lobsters nest. There are clams on the sludgy bottom, and mussels and mud shrimp and conchs and crabs and sea worms and sea plants. Bedloe's Island, the Statue of Liberty island, is in a part of the harbor that is grossly polluted, but there is a sprinkling of soft-shell clams in the mud beneath the shallow water that surrounds it. The ebb of a spring tide always draws the water off a broad strip of this mud, and then flocks of gulls appear from all over the Upper Bay and light on it and thrash around and scratch for clams. They fly up with clams in their beaks and drop them on the concrete walk that runs along the top of the island's sea wall, and then they swoop down and pluck the meats out of the broken shells. Even in the Gowanus Canal, there are a few fish; the water is dead up at the head of it —only germs can live there—but from the crook at the Sixth Street Basin on down to the mouth there are cunners and tomcods and eels. The cunners nibble on the acorn barnacles on the piles under the old quays.

In the spring, summer, and fall, during the great coastwise and inshore and offshore migrations of fishes along the Middle Atlantic coast, at least three dozen species enter the harbor. Only a few members of some species show up. Every spring, a few long, jaggy-backed sea sturgeon show up. Every summer, in the Lower Bay, dragger nets bring up a few small, weird, brightly colored strays from southern waters, such as porcupine fish, scorpion fish, triggerfish, lookdowns, halfbeaks, hairtails, and goggle-eyed scad. Every fall, a few tuna show up. Other species show up in the hundreds of thousands or in the millions. Among these are shad, cod, whiting, porgy, blackback flounder, summer herring, alewife, sea bass, ling, mackerel, butterfish, and blackfish. Some years, one species, the mossbunker, shows up in the hundreds of millions. The mossbunker is a kind of herring that weighs around a pound when full-grown. It migrates in enormous schools and is caught in greater quantity than any other fish on the Atlantic Coast, but it is unfamiliar to the general public because it isn't a good table fish; it is too oily and bony. It is a factory fish; it is converted into an oil that is used in making soaps, paints, and printing inks (which is why some newspapers have a fishy smell on damp days), and into a meal that is fed to pigs and poultry. In the summer and fall, scores of schools of mossbunkers are hemmed in and caught in the Lower Bay, Sandy Hook Bay, and Raritan Bay by fleets of purse seiners with Negro crews that work out of little fishing ports in North Carolina, Virginia, Delaware, New Jersey, and Long Island and rove up and down the coast, following the schools.

The migratory fishes enter the harbor to spawn or to feed. Some mill around in the bays and river mouths for a few days and leave; some stay for months. Only one fish, the eel, is present in great numbers in all seasons. Eels are nocturnal scavengers, and they thrive in the harbor. They live on the bottom, and it makes no difference to them how deep or dirty it is. They live in ninety feet of water in the cable area of the Narrows and they live in a foot of water in tide ditches in the Staten Island marshes; they live in clean blue water in Sandy Hook Bay and they live around the outfalls of sewers in the East River. There are eight or nine hundred old hulks in the harbor. A few are out in the bays, deeply submerged, but most of them lie half sunk behind the pierhead line in the Jersey Flats and the flats along the Arthur Kill and the Kill van Kull — old scows and barges, old boxcar floats, old tugs, old ferryboats, old sidewheel excursion steamers, old sailing ships. They were towed into the flats and left to rot. They are full of holes; the water in the hulls of many of them rises and falls with the tides. Some are choked with sea lettuce and sea slime. In the summer, multitudes of eels lay up in the hulks during the day and wriggle out at night to feed. In the winter, they bed down in the hulks and hibernate. When they begin to hibernate, usually around the middle of December, they are at their best; they are fleshy then, and tender and sweet. At that time, Italian-Americans and German-Americans from every part of Staten Island go to certain old scows in the flats along the kills and spear so many eels that they bring them home in washtubs and potato sacks. The harbor eels — that is, the eels that live in the harbor the year round — are all males, or bucks. The females, or roes, until they become mature, live in rivers and creeks and ponds, up in fresh water. They become mature after they have spent from seven to thirteen years in fresh water. Every fall, thousands upon thousands of mature females run down the rivers that empty into the harbor — the Hudson, the Hackensack, the Passaic, the Elizabeth, the Rahway, and the Raritan. When they reach salt water, they lie still awhile and rest. They may rest for a few hours or a few days. Divers say that some days in October and November it is impossible to move about anywhere on the harbor bottom without stirring up throngs of big, fat, silver-bellied female eels. After resting, the females congregate with the mature harbor males, and they go out to sea together to spawn.

Hard-shell clams, or quahogs, the kind that appear on menus as littlenecks and cherrystones, are extraordinarily abundant in the harbor. Sanitary engineers classify the water in a number of stretches of the Lower Bay and Jamaica Bay as "moderately polluted." In these stretches, on thinly sludge-coated bottoms, under water that ranges in depth from one to thirty-five feet, are several vast, pullulating, mazy networks of hard-shell-clam beds. On some beds, the clams are crowded as tightly together as cobblestones. They are lovely clams — the inner lips of their shells have a lustrous violet border, and their meats are as pink and plump as rosebuds — but they are unsafe; they sometimes contain the germs of a variety of human diseases, among them bacillary and protozoal dysentery and typhoid fever, that they collect in their systems while straining nourishment out of the dirty water. The polluted beds have been condemned for over thirty years, and are guarded against poachers by the city Department of Health and the state Conservation Department. Quite a few people in waterfront neighbor-hoods in Staten Island, Brooklyn, and Queens have never been fully convinced that the clams are unsafe. On moonless nights and foggy days, they slip out, usually in rowboats, and raid the beds. In the course of a year, they take tons of clams. They eat them in chowders and stews, and they eat them raw. Every once in a while, whole families get horribly sick.

Just west of the mouth of the harbor, between Sandy Hook and the south shore of Staten Island, there is an area so out-of-the-way that anchorage grounds have long been set aside in it for ships and barges loaded with dynamite and other explosives. In this area, there are three small tracts of clean, sparkling, steel-blue water, about fifteen square miles in all. This is the only unpolluted water in the harbor. One tract of about five square miles, in Raritan Bay, belongs to the State of New York; the others, partly in Raritan Bay and partly in Sandy Hook Bay, belong to New Jersey. The bottoms of these tracts are free of sludge, and there are some uncontaminated hard-shell-clam beds on them. They are public beds; after taking out a license, residents of the state in whose waters they lie may harvest and sell clams from them. The New York beds are clammed by about a hundred and fifty Staten Islanders, most of whom live in or near the sleepy little south-shore ports of Prince's Bay and Great Kills. Some do seasonal work in shipyards, on fishing boats, or on truck farms, and clam in slack times, and some — thirty or so, mostly older men — clam steadily. They go out at dawn in sea skiffs and in rowboats equipped with outboard motors. When they reach the beds, they scatter widely and anchor. They lean over the sides of their boats and rake the bottom with clumsy rakes, called Shinnecock rakes, that have twenty-four-foot handles and long, in-turned teeth. Last year, they raked up eighteen thousand bushels. A soup factory in New Jersey bought about half of these, and the rest went to fish stores and hotels and restaurants, mainly in New York City. Every New Yorker who frequently eats clams on the half shell has most likely eaten at least a few that came out of the harbor.

In Dutch and English days, immense beds of oysters grew in the harbor. They bordered the shores of Brooklyn and Queens, and they encircled Manhattan, Staten Island, and the islands in the Upper Bay; to the Dutch, Ellis Island was Oyster Island and Bedloe's Island was Great Oyster Island. One chain of beds extended from Sandy Hook straight across the harbor and up the Hudson to Ossining. The Dutch and the English were, as they still are, gluttonous oyster eaters. By the end of the eighteenth century, all but the deepest of the beds had been stripped. Oysters, until then among the cheapest of foods, gradually became expensive. In the eighteen-twenties, a group of Staten Island shipowners began to buy immature oysters by the schooner load in other localities and bring them to New York and bed them in the harbor until they got their growth, when they were tonged up and shipped to the wholesale oyster market in Manhattan, to cities in the Middle West, and to London, where they were prized. This business was known as bedding. The bedders obtained most of their seed stock in Chesapeake Bay and in several New Jersey and Long Island bays. Some bought three-year-olds and put them down for only six or seven months, and some bought younger oysters and put them down for longer periods. At first, the bedders used the shoals in the Kill van Kull, but by and by they found that the best bottoms lay along the seaward side of Staten Island, in the Lower Bay and Raritan Bay. Back then, the inshore water in these bays was rich in diatoms and protozoa, the tiny plants and animals on which oysters feed. Spread out in this water, on clean bottoms, at depths averaging around thirteen feet, oysters matured and fattened much faster than they did crowded together on their shell-cluttered spawning grounds; a thousand bushels of three-year-olds from Chesapeake Bay, put down in April in a favorable season, might amount to fourteen hundred bushels when taken up in October. Bedding was highly profitable in good years and many fortunes were made in it. It was dominated by old-settler Staten Island families — the Tottens, the Winants, the De Harts, the Deckers, the Manees, the Mersereaus, the Van Wyks, the Van Duzers, the Latourettes, the Housmans, the Bedells, and the Depews. It lasted for almost a century, during which, at one time or another, five Staten Island ports — Mariner's Harbor, Port Richmond, Great Kills, Prince's Bay, and Tottenville — had oyster docks and fleets of schooners, sloops, and tonging skiffs. Prince's Bay had the biggest fleet and the longest period of prosperity; on menus in New York and London, harbor oysters were often called Prince's Bays. Approximately nine thousand acres of harbor bottom, split up into plots varying from a fraction of an acre to four hundred acres, were used for beds. The plots were leased from the state and were staked with a forest of hemlock poles; nowadays, in deepening and widening Ambrose Channel, Chapel Hills Channel, Swash Channel, and other ship channels in the Lower Bay, dredges occasionally dig up the tube-worm-incrusted stumps of old boundary poles. Bedding was most prosperous in the thirty years between 1860 and 1890. In good years in that period, as many as fifteen hundred men were employed on the beds and as many as five hundred thousand bushels of oysters were marketed. Some years, as much as a third of the crop was shipped to Billingsgate, the London fish market. For a while, the principal bedders were the richest men on Staten Island. They put their money in waterfront real estate, they named streets after themselves, and they built big, showy wooden mansions. A half dozen of these mansions still stand in a blighted neighborhood in Mariner's Harbor, in among refineries and coal tipples and junk yards. One has a widow's walk, two have tall fluted columns, all have oddly shaped gables, and all are decorated with scroll-saw work. They overlook one of the oiliest and gummiest stretches of the Kill van

Kull. On the south shore, in the sassafras barrens west of Prince's Bay, there are three more of these mansions, all empty. Their fanlights are broken, their shutters swag, and their yards are a tangle of weeds and vines and overturned birdbaths and dead pear trees.

After 1900, as more and more of the harbor became polluted, people began to grow suspicious of harbor oysters, and the bedding business declined. In the summer of 1916, a number of cases of typhoid fever were traced beyond all doubt to the eating of oysters that had been bedded on West Bank Shoal, in the Lower Bay, and it was found that sewage from a huge New Jersey trunk sewer whose outfall is at the confluence of the Kill van Kull and the Upper Bay was being swept through the Narrows and over the beds by the tides. The Department of Health thereupon condemned the beds and banned the business. The bedders were allowed to take up the oysters they had down and rebed them in clean water in various Long Island bays. They didn't get them all, of course. A few were missed and left behind on every bed. Some of these propagated, and now their descendants are sprinkled over shoaly areas in all the bays below the Narrows. They are found on West Bank Shoal, East Bank Shoal, Old Orchard Shoal. Round Shoal, Flynns Knoll, and Romer Shoal. They live in clumps and patches; a clump may have several dozen oysters in it and a patch may have several hundred. Divers and dredgemen call them wild oysters. It is against state and city laws to "dig, rake, tong, or otherwise remove" these oysters from the water. A few elderly men who once were bedders are still living in the old Staten Island oyster ports, and many sons and grandsons of bedders. They have a proprietary feeling about harbor oysters, and every so often, in cold weather, despite the laws, some of them go out to the old, ruined beds and poach a mess. They know what they are doing; they watch the temperature of the water to make sure that the oysters are "sleeping," or hibernating, before they eat any. Oysters shut their shells and quit feeding and begin to hibernate when the temperature of the water in which they lie goes down to forty-one degrees; in three or four days, they free themselves of whatever germs they may have taken in, and then they are clean and safe.

There is a physician in his late fifties in St. George whose father and grandfather were bedders. On a wall of his waiting room hangs an heirloom, a chart of oyster plots on West Bank Shoal that was made in 1886 by a marine surveyor for the state; it is wrinkled and finger-smudged and saltwater-spotted, and his grandfather's plot, which later became his father's — a hundred and two acres on the outer rim of the shoal, down below Swinburne Island — is bounded on it in red ink. The physician keeps a sea skiff in one of the south-shore ports and goes fishing every decent Sunday. He stores a pair of pole-handled tongs in the skiff and sometimes spends a couple of hours hunting for clumps of harbor oysters. One foggy Sunday afternoon last March, he got in his skiff, with a companion, and remarked to the people on the dock that he was going codfishing on the Scallop Ridge, off Rockaway Beach. Instead, picking his way through the fog, he went to the West Bank and dropped anchor on one of his father's old beds and began tonging. He made over two dozen grabs and moved the skiff four times before he located a clump. It was a big clump, and he tonged up all the oysters in it; there were exactly sixty. All were mature, all were speckled with little holes made by boring sponges, and all were wedge-shaped. Sea hair, a marine weed, grew thickly on their shells. One was much bigger than the others, and the physician picked it up and smoothed aside its mat of coarse, black, curly sea hair and counted the ridges on its upper shell and said that it was at least fourteen years old. "It's too big to eat on the half shell," he told his companion. He bent over the gunnel of the skiff and gently put it back in the water. Then he selected a dozen that ranged in age from four to seven years and opened them. Their meats were well developed and gray green and glossy. He ate one with relish. "Every time I eat harbor oyster," he said, "my childhood comes floating up from the bottom of my mind." He reflected for a few moments. "They have a high iodine content," he continued, "and they have a characteristic taste. When I was a boy in Prince's Bay, the old bedders used to say that they tasted like almonds. Since the water went bad, that taste has become more pronounced. It's become coppery and bitter. If you've ever tasted the little nut that's inside the pit of a peach, the kernel, that's how they taste."

The fish and shellfish in the harbor and in the ocean just outside provide all or part of a living for about fifteen hundred men who call themselves baymen. They work out of bays and inlets and inlets within inlets along the coasts of Staten Island, Brooklyn, and Queens. Some baymen clam on the public beds. Some baymen set eelpots. Some baymen set pound nets, or fish traps. Pound nets are strung from labyrinths of stakes in shoal areas, out of the way of the harbor traffic. Last year, during the shad, summer herring, and mossbunker migrations, forty-one of them were set off the Staten Island coast between Midland Beach and Great Kills, in an old oyster-bedding area. Some baymen go out in draggers, or small trawlers, of which there are two fleets in the harbor. One fleet has sixteen boats, and ties up at two shaky piers on Plumb Beach Channel, an inlet just east of Sheepshead Bay, on the Brooklyn coast. The other has nine boats, and ties up alongside a quay on the west branch of Mill Basin, a three-branched inlet in the bulrush marshes in the Flatlands neighborhood of Brooklyn. The majority of the men in both fleets are Italian-Americans, a few of whom in their youth fished out of the Sicilian ports of Palermo and Castellammare del Golfo. Some of them tack saints' pictures and miraculous medals and scapular medals and little evil-eye amulets on the walls of their pilothouses. The amulets are in the shape of hunchbacks, goat horns, fists with two fingers upraised, and opened scissors; they come from stores on Mulberry Street and are made of plastic. The harbor draggers range from thirty to fifty feet and carry two to five men. According to the weather and the season, they drag their baglike nets in the Lower Bay or in a fishing ground called the Mud Hole, which lies south of Scotland and Ambrose lightships and is about fifteen miles long and five to ten miles wide. The Mud Hole is the upper part of the Old Hudson River Canyon, which was the bed of the river twenty thousand years ago, when the river flowed a hundred and twenty-five miles past what is now Sandy Hook before it reached the ocean. The draggers catch lower-depth and bottom feeders, chiefly whiting, butterfish, ling, cod, porgy, fluke, and flounder. They go out around 4 A.M. and return around 4 P.M., and their catches are picked up by trucks and taken to Fulton Market.

Some baymen set lines of lobster pots. In days gone by, there was a bountiful stock of lobsters in the harbor. Be tween 1915 and 1920, owing to pollution and overfishing and the bootlegging of berries, which are egg-carrying lobsters, and shorts and crickets, which are undersized lobsters, the stock began dwindling at a rapid rate. As late as 1920, forty-five lobstermen were still working the Upper Bay, the Narrows, and the Lower Bay. They ran out of seven inlets in Brooklyn and Staten Island, and their buoys dipped and danced all the way from the Statue of Liberty to the Hook.

Every year in the twenties, a few of them either dropped out for good or bought bigger boats and forsook the bays and started setting pots out beyond the three-mile limit, in the harbor approaches. By 1930, only one lobsterman of any importance, Sandy Cuthbert, of Prince's Bay, continued to work the bays. In the fall of that year, at the close of the season, Mr. Cuthbert took up his pots — he had two hundred and fifty — and stacked them on the bank of Lemon Creek, an inlet of Prince's Bay, and went into the rowboat-renting and fish-bait business. His pots are still there, rotting; generations of morning-glory and wild-hop vines are raveled in their slats and hold them together. During the thirties and forties, the lobsters began coming back, and divers say that now there are quite a few nests in the Upper Bay and many nests in the Lower Bay. However, they are still too scarce and scattered to be profitable. Sometimes, while repairing cables or pipelines on the bottom in parts of the Lower Bay where the water is clear and the visibility is good, divers turn over rocks and pieces of waterlogged driftwood and lobsters scuttle out and the divers pick them up and put them in the tool sacks hooked to their belts.

At present, there are nine lobster boats working out of the harbor — six out of Plumb Beach; two out of Ulmer Park, on Gravesend Bay; and one out of Coney Island Creek. They are of the sea-skiff type. They range from twenty-six to twenty-eight feet, they are equipped with gasoline engines that are strong enough for much bigger boats, and, except for canvas spray hoods, they are open to the weather. The men on these boats are Scandinavians and Italians. They set their pots in a section of the Mud Hole southeast of Ambrose lightship where the water in most places is over a hundred feet deep. They use the trawl method, in which the pots are hung at intervals from thick, tarred lines half a mile long; as a rule, thirty-five pots are hung from each line. The lines are buoyed at both ends with bundles of old, discarded ferryboat life preservers, which the lobstermen buy from a ship chandler in Fulton Market, who buys them from the Department of Marine and Aviation. Once a day, the lines are lifted, and each pot is pulled up and emptied of lobsters and chewed-up bait and stray crabs and fish, and rebaited with three or four dead mossbunkers. The coastwise and South American shipping lanes cross the lobster grounds in the Mud Hole, and every now and then a ship plows into a line and tears it loose from its buoys. Dump scows with rubbish from the city sometimes unload on the grounds and foul the lines and bury the pots. Mud Hole lobsters are as good as Maine lobsters; they can't be told apart. Some are sold to knowledgeable Brooklyn housewives who drive down to the piers in the middle of the afternoon, when the boats come in, and take their pick, but most are sold to Brooklyn restaurants. A boat working seven lines, which is the average, often comes in with around two hundred and fifty pounds.

A good many baymen work on public fishing boats that take sports fishermen out to fishing grounds in the harbor, in the harbor approaches, and along the Jersey coast. These boats are of two types — charter and party. Charter boats are cabin cruisers that may be hired on a daily or weekly basis. They are used for going after roaming surface feeders, big and small. Most of them are equipped with fighting chairs, fish hoists, and other contrivances for big-game fishing. They go out in the Lower Bay, Sandy Hook Bay, and Raritan Bay for striped bass, bluefish, and mackerel, and they go out to the Mud Hole and the Jersey grounds for tuna, albacore, bonito, and skipjack. They carry a captain and a mate, who baits and gaffs. Great Kills, which has fifteen boats, and Prince's Bay, which has eight, are the principal charter-boat ports in the harbor.

Party boats, also called open boats, are bigger boats, which operate on regular schedules and are open to anyone who has the fare; it varies from three and a half to five dollars a day. Sheepshead Bay is the principal party-boat port. It has over fifty boats. All of them leave from Emmons Avenue, which many people consider the most attractive waterfront street in the city. Emmons is a wide street, with a row of fluttery-leaved plane trees down the middle of it, that runs along the north shore of the bay. It smells of the sea, and of beer and broiled fish. On one side of it, for a dozen blocks, are bar-and-grills, seafood restaurants, clam stands, diners, pizza parlors, tackle and boat-gear stores, and fish markets, one of which has a cynical sign in its show window that says, "Catch your fish on the never-fail banks. Use a silver hook." The party-boat piers — there are ten of them, and they are long and roomy — jut out diagonally from the other side. Retired men from all over Brooklyn come down to the piers by bus and subway on sunny days and sit on the stringpieces and watch the boats go out, and rejuvenate their lungs with the brine in the air, and fish for blue-claw crabs with collapsible wirework traps, and quarrel with each other over the gulls; some bring paper bags of table scraps from home and feed the gulls and coo at them, and some despise the gulls and shoo them away and would wring their necks if they could get their hands on them. Among the boats in the Sheepshead Bay fleet are stripped-down draggers, converted yachts, and converted subchasers from both world wars. The majority carry a captain and a mate and take around thirty passengers; the old subchasers carry a captain, a mate, an engineer, a cook, and a deckhand and take up to a hundred and ten passengers. Some have battered iceboxes on their decks and sell beer and pop and sandwiches, and some have galleys and sell hot meals. Some have conventional fishing-boat names, such as the *Sea Pigeon*, the *Dorothy B,* and the *Carrie D II*, and some have strutty names, such as the *Atomic*, the *Rocket*, and the *Glory*. Most of them leave at 5, 6, 7, 8, 9, or 10 A.M. and stay out the better part of the day. The passengers bring their own tackle, and fish over the rails. Bait is supplied by the boats; it is included in the fare. In most seasons, for most species, shucked and cut-up skimmer clams are used. These are big, coarse, golden-meated ocean clams. Cut-up fish, live fish, fiddler crabs, calico crabs, sand worms, and blood worms are also used. There are two dozen baymen in Sheepshead Bay who dig, dredge, net, and trap bait. They deliver it to three bait barges moored in the bay, and the bargekeepers put it into shape and sell it to the party boats by the tubful. For five weeks or so in the spring and for five weeks or so in the fall, during the mackerel migrations, the party boats go out and find schools of mackerel and anchor in the midst of them. The rest of the year, they go out and anchor over wrecks, reefs, scow dumps, and shellfish beds, where cod, ling, porgy, fluke, flounder, sea bass, blackfish, and other bottom feeders congregate.

There are many wrecks — maybe a hundred, may be twice that; no one knows how many — lying on the bottom in the harbor approaches. Some are intact and some are broken up. Some are out in the Old Hudson River Canyon, with over two hundred feet of water on top of them. Some are close to shore, in depths of only twenty to thirty feet; around noon, on unusually clear, sunny fall days, when there is not much plankton in the water and the turbidity is low, it is possible to see these and see schools of sea bass streaming in and out of holes in their hulls. The wrecks furnish shelter for fish. Further-more, they are coated, inside and out, with a lush, furry growth made up of algae, sea moss, tube worms, barnacles, horse mussels, sea anemones, sea squirts, sea mice, sea snails, and scores of other organisms, all of which are food for fish. The most popular party boats are those whose captains can locate the fishiest wrecks and bridle them. Bridling is a maneuver in which, say the wreck lies north and south, the party boat goes in athwart it and drops one anchor to the east of it and another to the west of it, so that party boat and wreck lie crisscross. Held thus, the party boat can't be skewed about by the wind and tide, and the passengers fishing over both rails can always be sure that they are dropping their bait on the wreck, or inside it. Good party-boat captains, by taking bearings on landmarks and lightships and buoys, can locate and bridle anywhere from ten to thirty wrecks. A number of the wrecks are quite old; they disintegrate slowly. Three old ones, all sailing ships, lie close to each other near the riprap jetty at Rockaway Point, in the mouth of the harbor. The oldest of the three, the *Black Warrior* Wreck, which shelters tons of sea bass from June until Novem-ber, went down in 1859. The name of the next oldest has been forgotten and she is called the Snow Wreck; a snow is a kind of square-rigged ship similar to a brig; she sank in 1886 or 1887. The third one is an Italian ship that sank in 1890 with a cargo of marble slabs; her name has also been forgotten and she is called the Tombstone Wreck, the Granite Wreck, or the Italian Wreck. Over to the east, off the Rockaways, there is another group of old ones. In this group, all within five miles of shore, are the steamship *Iberia*, which sank in a snowstorm in 1889, after colliding with the steamship *Umbria*; the Wire Wreck, a sailing ship that sank around 1895 while outbound with a cargo of bedsprings and other wire products; the *Boyle* Wreck, a tug that sank around 1900; and the East Wreck, three coal barges that snapped their tow in a storm in 1917 and settled on the bottom in an equilateral triangle. Several of these wrecks have been fished steadily for generations, and party-boat captains like to say that they would be worth salvaging just to get the metal in the hooks and sinkers that have been snagged on them.

There are stretches of reefy bottom in the harbor approaches that are almost as productive of fish as the wrecks, and for the same reasons. These stretches are easier to locate than the wrecks, and much easier to fish. All have been named. Some are natural rock ledges, and among these are the Shrewsbury Rocks, the Buoy Four Grounds, the Cholera Bank, the Klondike Banks, the Seventeen Fathoms, and the Farms. Some are artificial ledges, consisting of debris from excavations and torn-down buildings that was transported from the city in scows and dumped. One such is the Subway Rocks, a ridge of underwater hills beginning four miles south of Ambrose lightship and running south for several miles, that was made of rocks, bricks, concrete, asphalt, and earth excavated during the construction of the Eighth Avenue Subway. Another such is the New Grounds, or Doorknob Grounds, a stretch of bottom in the northwest corner of the Mud Hole that is used as a dump for slum-clearance projects. There are bricks and brownstone blocks and plaster and broken glass from hundreds upon hundreds of condemned tenements in the New Grounds. The ruins of the somber old red-brick houses in the Lung Block, which were torn down to make way for Knickerbocker Village, lie there. In the first half of the nineteenth century, these houses were occupied by well-to-do families; from around 1890 until around 1905, most of them were brothels for sailors; from around 1905 until they were torn down, in 1933, they were rented to the poorest of the poor, and the tuberculosis death rate was higher in that block than in any other block in the city. All the organisms that grow on wrecks grow on the hills of rubble and rubbish in the Subway Rocks and the New Grounds.

The comings and goings of the baymen are watched by a member of the staff of the Bureau of Marine Fisheries of the State

Conservation Department. His name is Andrew E. Zimmer, his title is Shellfish Protector, and his job is to enforce the conservation laws relating to marine shellfish and finfish. Mr. Zimmer is a Staten Islander of German descent. He is muscular and barrel-chested and a bit above medium height. He is bald and he is getting jowly. The department issues him a uniform that closely resembles a state trooper's uniform, but he seldom wears it. On duty, he wears old, knockabout clothes, the same as a bayman. He carries a pair of binoculars and a .38 revolver. He is called Happy Zimmer by the baymen, some of whom grew up with him. He is a serious man, a good many things puzzle him, and he usually has a preoccupied look on his face; his nickname dates from boyhood and he has outgrown it. He was born in 1901 on a farm in New Springville, a truck-farming community on the inland edge of the tide marshes that lie along the Arthur Kill, on the western side of Staten Island. In the front yard of the farmhouse, his father ran a combined saloon and German home-cooking restaurant, named Zimmer's, that attracted people from the villages around and about and from some of the Jersey towns across the kill. Picnics and clambakes and lodge outings were held in a willow grove on the farm. His father had been a vaudeville ventriloquist, and often performed at these affairs. Specialties of the restaurant were jellied eels, clam broth with butter in it, and pear conchs from the Lower Bay boiled and then pickled in a mixture of vinegar and spices and herbs. As a boy, Mr. Zimmer supplied the restaurant with eels he speared in eel holes in the marshes and with soft-shell clams that he dug in the flats along the kill. Until 1916, when the harbor beds were condemned, Prince's Bay oysters were sold from the barrel in the saloon side of the restaurant. Friday afternoons, he and his father would drive down to the Oyster Dock in Prince's Bay in the farm wagon and bring back three or four barrels of selects for the week-end trade. In 1915, after completing the eighth grade, Mr. Zimmer quit school to help his father in the restaurant. In 1924, he took charge of it. In his spare time, mainly by observation in the marshes, he became a good amateur naturalist. In 1930, he gave up the restaurant and went to work for the Conservation Department.

Mr. Zimmer patrols the harbor in a lumbering, rumbly old twenty-eight-foot sea skiff. It has no flag or markings and looks like any old lobster boat, but the baymen can spot it from a distance; they call it the State Boat. Some of Mr. Zimmer's duties are seasonal. From March 15th to June 15th, when pound-netting is allowed, he makes frequent visits to the nets at pull-up time and sees to it that the fishermen are keeping only the species they are licensed for. When the mossbunker seiners come into the harbor, he boards them and looks into their holds and satisfies himself that they are not taking food fishes along with the mossbunkers. Now and then during the lobstering season, he draws up alongside the lobster boats inbound from the grounds and inspects their catches for shorts. Several times a year, he bottles samples of the water in various parts of the harbor and sends them to the department's laboratory. His principal year-round duty is to patrol the shellfish beds. He runs down and arrests poachers on the polluted beds, and he keeps an eye on the clammers who work the legal beds in Raritan Bay. It is against the law to do any kind of clamming between sundown and sunup, and he spends many nights out on the beds. He is a self-sufficient man. He can anchor his skiff in the shadow of a cattail hassock in Jamaica Bay and, without ever getting especially bored, sit there the whole night through with an old blanket over his shoulders, listening and watching for poachers and looking at the stars and the off-and-on lights on airplanes and drinking coffee out of a thermos jug. The legal beds in New Jersey territory in the harbor have been over-worked and are not as fertile as the legal beds in New York territory. In recent years, allured by high clams prices, some of the Jersey clammers have become pirates. They tantalize Mr. Zimmer. On dark nights, using Chris Craft cruisers, they cross the state line, which bisects Raritan Bay, and poach on the New York beds. When they hear the rumble of Mr. Zimmer's skiff, they flee for Jersey. Mr. Zimmer opens his throttle and goes after them, shouting at them to halt and sometimes firing his revolver over their heads, but their cruisers draw less water than his skiff and at the end of the chase they are usually able to shoot up into one of the shallow tide creeks between South Amboy and the Hook and lose him. Mr. Zimmer keeps his skiff in Prince's Bay. Prince's Bay has gone down as a port since his boyhood. Not a trace of the oyster-bedding business is left there. It has a clam dock, a charter-boat pier, and two boatyards, and it has Sandy Cuthbert's rowboat livery and bait station, but its chief source of income is a factory that makes tools for dentists; the factory is on Dental Avenue. The old Prince's Bay Lighthouse still stands on a bluff above the village, but it is now a part of Mount Loretto, a Catholic home for children; it is used as a residence by the Monsignor and priests who run the home. The light has been taken down and supplanted by a life-size statue of the Virgin Mary. The Virgin's back is to the sea.

Once in a while, Mr. Zimmer spends a day patrolling the Staten Island tide marshes on foot. He feels drawn to the marshes and enjoys this part of his job most of all. A good many people wander about in the marshes and in the meadows and little woods with which they are studded. He is acquainted with scores of marsh wanderers. In the fall, old Italians come and get down on all fours and scrabble in the leaves and rot beneath the blackjack oaks, hunting for mushrooms. In the spring, they come again and pick dandelion sprouts for salads. In midsummer, they come again, this time with scap nets, and scoop tiny mud shrimp out of the tide ditches; they use them in a fried fish-and-shellfish dish called *frittura di pesce*. On summer afternoons, old women from the south-shore villages come to the fringes of the marshes. They pick herbs, they pick wild flowers, they pick wild grapes for jelly, and in the fresh-water creeks that empty into the salt-water creeks they pick watercress. In the fall, truck farmers come with scythes and cut salt hay. When the hay dries, they pack it around their cold frames to keep the frost out. Bird watchers and Indian-relic collectors come in all seasons. The relic collectors sift the mud on the banks of the tide ditches. Mr. Zimmer himself sometimes finds arrowheads and stone net-sinkers on the ditchbanks. Once, he found several old English coins. In September or October, the rabbis and elders come. On Hoshanna Rabbah, the seventh day of the Festival of Succoth, an ancient fertility rite is still observed in a number of orthodox synagogues in the city. The worshipers who take part in the rite are given bunches of willow twigs; each bunch has seven twigs and each twig has seven leaves. After marching in procession seven times around the altar, chanting a litany, the worshipers shake the bunches or strike them against the altar until the leaves fall to the floor. The twigs must be cut from willows that grow beside water, the buds on the ends of the twigs must be unblemished, and the leaves must be green and flawless. For generations, most of the willow bunches have come from black willows and weeping willows in the Staten Island tide marshes.. In the two or three days preceding Hoshanna Rabbah — it usually falls in the last week of September or the first or second week of October — rabbis and trusted elders go up and down the ditchbanks, most often in pairs, the rabbi scrutinizing twigs and cutting those that pass the test, and the elder trimming and bunching them and stowing them gently in brown-paper shopping bags.

There is much resident and migratory wildlife in the marshes. The most plentiful resident species are pheasants, crows, marsh hawks, black snakes, muskrats, opossums, rabbits, rats, and field mice. There is no open season on the pheasants, and they have become so bold that the truck farmers look upon them as pests. One can walk through the pokeweed and sumac and blue-bent grass on any of the meadow islands at any time and put up pair after pair of pheasants. At the head of a snaky creek in one of the loneliest of the marshes, there is an old rickamarack of a dock that was built by rumrunners during Prohibition. One morning, hiding behind this dock, waiting for some soft-shell-clam poachers to appear, Mr. Zimmer saw a hen pheasant walk across a strip of tide flat, followed by a brood of seventeen. At times, out in the marshes, Mr. Zimmer be comes depressed. The marshes are doomed. The city has began to dump garbage on them. It has already filled in hundreds of acres with garbage. Eventually, it will fill in the whole area, and then the Department of Parks will undoubtedly build some proper parks out there and put in some concrete highways and scatter some concrete benches about. The old south-shore secessionists — they want Staten Island to secede from New York and join New Jersey, and there are many of them — can sit on these benches and meditate and store up bile.

Mr. Zimmer is a friend of mine, and I sometimes go out on patrols with him. One cold, windy, spitty morning, we made a patrol of the polluted skimmer-clam beds in the ocean off Rockaway Beach. On the way back to Staten Island, he suggested that we stop in Sheepshead Bay and get some oyster stew to warm us up. We turned in to the bay and tied the skiff to the Harbor Police float and went across the street to Lundy's, the biggest and best of the Emmons Avenue seafood restaurants. We went into the oyster-bar side and took a table, and each of us ordered a double stew. Mr. Zimer caught sight of a bayman named Leroy Poole, who was standing at the bar, bent over some oysters on the half shell. Mr. Poole is captain and owner of the party boat *Chinquapin*. Mr. Zimmer went over to the bar, and he and Mr. Poole shook hands and talked for a minute or two. When he returned, he said that Mr. Poole would join us as soon as he'd finished his oysters. He told the waiter to set another place and add another double stew to the order. "Do you know Roy?" Mr. Zimmer asked me. I said that I had often seen him around the party-boat piers but that I knew him only to speak to.

"Roy's a south-shore boy," Mr. Zimmer said. "His father was one of the biggest oyster-bedders in Prince's Bay — lost everything when they condemned the beds, and took a bookkeeping job in Fulton Market and died of a stroke in less than a year;

died on the Staten Island ferry, on the way to work. After Roy finished grade school, one of his father's friends got him a job in the market, and he became a fish butcher. When the carcass of a three- or four-hundred pound swordfish is cut into pieces that the retail trade can handle, it's about the same as dressing a steer, and Roy had a knack for that type of work. He got to be an expert. When he cut up a swordfish, or a tuna, or a sturgeon, or a big West Coast halibut, he didn't waste a pound. Also, he was a good fillet man, and he could bone a shad quicker and cleaner than any man in the market. He made good money, but he wasn't happy. Every now and then, he'd quit the market for a year or so and work on one of the government dredges that dredge the sludge out of the ship channels in the harbor. He generally worked on a dredge named the *Goethals*. He made better pay in the market, but he liked to be out in the harbor. He switched back and forth between the market and the Goethals for years and years. Somewhere along the line, he got himself tattooed. He's got an oyster tattooed on the muscle of his right arm. That is, an oyster shell. On his left arm, he's got one of those tombstone tattoos — a tombstone with his initials on it and under his initials the date of his birth and under that a big blue question mark. Six or seven years ago, he turned up in Sheepshead Bay and bought the *Chinquapin*. Roy's a good captain, and a good man, but he's a little odd. He says so himself. He's a harbor nut. Most of the baymen, when they're standing around talking, they often talk about the bottom of the harbor, what's down there, but that's *all* Roy talks about. He's got the bottom of the harbor on the brain."

The waiter brought in the stews, and a moment later Mr. Poole came over and sat down. He is a paunchy, red-haired, freckled man. His hair is thinning and the freckles on his scalp show through. He has drooping eyelids; they make his eyes look sleepy and sad. He remarked on the weather; he said he expected snow. Then he tasted his stew. It was too hot for him, and he put his spoon down. "I didn't rest so good last night," he said. "I had a dream. In this dream, a great earthquake had shook the world and had upset the sea level and New York Harbor had been drained as dry as a bathtub when the plug is pulled. I was down on the bottom, poking around, looking things over. There were hundreds of ships of all kinds lying on their sides in the mud, and among them were some wormy old wrecks that went down long years ago, and there were rusty anchors down there and dunnage and driftwood and old hawsers and tugboat bumpers and baling wire and tin cans and bottles and stranded eels and a skeleton standing waist-deep in a barrel of cement that the barrel had rotted off of. The rats had left the piers and were down on the bottom, eating the eels, and the gulls were flopping about, jerking eels away from the rats. I came across an old wooden wreck all grown over with seaweed, an old, old Dutch wreck. She had a hole in her, and I pulled the seaweed away and looked in and I saw some chests in there that had money spilling out of them, and I tried my best to crawl in. The dream was so strong that I crawled up under the headboard of the bed, trying to get my hands on the Dutch money, and I damn near scraped an ear off.''

"Eat your stew, Roy," Mr. Zimmer said, "before it gets cold."

"Pass me the salt," said Mr. Poole. We ate in silence. It isn't easy to carry on a conversation while eating oyster stew. Mr. Poole finished first. He tilted his bowl and worked the last spoonful of the stew into his spoon. He swallowed it, and then he said, "Happy, you've studied the harbor charts a lot in your time. Where would you say is the deepest spot in the harbor?"

"Offhand," said Mr. Zimmer, "I just don't know."

"One of the deepest spots I know is a hole in the bed of the Hudson a little bit south of the George Washington Bridge," said Mr. Poole. "On the dredges, we called it the Gut. It's half full of miscellaneous junk. The city used to dump bargeloads of boulders in there, and any kind of heavy junk that wasn't worth salvaging. Private concerns dumped in there, too, years back, but it's against the harbor regulations now. During the worst part of the last war, when the dredges cleaned sludge out of the ship channel in the Hudson, they had the right to dump it in the Gut — save them from taking it out to sea. The old-timers say the Gut used to go down a hundred and eighty feet. The last sounding I heard, it was around ninety feet. I know where the shallowest spot in the harbor is. I've sounded it myself with a boat hook. It's a spot on Romer Shoal, out in the middle of the Lower Bay, that's only four feet deep at low tide."

"Oh, yes," said Mr. Zimmer. "I've seen it on the charts. It's called a lump."

"It's right on the edge of Ambrose Channel, the channel that the big liners use," continued Mr. Poole. "I told my mate I want him to take me out there someday when the *Queen Mary* is due to come upchannel, and leave me standing there with a flag in my hand."

"What in hell would you do that for?" asked Mr. Zimmer.

"I'd just like to," said Mr. Poole. "I'd like to wave the flag and make the people on the Queen Mary wonder what I was standing on — shoulder-deep, out there in the middle of the Lower Bay. I'd wear a top hat, and I'd smoke a big cigar. I'd like to see what would happen."

"I'll tell you what would happen," said Mr. Zimmer. "The wash from the *Queen Mary* would drown you. Did you think of that?"

"I thought of it," said Mr. Poole. "I didn't do it, did I?" He crumpled up his napkin and tossed it on the table. "Another queer spot in the harbor," he said, "is Potter's Field. It's in the East River, in between Williamsburg Bridge and Manhattan Bridge. The river makes a sharp bend there, an elbow. On an ebb tide, there's an eddy in the elbow that picks up anything loose coming downriver, afloat or submerged, and sweeps it into a stretch of backwater on the Brooklyn side. This backwater is called Wallabout Bay on charts; the men on the dredges call it Potter's Field. The eddy sweeps driftwood into the backwater. Also, it sweeps drowned bodies into there. As a rule, people that drown in the harbor in winter stay down until spring. When the water begins to get warm, gas forms in them and that makes them buoyant and they rise to the surface.,

Every year, without fail, on or about the fifteenth of April, bodies start showing up, and more of them show up in Potter' Field than any other place. In a couple of weeks or so, the Harbor Police always finds ten to two dozen over there — suicides, bastard babies, old barge captains that lost their balance out on a sleety night attending to towropes, now and then some gangster or other. The police launch that runs out of Pier A on the Battery — Launch One — goes over and takes them out of the water with a kind of dip-net contraption that the Police Department blacksmith made out of tire chains. I ride the Staten Island ferry a good deal, and I'm forever hearing the tourists remark how beautiful the harbor is, and I always wish they could see Potter's Field some mornings in April — either that or the Gowanus Canal in August, when the sludge bubbles are popping like whips; they'd get a brand-new idea how beautiful the harbor is."

"Oh, I don't know, Roy," said Mr. Zimmer. "They've stopped dumping garbage out in the harbor approaches, where the tide washes it right back, and they're putting in a lot of sewage-disposal plants. The water's getting cleaner every year."

"I've read that," said Mr. Poole, "and I've heard it. Only I don't believe it. Did you eat any shad last spring — Staten Island shad *or* Hudson River shad? They've still got that kerosene taste. It was worse last spring than it ever was. Also, have you been up the Gowanus Canal lately? On the dredges, they used to say that the smell in the Gowanus would make the flag on a mast hang limp in a high wind. They used to tell about a tug that was freshly painted yellow and made a run up the Gowanus and came out painted green. I was up there last summer, and I didn't notice any change."

"Seriously, Roy," said Mr. Zimmer, "don't you think the water's getting cleaner?"

"Of course it isn't," said Mr. Poole. "It's getting worse and worse. *Every*thing is getting worse *every*where. When I was young, I used to dream the time would come when we could bed oysters in the harbor again. Now I'm satisfied that that time will never come. I don't even worry about the pollution any more. My only hope, I hope they don't pollute the harbor with something a million times worse than pollution."

"Let's don't get on that subject," said Mr. Zimmer.

"Sometimes I'm walking along the street," continued Mr. Poole, "and I wonder why the people don't just stand still and throw their heads back and open their mouths and howl."

"Why?" asked Mr. Zimmer.

"I'll tell you why," said Mr. Poole, "On account of the God-damned craziness of everything."

"Oh, well," said Mr. Zimmer, glancing at the empty stew bowls, "we can still eat."

Mr. Poole grunted. He looked at his wristwatch. "Well," he said, "this ain't making me any money." He got up and put on his hat. "Thanks for the stew," he said. "I enjoyed it. My treat next time. Take care, all."

"That's right, Roy," said Mr. Zimmer. "You take care of your-self."

"Thanks again," said Mr. Poole. "Give my regards home. Take care. Take care. Take care."

CORAL REEFS AND TROPIC SEAS
by David K. Bulloch

From his book The Underwater Naturalist. *Bulloch worked as an industrial chemist, but his first love has been the sea, which he has watched with scuba and sampled with camera, shovel, and plankton net. He has been a president of the American Littoral Society and a prolific writer for its maga-zine. His books include* The Wasted Ocean *and* The American Littoral Society Handbook for the Marine Naturalist.

The Underwater Naturalist *is subtitled "a layman's guide to the vibrant world beneath the sea." Here, Bulloch takes us to coral reefs.*

⚓

CONJURE UP A VISION OF A BRIGHT BLUE SKY ABOVE A WARM turquoise sea. Edged by the glaring white sand of a palm-lined beach, green water extends offshore, then abruptly changes to deep blue beyond the breakers. This is the realm of the coral reef. The life within it is the richest and most beautiful in the sea. No more diverse and prolific region can be found underwater. Once you have visited, you will be drawn back time and again, for few places can rival its attractions.

Although the southern tip of the continental United States lies above the Tropic of Cancer, the Florida Current bathes the east-ern side of southern Florida in waters warm enough for reefs to flourish. From Fowley Rocks in Biscayne Bay to the Dry Tortugas, corals grow fast enough to sustain and enlarge the limestone monuments that harbor so many creatures.

The Keys, its reefs, Florida, and the Bahamas all sit atop a broad limestone base shaped by reef growth eons ago, the product of emergence, erosion, and resubmergence over geo-logical time. The Florida Reef Tract, as the underwater region is known, lies in the ocean side of the Florida Keys, eight to eleven kilometers offshore. To the north, off Key Largo, lies John Pennecamp Coral Reef Preserve, which extends from Turtle Reef at its northernmost end to Molasses Reef twenty-nine kilometers to the south. Between the two lie well-known diving locations that draw hundreds of thousands of scuba divers and snorklers each year: the Elbow, Grecian Rocks, and French Reef. Grecian Rocks is shallow and suitable for snorkling.

South of Pennecamp Park, Alligator Reef, Sombrero Key, Looe Key, and American Shoals form a sea chain that parallels the Keys as far south as Key West. Midkey reefs are not as well developed as those either to the north or south; cold winter water from Florida Bay discourages their growth. From Marathon Key southward, offshore reefs are much like those in the Caribbean, with well-developed fore-reefs, and buttress and breaker zones.

STRUCTURE OF THE REEF

Reef-building corals thrive in shallow tropic seas where the water is clear, salty, sunlit, and warm. Although some species of coral grow in temperate waters, they only grow fast enough to create reefs in waters where the temperature does not fall below 18°C year-round. Water temperatures around 24°C are ideal. Growth can occur in water as low as 20°C and as high as 36°C, but much less vigorously. Thus, the majority of the world's reefs lie between the Tropic of Cancer and the Tropic of Capricorn.

Corals grow best in waters whose salinity is thirty-four parts per thousand — open ocean. The waters must be free of silt, although a few corals can tolerate some silt and low salinity well enough to grow close to shore.

The coral reef is a living veneer of animals actively growing on a base of the remains of earlier colonies. Over geological time, large land masses have been created by these endless replications. Islands and continental margins have been shaped by their ceaseless activity over millions of years.

Charles Darwin was the first to describe classic reef forms: fringing reefs, barrier reefs, and atolls. *Fringing reefs* build on and extend out from a rocky shoreline. *Barrier reefs* build up parallel to the coast in a shallow sea, often at a considerable distance from land. For example, the Great Barrier Reef off northeastern Australia parallels its coastline for nearly 1600 kilometers and lies 50 to 240 kilometers offshore. *Atolls* are a ring of reefs in open ocean surrounding a shallow lagoon. Darwin speculated that atolls begin as fringing reefs around a subsiding volcanic cone. As the mountain of basalt slowly sinks over thousands of years, the corals grow upward fast enough to keep pace with the submergence. The net result is a circular chain of reefs. Similarly, he reasoned, barrier reefs form by slowly subsiding coastland.

Most of Darwin's ideas were drawn from Indo-Pacific examples and without the benefit of later findings of geologists. He classified Floridian and Caribbean reefs as fringing reefs, but their origins, like those of many Pacific reefs, have proved to be more complex than he thought. He did prove correct about the origin of atolls.

West Indian reefs have a typical architecture, but it is often highly modified from one place to another by underwater topography, current flow, wave action, suspended sediments, and a host of other extenuating circumstances. The best example of an archetypical West Indies reef is found along the north shore of Jamaica. A breaker zone runs parallel to the coast where the sea crests and spills over into the shoreward shoals beyond the reef flat; it is so shallow that it may be partly exposed at low tide. Further landward lies a rubble field: coral debris thrown shoreward by waves. Very little coral grows there, but patches of algae and expanses of the green colonial anemone *Zooanthus* prosper; so much so that the region is called the *Zooanthus* zone. Between land and the *Zooanthus* zone lies the lagoon.

The crest of the reef at the breaker line is dominated by elkhorn coral, *Acropora palmata*, to such an extent it is called the *palmata* zone. These corals take the full brunt of the surf, a place where few other corals can grow.

Seaward, below the *palmata* zone, lies a gently sloping area filled with loose rubble and occasional stands of elkhorn coral. Farther below, coral-covered mounds, called spurs or buttresses, rise from the bottom and extend seaward perpendicular to the reef crest. These mounds can be thirty meters long, three to ten meters high, and are rarely narrower than three meters. Between their parallel walls lie narrow coral sand canyons one to two meters wide, called grooves or channels. They are often close enough that corals from adjacent buttresses extend out and roof over portions, turning them into tunnels or caves. How this spur-and-groove (or buttress-and-channel, as it is alternatively called) arrangement comes about isn't known, but the likely explanation lies in the great volume of sediment formed in the *palmata* zone. The return water from the breaker zone carries the coral sand seaward along the bottom through these channels. If the channels were not there, the sediment would soon scour and choke the buttress reefs out of existence.

Although the buttresses are constructed by the growth, death, and compaction of a great many coral species, the massive-wall-builder *Montastrea annularis* does most of the work. Below the buttress-and-channel zone, which typically ends at a depth of eight meters, a tract of sand and coral rock begins and gently slopes seaward for thirty to ninety meters to a depth of fifteen meters or so. Immense heaps of antler or staghorn coral, *Acropora cervicornis*, litter this bottom.

Around a depth of twenty meters, the bottom sharply rises, staghorn coral disappears, and *M. annularis* codominates with *Agaricia agaricites*, lettuce coral, whose leafy plates cover wide expanses of this fore-reef. The seaward side of the fore-reef is the edge of the escarpment, the "wall" or "drop-off" in diver's parlance. As the gradient steepens, hard corals give way to soft corals — sea whips and sea fans.

Other places show other arrangements. Where the seaward

slope is long and waves are moderate, *Acropora palmata* may dominate the breaker zone both on the seaward side and well inshore of the surf line. Seaward of the elkhorn coral, heaps of staghorn coral often intermix with it and the buttress zone is confined to deeper water. In other areas, clear-cut zonation is muted or nonexistent

West Indian and Floridian reefs do not always follow predictable sequences. Lagoons may either be barren or filled with small reefs surrounded by limey sands, grass flats, or hard bottom. In deeper water, fifteen meters or so, the bottom may not follow the Jamaican example but simply be littered with mixed patch reefs separated by narrow sediment beds. These mixed patch reefs go through cycles of growth and decay that leave them pockmarked with holes, interconnecting passages, overhangs, and minicaverns.

THE CORAL ANIMAL

Corals are kin to the sea anemones. Hard-coral polyps are ringed with six or a multiple of six (usually twelve or twenty-four) tentacles that sit atop a contractable sac. The tentacles are lobed with stinging cells. When chemically stimulated, they discharge a barb filled with a paralyzing toxin that stuns and holds microscopic prey.

The tissue in the sac is folded and follows the outline of the skeletal cup, which the polyp builds by secreting calcium carbonate at the floor and sides of the cup. Within the sac, the tissues specialize in digestion and reproduction. Threadlike filaments with powerful digestive capabilities also originate here and extend into the interior of the sac and out through pores in the walls into the spaces between the polyps.

Certain hard corals have a symbiotic relationship with chlorophyll-bearing algae, called *zooxanthellae*, that live within the corals' tissues. They convert sunlight into nutrients, thus helping the coral to prosper. In the Caribbean, most reef-building corals are limited to depths no greater than twenty-seven meters, although slow-growers exist down to sixty meters.

The zooxanthellae are stored inside the cells of the coral polyp; their numbers are in proportion to the amount of light the coral receives. If the coral is blocked off from light for a few months, it will expel the zooxanthellae, presumably to lighten the metabolic load these tiny cells impose in continuous darkness.

Zooxanthellae are passed on to future coral offspring through the planula, the free-swimming larval stage of the coral. Specific species of zooxanthellae have adapted to specific corals.

Considerable controversy rages over the role of zooxanthellae as a source of food for corals. They are not digested directly; that is, the coral does not farm and harvest them, but they do supply soluble nutrients to the coral and use waste products of coral metabolism such as ammonia and carbon dioxide. Zooxanthellae also aid reef-building. They consume phosphorus, which otherwise would inhibit calcification. Calcium carbonate is secreted as the mineral aragonite by the polyps onto an organic interlayer that provides sites for mineral growth. Organic phosphorus compounds stifle mineral formation.

A coral colony does not continue to grow indefinitely, but reaches a maximum size. The hemispherical brain corals rarely exceed two meters in diameter. Elkhorn coral rarely fans out wider than three meters. Mounds of *Montastrea* become more and more bumpy as they expand, and finally evolve into a series of separate lumps. *Montastrea* also change form with depth, becoming more platelike as the light fails.

The growth rate of corals varies from ten to twenty-five centimeters per year in length for staghorn coral, to one centimeter in diameter per year for brain and finger corals. The remains of shipwrecks on reefs have helped establish average growth rates; corals attached to the ships' steel obviously can be no older than the date of the vessel's demise.

Corals are excellent microcarnivores, catching just about

everything that settles on them. They trap plankton by stinging them or entangling them in mucus. Polyps feed at night when plankton rise to the surface from the deeps. Corals with large polyps trap more plankton and have fewer zooxanthellae than do smaller-polyped corals.

The first impression of a coral reef is one of rampant animal life. Where are the plants to feed them all? Very little green shows anywhere, and tropic waters don't hold enough plankton to provide for such abundance. To measure the net productivity of the reef—the excess of plant growth over animal uptake—biologists measure the increase in oxygen over the reef during the day and compare it to its decline during the night. The day-to-night change can be converted into net photosynthesis, which is expressed as the amount of carbon "locked up" in converting carbon dioxide into life. The figures are staggering. Open-sea productivity in the tropics averages forty grams of carbon per square meter per year, but the waters around the reef may be as high as thirty-five hundred grams per year. Where is all the plant life located?

Zooxanthellae account for some of it. Encrusting algae growing on dead coral and among the grains of the coarse coral sediments account for most of the rest. Constant close cropping by fishes and urchins keep the algae inconspicuous. If you remove the major reef grazer, the spiny sea urchin, *Diadema antillarum*, algal mats will quickly appear. Unchecked, these mats will overgrow sessile creatures, including the corals, and destroy them.

Corals suffer continual predation. The parrotfishes and the surgeonfishes nip off live coral in their search for algae. In parrotfish, the teeth have fused into a beak that can scrape a sizable chunk from a coral head. You will see the white scars on almost all coral surfaces. The ingested coral is crushed, the organic material absorbed, and the remains defecated as a fine silt. This silt settles and eventually consolidates into a hard bottom sediment. The coral's scars either heal over with new coral growth or become the points of entry for colonists such as boring sponges, tube-building worms, or algae.

Dead coral is continually scraped by urchin, *Diadema* for one, and *Echinometra viridis* for another. Scraping prevents new organisms from gaining a foothold, but also wears depressions in the coral that weaken their structural integrity. Boring sponges dissolve both living and dead coral: *Siphonodictyon coralliphagum*, a yellow, tubed type, and *Cliona delitrix*, a red incruster often dotted with *Parazoanthus* anemone, burrow, riddle, overgrow, and kill large corals. They also weaken the base of the coral and destroy it by detaching the main body from the base.

Most tropic sponges are benign, simply using the dead coral as a foothold. In deep water, *Mycale laeris* can be downright helpful. Growing in a flattened form under the leaf coral, *Agaricia agaricites*, it crowds out boring forms and cushions the coral in an upright horizontal position if its small stalk cracks off from storm surges.

Sponges add bright color and contrast to the reef scene and harbor their own commensals and parasites. The interstices of the common loggerhead sponge, *Speciospongia vesparium*, a barrel-sized black mass with a flattened top and large circular openings, provides a home for a great many porcellanid crabs and pistol shrimp. The snapping shrimp, *Synalpheus*, is one such tenant. Like other pistol shrimps, it has one enlarged claw that slams shut with an audible click.

The mantis shrimp, *Gonodactylus*, sometimes lives in the loggerhead sponge, but is more commonly found in coral crevices, where it lies in wait for its prey. Armed with two unusual forelimbs, it is a formidable predator. The forelimbs are hinged and fold back like those of a praying mantis. The inside edges of the forelimbs are lined with sharp spines that initially impale, then snap shut like an iron maiden, sometimes cutting the victim in two.

The fronts of the forelimbs of these species can be shaped either like a spear or a hammer. Their strike is one of the fastest blows in nature, taking only four to eight milliseconds to deliver. In those shrimp with limbs built for smashing, the forelimbs can split a crab with a single thwack. *Hemisquilla ensigera*, twenty-five centimeters in length, can deliver a punch with a force nearly equal to a small-caliber bullet. They are nicknamed "thumb busters" for good reason.

Totally passive and apparently defenseless, what protects sponges from depredation? Neither their fibrous inner structure nor the spicules that frame their inner walls are decisive deterrents. The answer lies within the fleshy tissue, which ranges from terribly distasteful to downright poisonous. Both the massive brick-red touch-me-not sponge, *Neofibularia nolitangere*, and the bright-orange-to-red *Tedania ignis* are so toxic that a diver will develop blisters from handling them. Most tropic sponges are not dangerous to the touch, but enough red ones are that it's wise to avoid them until you know your species well enough to tell the innocuous from the harmful.

The surface settlers on the massive corals include the Christmas tree worm, *Spirobranchus giganteus*, one of the many fan and feather-duster worms whose bright gills sweep the waters for plankton. When disturbed, it retreats into its tube in a wink. As the coral grows, these polychaetes add new tubing, giving the impression the worm burrows in, which it does not. Date mussels, *Lithophaga*, bore into coral, living or dead, until all that is seen of them is a dumbbell-shaped opening. If the coral is alive, they must continually bore outward to keep from being overgrown.

Gall crabs, settling on coral, dig their own specialized accommodations. *Domecia acanthophora*, a little one-centimeter-long crab, lives within a chamber on elkhorn coral. Its relationship with the coral is more commensal (sharing) than parasitic. The crabs *Cryptochirus* and *Pseudocryptochirus* settle in pits on lettuce corals and the growing coral all but encloses them. Often a male and female are found together. When abandoned, these minicaves in the coral are quickly occupied by gobies.

Living associations within the reef are legion. Some are obvious, others more subtle. Between coral polyps, ciliated protozoans, flatworms, copepods, and other tiny crustaceans live and prosper no worse for wear either from the coral's feeding tentacles or mucous strands. Collectively, they look like pieces of sand on the polyps, quiet most of the time but occasionally making quick, erratic movements, then lying low again. Some can be found in the polyps, perhaps feeding on indigestible bits of food not yet expelled by the polyp. Many are species-specific: found nowhere else except within the confines of one kind of coral. To see them requires a low-power microscope. To separate them from the coral, immerse a small fragment of coral in seawater containing five percent alcohol, wait seven to fourteen hours, then collect and examine the sediment that has fallen off the coral. Rubbing alcohol will do; so will gin or vodka, which is sometimes more readily available. Remember that the proof is twice the percentage of the alcohol content, so make the concoction about one part gin to nine parts seawater.

The free-swimming bristleworm, *Hemodice carunculata*, larger than the northern clam worm but structurally much the same, feeds voraciously on clubbed finger coral, *Porites porites*, and staghorn coral. Be careful handling this worm. Its *setae*, the hairs along the sides of its body, stick into flesh easily and are irritating and painful.

Physical damage to a reef, although sporadic, can be catastrophic. West Indian hurricanes strike with a fury few people comprehend. Crashing seas loosen and topple both elkhorn coral and brain corals, sending them crashing down on more fragile fore-reef species, burying them and hardier species in their path. The great clouds of sediment stirred up by the violent wave action resettle and choke out those corals not physically destroyed, adding significantly to the carnage. A hurricane may only strike a reef once in fifty years, but it may take half that long to repair the damage one leaves behind.

In 1961, a hurricane off Belize decimated its barrier reef. Regrowth took nearly twenty years to cover the debris left by that great storm. The north shore of Jamaica was severely battered by Hurricane Carmen in the autumn of 1974, by Hurricane Allen in August 1980, and again by Hurricane Gilbert in 1988. Extensive damage was done to corals as deep as forty-five meters, and the surf zone turned into piles of broken rubble.

Both physical violence and biological degradation are essential in reef-building, for the reef is a cemented conglomerate of large chunks and small particles. Some of the finer particles are carried away by heavy wave action, but enough rubble and sediment remain to build up the bottom at rates varying between .5 to 5 meters every thousand years. The pace of the fastest-growing reefs in the West Indies is fifteen meters per thousand years.

Over sixty species of corals grow in the West Indies. In quiet waters, *Oculina* species grow from a single stem into a branched bushlike shape. *Favia fragum* form small, encrusting, cobbled knobs. *Astrangia solitaria* occurs in single cups, *Cladocora arbuscula* in tubed, irregular clumps, and *Madracis mirabilis* in tangles of tightly grouped branches in which small invertebrates hide.

But the corals we are most familiar with form massive stands or single structures. The brain coral, *Diploria labyrinthiformis*, forms giant boulders up to three meters in diameter. *Montastrea annularis* grows in enormous vertical and horizontal sheets, often forming horizontal plates layered in tiers. It cloaks the buttress walls of old coral stacks in knobby, irregular, and discontinuous growth that looks like so many errant roof tiles.

In between and among both the hard and soft corals there grows a false coral, called fire coral, *Millepora alcicornis*. It comes in a bewildering array of shapes but all are a light mustard brown often tipped in white. Beware! On tender portions of human skin it packs the wallop of a hot soldering iron and raises a welt that lasts for weeks. It is not a true coral, but a hydrozoan. Although it can encrust anything firm, it also can be found free-standing in flattened or folded sheets, like drapes or wrinkled curtains that rise vertically from a lumpy, encrusting base.

Common corals can be identified by sight but some lookalikes must be sorted out by a few simple measurements and a closer look. When coral-watching, carry a short plastic metric ruler with you. Measure the average diameter of the cup in which the polyp sits. If the cups join together to form valleys, as they do in brain corals, measure the width from wall to wall. Partitions radiate from the walls of the cup into its interior and, occasionally, out beyond its periphery. The numbers and distance between these partitions also aid in identification, as does noting the absence or presence of a center structure, the columella, in the cup and its shape.

If you have access to a rock saw with a water-cooled carbide blade, cross-section a piece of dead brain coral and see for yourself how the polyps have built cup upon cup, outward radially. Don't pick live coral. It is illegal in Florida, will impoverish the reef, and the coral serves very little purpose when dead.

The undersides of loose dead coral are worth a look; aside from the vacant homes of tube worms and boring clams, they often contain small, bright red, knobby protuberances of the foraminiferan *Homotrema rubrum*. This shelled protozoan can be so abundant that it colors the coral sands a light pink, as it has done on the beaches of Bermuda.

Tropical-coral polyps close during the day. At night they open in full display, combing the waters for a tiny meal. Look closely at their tentacles, especially those of *Montastrea cavernosa*, whose cups are nearly one centimeter (nearly half an inch) in diameter. All its tentacles are about the same in length save one, the sweeper tentacle, which is ten times longer than its neighbors. This tentacle can reach over several polyps and will attack alien coral encroaching on its borders.

As two corals of different species grow toward each other, there comes a time when they compete for the same space. You might expect the faster-growing species to win out by simply overwhelming the other, but the slow-grower can alter the odds by fighting back. When *M. annularis* and *M. cavernosa* meet, the sweeper tentacles of *M. cavernosa* attack and kill the polyps of *M. annularis*, leaving a no-man's-land between, where nothing grows.

Those that have no sweeper tentacles do battle with the long, threadlike digestive filaments they extend outside the polyp into the polyp of the enemy. A hierarchy of winners and losers — the smaller flower corals among the winners and the club finger corals with the losers — has been established by tank experiments. However, the pecking order in the laboratory has not always corresponded with observations in the field.

REEF FISHES

All the spaces in a coral reef make marvelous havens for hundreds of species of reef fish, who range from thumbnail size to more than a meter long. A busy reef will have a cloud of hundreds of small fishes swimming over it. The value of the nooks and crannies below them becomes quite apparent when a predator approaches. The cloud of fish shrinks as the hunter cruises in and, if frightened by sudden movement, vanishes instantly into the protective coral cavities. As the threat passes, the little fish quickly emerge and go about business as usual.

Identifying all these fish is far easier than recognizing cold-water species. Their shapes, colors, and color patterns are distinctive enough to remember while thumbing through a guidebook after a dive. The common ones will be seen on every dive, and every visit to the reef will add more to your species list. A week of visits should net over fifty species positively identified and dozens more tentatively so.

But if you have an initially high success rate, don't be lulled into careless observation. Among some fish, color patterns are quite variable. In some closely related species, color patterns and other differences can be slight. Note color, size, shape, and specific markings. Does the fish have a distinct spot? Is it all one color or multicolored? If it is striped, how many are there and what is the color sequence of the stripes? Is it barred (vertical stripes)? Is the body slender, exceptionally thin, unusually long, boxlike? Are the fins unusual: prominent spines, thread-finned, fanlike, or stalked? Where did you see the fish? Very close to the surface, midwater, or on the bottom? Sitting on the bottom, in a burrow or a coral crevice? How big is the fish, a half centimeter or one meter? How does it behave? Does it school, mix in with others, or is it a lone swimmer? Does it lay still, walk on the bottom with its pectoral fins, wriggle into the loose bottom sediments? Is it associated with an invertebrate?

Look and read, then look and read again. Within a few dives you will recognize the differences between French grunt, *Haemulon flavolineatum*, and the similarly colored porkfish, *Anisotremus virginicus*, who has two black vertical bars on its head. Keep the Latin names in your notes, for if you decide to find e about them, the Latin name is the key to the scientific literature.

After a few tropic trips, you will become aware of the typical body shapes of the common fish families; that is, you will recognize a parrotfish from a snapper or a grouper even though you do not recognize.the exact species. There really isn't any reason to try and identify every fish you see. What is more important is the variety of ways each makes its living and how it interacts with others in its world. If that interests you, your lifetime isn't long enough to take in the half of it.

The behavior of reef fishes is as intriguing as their splashy coloration and bizarre shapes. Many divers are in such a hurry to see another part of the reef that they move on long before they have had a chance to absorb the rhythm of the life before their eyes. As Yogi Berra once said "You can see a lot just by lookin'," and if you settle down and watch, you will.

Some fish stake a claim to specific territory and defend it with a belligerence that belies their small size. For the damselfishes, no challenger seems too large. Algae-eaters, they will vigorously defend areas of dead coral on which algae rapidly proliferate. Charging, retreating, then charging again at all comers, large grazing fish — tang, surgeonfishes, and parrotfish — retreat after barely a brief nibble.

Some damselfishes are said to bite off coral in order to "farm" the ensuing growth on the broken surface. Most are plankton feeders. They snatch copepods from the water with a curious snap of the head. When feeding on plankton, the damsels suffer a curious angst: Pickings are better the farther away they get from the reef, but their uneasiness grows rapidly with the distance from home.

Other territorial fish patrol a set pathway in the reef, weaving in and out of crevices and only abandoning the outside leg of the circuit when faced by imminent threat. Some hover in reef recesses and simply withdraw deeper if intimidated. Many are awaiting the night shift. Squirrelfishes feed at night, venturing away from the reef only under cover of darkness. Day-feeders replace them, resting in the very same holes vacated by the night foragers.

So many reef species share the same digs and appear to make a living in similar ways that biologists have been puzzled by this seeming contradiction of the ecologist's dictum that says no two species will occupy the same niche at the same time for too long; one of the competing species will gain a competitive edge and displace the other. How then does the reef support hundreds of species with such similar lifestyles without the rise of a few dominant species? Some experts claim each species is specialized enough to exert a subtle claim to its own turf. Others argue that all are so well suited to their environment that space and successful existence is allotted by an "endless lottery" determined by chance.

Mimicry and subterfuge are common ploys among reef fish. Less aggressive fish cloaked in the colors of a more aggressive species gain an important margin of safety as a predator hesitates, unsure of his victim. This gives his intended prey an opportunity to widen the striking distance beyond the predator's rushing range. Such disguise can be as simple as spots on the flanks. Members of the butterfly fishes have spots that may appear like large eyes to a following fish. Is the predator really put off by this elementary ruse, or is this explanation of the purpose of the spots the figment of some biologist's imagination? It is hard to say. Fish obviously don't like approaching "eyes," and will back off — that is easy to observe on nearly every dive — but whether this observed behavior specifically protects those butterfly fishes with spots may be an unwarranted assumption.

And the game cuts both ways. An aggressor who mimics a benign species, either by taking on its color patterns or imitating its behavior, can narrow the gap between itself and its intended victim.

The clever use of cover also gets results. The trumpetfish, *Aulostomus maculatus*, a long, slender fish-eater, will swim alongside algae grazers such as parrotfish, using them as a blind to get within striking distance of small wrasse, who are unperturbed by the parrotfish's approach. It will also hover vertically, head down, aligned with a sea fan, and wait for passing prey. The trumpetfish's strike is short and sure, and so fast your eyes cannot follow it. One second earlier the little fish is there, and in the next instant, gone.

Not all relationships are so ruthless; many are distinctly cooperative. Cleaning, one species picking parasites or dead matter off another, exists between fish and fish, shrimp and fish, and crabs and fish. Most of the cleaner-fish are small gobies, blennies, and wrasses. The neon goby, *Gobiosoma oceanops*, electric blue with black stripes, the cleaner goby, *G. genie*, and the juvenile bluehead wrasse, *Thalassoma bifasciatum*, congregate at work stations and signal their services by an undulating display dance, weaving back and forth over their favorite coral head, awaiting customers. The approaching host must also act its part by flaring its pectoral fins, aligning its body head-up or -down, or holding its body diagonally.

The cleaner will then approach the host, lightly butting its flanks. The host responds by holding still in whatever odd position it had earlier assumed. Creole wrasse, *Clepticus parrai*, align head-down, as does the queen parrotfish, *Scarus vetula*.

Other parrotfish angle their bodies head-up, while the doctor fish, *Acanthurus chirurgus*, turns sideways, not quite horizontally but close to it. Just how variable or universal these postures are within a given species is an open question. Once you get to know these fish, keep notes of your observations at different cleaning stations. You may be able to shed some light on this behavior pattern.

The cleaners work on one fish at a time, sometimes concentrating on mouth and gills; sometimes on flanks and tail. When the host has had enough, a few shakes of its body sends the cleaners away, who wait for the next customer to move up in the queue. As each fish awaits its turn, now and then a cleaner will break away from the main group and briefly butt its flanks as if to assure it that it is next in line.

Every reef of reasonable size has a cleaner station centrally located, but not necessarily at its crest. To find it, simply watch the parade of passing foragers. Should a few stop their swim-and-peck routine and assume an awkward stance, you will soon see the cleaners appear. You can approach the group, but the cleaners may get nervous and leave if you come too dose.

Small fish often follow large grazing fish for short distances, gobbling up whatever invertebrates are uncovered by their foragings. Uprooted and momentarily out in the open, they are easy pickings for the wrasses and blennies who tag along until the larger fish move too far into unfamiliar territory. For the wrasses, gobies, blennies, and even butterfly fish, getting too far away from home may mean not being able to navigate back.

On home ground, small fish behave more opportunistically than do larger ones. Break open an urchin and watch the local juveniles arrive first. The bluehead wrasse, slippery dick, *Halichoeres bivittatus*, and other small residents are the first on the scene, grabbing what they can before bigger fish butt in and hog the meal.

Even large reef fish keep to a limited home range. Tagged groupers and snappers have been recaptured where they were first caught as much as three years later. Parrotfishes return to their favorite caves to spend the night, but may roam considerable distances during the day.

THE REEF AT NIGHT

At night, the cryptic life of the reef emerges. Shrimp and crab venture out to feed. Urchins leave their crevices to graze on algae in nearby sandy bottoms. The basket stars, whose days are spent balled up in a crevice or wrapped around a sea fan, unwind, spread their tentacles out, and hunt for plankton. Brittle stars also seek the passing plankton by raising three of their five arms.

The moray eels go hunting. The spiny lobster, *Panulirus argus*, emerges, as does the common Atlantic octopus, *Octopus vulgaris*. If you come across an octopus at night, you will find it totally bedazzled by your dive light. You can pick it up (gently) and it will offer little or no resistance and will not attempt to bite you. If you play too rough, it will discharge a cloud of ink and flee, a not too unexpected reaction. During the day you can tell if its den is close by if you come across a grouping of clean conch shells. Conch is a favorite food of the octopus, and invariably it brings the conch to its doorstep before eating it.

Some fish change color at night. The spotfin butterfly fish, *Chaetodon ocellatus*, develops a dark, smeary blotch on its white flanks. The color of the blue tang, *Acanthurus coeruleus*, a deep blue by day, fades at night, and four vertical gray bars appear on its side. The bright red cardinal fish, *Apogon planifrons*, turns to a dull pink.

Divers' lights at night alter fish behavior. The spotted goatfish, *Pseudupeneus maculatus*, has three or four dark brown blotches down its flanks by day, but variegated red blotches at night. Or are the night colors caused by a fright reaction to the blinding lights of the diver? Stress induced by light causes red blotches in the Pacific goatfish, *Mulloidichthys dentatus*. Is the same true for its Caribbean relative?

Lights in or on the water at night attract hordes of plankton, who are quickly followed by bigeye scad, *Selar crumenophthalmus*, who home in on the life dancing in the beam. Needlefish and herrings also join the fray. If the beam is on long enough, squid will dart in for a meal, as will an occasional barracuda.

Night dives are best made from an anchored boat. If it is your first night trip, buddy up with someone you know and trust. Don't stray too far from the boat. It isn't that the blackness holds long-leggity beasties, or ghosties and ghoulies, but the fear of what you can't see may induce a claustrophobic response. If apprehension *does* sweep over you, don't fight it. Go back to the boat and await another time. Try again, and next time start in more benign surroundings. Once you are caught up by it, the beauty of the reef at night will draw you back just as its beauty by day will entice you to it whenever you have the opportunity to return.

EXPLORING THE REEF

A word of caution when exploring the breaker zone of the coral reef: The inner fringes of elkhorn coral create a maneuverability problem for the diver. An errant surge of water can hurl you into the crest of the reef with unanticipated suddenness.

Never swim over the top of a shoal reef. Doing so is a prelude to grief. If you are dropped into the trough of a passing wave, the power of the following sea will push you farther aground, scraping your hull from stem to flipper. Deep coral cuts and abrasions head to foot will ruin your whole day, to say nothing of the damage you may do to the reef. And if fire coral is part of the fauna in the breaker zone, you may spend the next few days in a hospital ward.

Skirt shallow zones carefully, penetrating inward only where a wide stretch of open deep water abuts the shoals so that you have plenty of time and water in which to execute a tuck turn. If carried by a wave, meet the shallows fins-first, then beat to sea as the wave passes and its energy slackens. At worst, you will only suffer scratched ankles.

Unfortunately, many reefs are not what they were a mere forty years ago. Silt drifting seaward from construction projects, sediment stirred up by boats, overnutrification from sewage — in short, the depredations of man — have left the waters cloudier and the reefs poorer every year. You can help preserve what remains: Take only pictures, don't let your fins stir up sediments or break off coral, and don't let your boat anchor scrape over the reef.

Plan in advance how you intend to get to the reef and safely back. Charter trips are available throughout the Keys and the Caribbean. Should you bring your own boat or rent a bare boat, consider three important elements to a successful day of exploration: the weather, the sun, and finding your way home. Strong winds off the Atlantic can kick up a wicked chop in reef-filled shallows, making it unsafe to navigate among coral heads, yet difficult to remain anchored.

For the untanned, the sun's intensity, even in winter, is a serious threat. A day of overexposure can mean a week's incapacitation. To solve the problem and at the same time protect your skin from coral abrasions, consider wearing a lightweight full-sleeved shirt and pants over your swim suit. Add a pair of light cotton gloves to protect your hands. You won't look the height of fashion, but at the end of the day you will be in one piece, unburned and unscraped.

Then there is the problem of finding your way back to the dock. Obviously, in the Keys, west is home, but finding a channel into a mangrove with the setting sun in your face is not often easy. Off Florida, the mainland Keys are low with few prominent landmarks, so keep track of every useful bearing you can. A chart is a must and a VHF radio a wise complement. These waters look benign and inviting, but have created their share of grief for sailors over the years.

Coral reefs contain so much exhilarating life that the urge to hold in your memories is bound to lead you to underwater photography. No other place holds so many photogenic possibilities, and no other way allows you to harvest its bounty so easily without doing harm. Those photographs and your log, years hence and perhaps in less propitious circumstances, will remind you of blissful times past and the beauty you were once privileged to see.

THE LOG FROM THE SEA OF CORTEZ
by John Steinbeck and Edward K. Ricketts

From their book by the same name. In 1940 Ricketts, a marine biologist and specimen collector, set out from California in an old sardine boat to sample the biota on the shores of the Gulf of California. Along with him went John Steinbeck, who later won the Nobel Prize for such works as The Grapes of Wrath *and* Cannery Row *(which dealt with the life of a marine specimen collector named Doc).*

The log records the days of the trip, sometimes a mere cataloguing of the specimens, other times Steinbeck being macho or introspective. The selections below describe some of the collecting problems and techniques, plus the joy of discovery.

⚓

ABOUT NOON we sailed and moved out of the shrouded and quiet Amortajada Bay and up the coast toward Marcial Reef, which was marked as our next collecting station. We arrived in mid-afternoon and collected on the late tide, on a northerly pile of boulders, part of the central reef. This was just south of Marcial Point, which marks the southern limit of Agua Verde Bay.

It was not a good collecting tide, although it should have been according to the tide chart. The water did not go low enough for exhaustive collecting. There were a few polyclads which here were high on the rocks. We found two large and many small chitons — the first time we had discovered them in numbers. There were many urchins visible but too deep below the surface to get to. Swarms of larval shrimps were in the water swimming about in small circles. The collecting was not successful in point of view of numbers of forms taken.

That night we rigged a lamp over the side, shaded it with a paper cone, and hung it close down to the water so that the light was reflected downward. Pelagic isopods and mysids immediately swarmed to the illuminated circle until the water seemed to heave and whirl with them. The small fish came to this horde of food, and on the outer edges of the light ring large fishes flashed in and out after the small fishes. Occasionally we interrupted this mad dance with dip-nets, dropping the catch into porcelain pans for closer study, and out of the nets came animals small or transparent that we had not noticed in the sea at all.

Having had no good tide at Marcial Reef, we arose at four o'clock the following morning and went in the darkness to collect again. We carried big seven-cell focusing flashlights. In some ways they make collecting in the dark, in a small area at least, more interesting than daytime collecting, for they limit the range of observation so that in the narrowed field one is likely to notice more detail. There is a second reason for our preference for night collecting — a number of animals are more active at night than in the daytime and they seem to be not much disturbed or frightened by artificial light. This time we had a very fair tide. The light fell on a monster highly colored spiny lobster in a crevice of the reef. He was blue and orange and spotted with brown. The taking of him required caution, for these big lobsters are very strong and are so armed with spikes and points that in struggling with one the hands can be badly cut. We approached with care, bent slowly down, and then with two hands grabbed him about the middle of the body. And there was no struggle whatever. He was either sick or lazy or hurt by the surf, and did not fight at all.

The cavities in Marcial Reef held a great many club-spined urchins and a number of the sharp-spined purple ones which had hurt us before. There were numbers of sea fans, two of the usual starfish and a new species which later we were to find common farther north in the Gulf. We took a good quantity of the many-rayed sunstars, and a flat kind of cucumber which was new to us. This was the first time we had collected at night, and under our lights we saw the puffer fish lazily feeding near the surface in the clear water. On the bottom, the brittle stars, which we had always found under rocks, were crawling about like thousands of little snakes. They rarely move about in the daylight. Wherever the sharp, powerful rays of the flashlight cut into the water we could see the moving beautiful fish and the bottoms alive with busy feeding invertebrates. But collecting with a flashlight is difficult unless it is arranged that two people work together — one to hold the light and the other to take the animals. Also, from constant wetting in salt water the life of a flashlight is very short.

The one huge and beautiful lobster was the prize of this trip. We tried to photograph him on color film and as usual something went wrong but we got a very good likeness of one end of him, which was an improvement on our previous pictures. In most of our other photographs we didn't get either end.

We took several species of chitons and a great number of tunicates. There were several turbellarian flatworms, but these are so likely to dissolve before they preserve that we had great difficulties with them. There were in the collecting pans several species of brittle stars, numbers of small crabs and snapping shrimps, plumularian hydroids, bivalves of a number of species, snails, and some small sea urchins. There were worms, hermit crabs, sipunculids, and sponges. The pools too had been thick with pelagic larval shrimps, pelagic isopods — tiny crustacea similar to sow bugs — and tiny shrimps (mysids). In this area the water seemed particularly peopled with small pelagic animals — "bugs," so the boys said. Everywhere there were bugs, flying, crawling, and swimming. The shallow and warm waters of the area promoted a competitive life that was astonishing.

After breakfast we pulled up the anchor and set out again northward. The pattern of the technique of the trip had by now established itself almost as a habit with us; collecting, running to a new station, collecting again. The water was intensely blue on this run, and the fish were very many. We could see the splashing of great schools of tuna in the distance where they beat the water to spray in their millions. The swordfish leaped

all about us, and someone was on the bow the whole time trying to drive a light harpoon into one, but we never could get
close enough. Cast after cast fell short.

We preserved and labeled as we went, and the water was so
smooth that we had no difficulty with delicate animals. If the
boat rolls, retractile animals such as anemones and sipunculids
are more than likely to draw into themselves and refuse to relax
under the Epsom-salts treatment, but this sea was as smooth as
a lawn, and our wake fanned out for miles behind us.

The fish-lines on the stays snapped and jerked and we
brought in skipjack, Sparky's friend of the curious name, and
the Mexican sierra. This golden fish with brilliant blue spots is
shaped like a trout. In size it ranges from fifteen inches to two
feet, is slender and a very rapid swimmer. The sierra does not
seem to travel in dense, surface-beating schools as the tuna
does. Although it belongs with the mackerel-like forms, its meat
is white and delicate and sweet. Simply fried in big hunks, it is
the most delicious fish of all.

The shallow water along the shore at Concepción Bay was
littered with sand dollars, two common species and one very
rare. And in the same association, brilliant-red sponge arbores-
cences grew in loose stones in the sand or on the knobs of old
coral. These are the important horizon markers. On other
rocks, imbedded in the sand, there were giant hachas, clustered
over with tunicates and bearing on their shells the usual small
ophiurans and crabs. One of the masked rock clams had on it a
group of solitary corals. Close inshore were many brilliant large
snails, the living animals the shells of which had so moved
Sparky. In this area we collected from the skiff, leaning over the
edge, bringing up animals in a dip-net or spearing them with a
small trident, sometimes jumping overboard and diving for a
heavier rock with a fine sponge growing on it.

The ice we had taken aboard at La Paz was all gone now. We
started our little motor and ran it for hours to cool the
ice-chest, but the heat on deck would not permit it to drop the

temperature below about thirty-eight degrees F, and the little motor struggled and died often, apparently hating to run in such heat. It sounded tired and sweaty and disgusted. When the evening came, we had fried fish, caught that day, and after dark we lighted the deck and put our reflecting lamp over the side. We netted a serpent-like eel, thinking from its slow, writhing movement through the water that it might be one of the true viperine sea-snakes which are common farther south. Also we captured some flying fish.

We used long-handled dip-nets in the lighted water, and set up the enameled pans so that the small pelagic animals could be dropped directly into them. The groups in the pans grew rapidly. There were *heteronereis* (the free stages of otherwise crawling worms who develop paddle-like tails upon sexual maturity). There were swimming crabs, other free-swimming annelids, and ribbonfish which could not be seen at all, so perfectly transparent were they. We should not have known they were there, if they had not thrown faint shadows on the bottom of the pans. Placed in alcohol, they lost their transparency and could easily be seen. The pans became crowded with little skittering animals, for each net brought in many species. When the hooded light was put down very near the water, the smallest animals came to it and scurried about in a dizzying dance so rapidly that they seemed to draw crazy lines in the water. Then the small fishes began to dart in and out, snapping up this concentration, and farther out in the shadows the large wise fishes cruised, occasionally swooping and gobbling the small fishes. Several more of the cream-colored spotted snake eels wriggled near and were netted. They were very snake-like and they had small bright-blue eyes. They did not swim with a beating tail as fishes do, but rather squirmed through the water.

While we worked on the deck, we put down crab-nets on the bottom, baiting them with heads and entrails of the fish we had had for dinner. When we pulled them up they were loaded with large stalk-eyed snails and with sea urchins having long vicious spines. The colder-water relatives of both these animals are very slow-moving, but these moved quickly and were completely voracious. A net left down five minutes was brought up with at least twenty urchins in it, and all attacking the bait. In addition to the speed with which they move, these urchins are clever and sensitive with their spines. When approached, the long sharp little spears all move and aim their points at the approaching body until the animal is armed like a Macedonian phalanx. The main shafts of the spines were cream-yellowish-white, but a half-inch from the needle-points they were blue-black. The prick of one of the points burned like a bee-sting. They seemed to live in great numbers at four fathoms; we do not know their depth range, but their physical abilities and their voraciousness would indicate a rather wide one. In the same nets we took several dromiaceous crabs, reminiscent of hermits, which had adjusted themselves to life in half the shell of a bivalve, and had changed their body shapes accordingly.

It is probable that no animal tissue ever decays in this water. The furious appetites which abound would make it unlikely that a dead animal, or even a hurt animal, should last more than a few moments. There would be quick death for the quick animal which became slow, for the shelled animal which opened at the wrong time, for the fierce animal which grew timid. It would seem that the penalty for a mistake or an error would be instant death and there would be no second chance.

It would have been good to keep some of the sensitive urchins alive and watch their method of getting about and their method of attack. Indeed, we will never go again without a full-sized observation aquarium into which we can put interesting animals and keep them for some time. The aquaria taken were made with polarized glass. Thus, the fish could look out but we could not look in. This, it turned out, was an error on our part.

There are three ways of seeing animals: dead and preserved; in their own habitats for the short time of a low tide; and for long periods in an aquarium. The ideal is all three. It is only after long observation that one comes to know the animal at all.

In his natural place one can see the normal life, but in an aquarium it is possible to create abnormal conditions and to note the animal's adaptability or lack of it. As an example of this third method of observation, we can use a few notes made during observation of a small colony of anemones in an aquarium. We had them for a number of months.

In their natural place in the tide pool they are thick and close to the rock. When the tide covers them they extend their beautiful tentacles and with their nettle-cells capture and eat many micro-organisms. When a powerful animal, a small crab for example, touches them, they paralyze it and fold it into the stomach, beginning the digestive process before the animal is dead, and in time ejecting the shell and other indigestible matter. On being touched by an enemy they fold in upon themselves for protection. We brought a group of these on their own stone into the laboratory and placed them in an aquarium. Cooled and oxygenated sea water was sprayed into the aquarium to keep them alive. Then we gave them various kinds of food, and found that they do not respond to simple touch-stimulus on the tentacles, but have something which is at least a vague parallel to taste-buds, whatever may be the chemical or mechanical method. Thus, protein food was seized by the tentacles, taken and eaten without hesitation; fat was touched gingerly, taken without enthusiasm to the stomach, and immediately rejected; starches were not taken at all — the tentacles touched starchy food and then ignored it. Sugars, if concentrated, seemed actually to burn them so that the tentacles moved away from contact. There did really appear to be a chemical method of differentiation and choice. We circulated the same sea water again and again, only cooling and freshening it. Pure oxygen, introduced into the stomach in bubbles, caused something like drunkenness; the animal relaxed and its reaction to touch was greatly slowed, and sometimes completely stopped for a while. But the reaction to chemical stimulus remained active, although slower. In time, all the microscopic food was removed from the water through constant circulation past the anemones, and then the animals be-gan to change their shapes. Their bodies, which had been thick and fat, grew long and neck-like; from a normal inch in length, they changed to three inches long and very slender. We suspected this was due to starvation. Then one day, after three months, we dropped a small crab into the aquarium. The anemones, moving on their new long necks, bent over and at-tacked the crab, striking downward like slow snakes. Their nor-mal reaction would have been to close up and draw in their tentacles, but these animals had changed their pattern in hunger, and now we found that when touched on the body, even down near the base, they moved downward, curving on their stalks, while their tentacles hungrily searched for food. There seemed even to be competition among the individuals, a thing we have never seen in a tide pool among anemones. This versatility had never been observed by us and is not mentioned in any of the literature we have seen.

The aquarium is a very valuable extension of shore obser-vation. Quick-eyed, timid animals soon become used to having humans about, and quite soon conduct their business under lights. If we could have put our sensitive urchins in an aquarium, we could have seen how it is that they move so rap-idly and how they are stimulated to aim their points at an ap-proaching body. But we preserved them, and of course they lost color and dropped many of their beautiful sharp spines. Also, we could have seen how the great snails are able to consume animal tissue so quickly. As it is, we do not know these things.

GEORGIA'S MARSHES
by George Reiger

From his book Wanderer on My Native Shore. *From his pulpit as conservation editor of* Field & Stream *(but written on his saltwater farm in Virginia), Rieger inveighs against lazy bureaucrats, selfish landowners, antihunters, developers — you name them, they have felt Rieger's barb. Rieger is big of frame and loud of voice, but he is gentle with the land and its creatures and he would have us be the same.*

⚓

GEORGIA SCHOOLCHILDREN MUST STILL MEMORIZE some of the verses of Sidney Lanier, but most young Americans have never heard of him. And little wonder. Southerners once read Lanier less because of the sentiments he expressed than because he had been a soldier in the lost Confederate cause. And because he had been a Confederate, many Northerners dismissed him as a "regional poet." Yet there are few sweeter testaments to nature's paradoxical combinations of delicacy and power, of life and death, than in the verses of Sidney Lanier. And there is no more compelling psalm to the beauty of the merging sea and shore than "Marshes of Glynn."

> *A league and a league of marsh grass,*
> *waist-high, broad in the blade,*
> *Green, and all of a height, and unflecked with*
> *a light or a shade,*
> *Stetch leisurely off, in a pleasant plain,*
> *To the terminal blue of the main.*

Glynn County, Georgia, still has leagues of marsh grass stretching off in a pleasant plain. However, Interstate 95, the city of Brunswick, and the development of Jekyll, St. Simons, and Sea islands have cast shadows across the formerly unsullied sea marshes. Furthermore, the settlement of upland Georgia, with the consequent conversion of blackwater rivers like the Big Satilla and the Altamaha from occasionally muddy streams into waters orange with clay, has ensured that "the terminal blue of the main" now lies many miles east of where it might still have been seen from shore in Lanier's day. Still the peace and the healing quality of the salt marsh remain:

> *Somehow my soul seems suddenly free*
> *From the weighing of fate and the sad*
> *discussion of sin,*
> *By the length and the breadth and the sweep of*
> *the marshes of Glynn.*
> *Ye marshes, how candid and simple and*
> *nothing-withholding and free*
> *Ye publish yourselves to the sky and offer*
> *yourselves to the sea!*

The rocky coats of the North Atlantic have a more flamboyant beauty than our coastal marshlands. High winds create sound and light spectacles where jagged cliffs stand opposed to the thundering sea. The contrasts and leitmotifs are Wagner or Richard Strauss, but the music of the Georgia salt marshes is Brahms or Lanier or even Johnny Mercer, whose wistful whimsy was inspired in part by the marshy tidal creeks on which he grew up near Savannah, Georgia.

My wife was born in Savannah and her best friend's uncle was Johnny Mercer. Her generation, like his, still heard the daily cries of the Gulah women selling shrimp and crab cakes and other products of the coastal waters. Below Savannah are sea meadows through which freighters and tankers glide like ships in a prairie mirage. Despite pollution in the creeks and river so bad at times that not even barnacles can grow on the channel markers, striped bass — some up to fifty-five pounds — red and black drums, spotted sea trout and southern flounder move in with the flooding tide to pursue bait fish and shrimp. One lazy, hazy summer day, my wife, four friends, and I caught all these fishes anchored just downstream from Savannah while holding on for dear life every time a great ship passed and rolled enormous waves up at us out of the channel.

Savannah's ties to the sea are more substantial than many Northerners imagine. Ever since the heyday of the Yankee clipper and whaling ship, the nation has accepted the mostly-Massachusetts-made myth that our best sailors come principally from New England. Yet the history of the U.S. Navy, Merchant Marine, and Coast Guard is star-studded by senior officers from the South, and a boy who used to pedal over on his bike to teach my wife to play chess when they were youngsters growing up in Savannah successfully defended the America's Cup and the country's maritime honor as skipper of the *Courageous*. Ted Turner may be brash and arrogant, but those faults are intrinsic to a competitive spirit which sails circles around less intrepid yachtsmen.

Savannah is also headquarters for an organization which has helped educate the last three Washington administrations as to the recreational values of our sea resources and, in the process, helped write federal legislation affecting dozens of different coastal activities. The National Coalition for Marine Conservation was founded by Frank E. Carlton, a Savannah-based urologist, who converted his anger at the commercially biased way in which the National Marine Fisheries Service used to conduct its business into leadership of an action-oriented consortium of influential friends and fellow anglers who have succeeded in carrying a message to Congress that the nation's twenty million marine recreational fishermen have at least as great a stake in fisheries management as the few tens of thousands of commercial fish boat owners and operators.

While Dr. Carlton has tried to suppress his partiality for Georgia coast through his efforts in other areas, particularly the preservation of bluefin tuna and the restoration of Atlantic salmon to New England and eastern Canada, he fortunately could not forbear to include Gray's Reef, lying fifteen miles east of Sapelo Island, Georgia, in a proposal to expand the nation's marine sanctuary program — a proposal which in no way interferes with traditional uses of this area, such as recreational and commercial fishing, but which does raise storm signals if offshore drilling or mining industries show interest.

Gray's Reef is enriched by life and detritus flowing from the marshes of Glynn and McIntosh counties. Its biotic diversity encompasses species characteristic of both littoral and pelagic zones of northern waters as well as those of the tropics. Grouper and northern porgy may be found gliding through sea whips and around hard coral heads while above them, amberjack feed on butterfish. Over the surrounding sands, sometimes tens of thousands of wintering scoters dive for tiny *Crassinella* and *Cyclocardia* clams.

Gray's Reef and its vicinity are riddled with ecological anomalies and contradictions, and its wonders are not perceived by people with purely political outlooks. General James Edward Oglethorpe saw Georgia only as a front line between the British Carolinas and Spanish-held Florida. Disappointed that his colonists of 1733 were more interested in building homes and businesses in Savannah than in killing Spaniards, Oglethorpe was finally able to recruit some professional soldiers to annihilate a Spanish force on June 9, 1742, in the marshes of St. Simons Island. Although the general was ultimately frustrated in his efforts to drive the Spanish out of St. Augustine, he did enable Charleston to emerge as the foremost British colony in the South by using Brunswick and the marshes of Glynn as buffers between South Carolina and Florida less than a hundred miles apart as the Spanish warships sailed.

Today, while American history buffs make pilgrimages to the battlefields of Bloody Marsh near Fort Frederica National Monument on St. Simons, natural history buffs make comparable pilgrimages to Sapelo Island just up the coast, where much of our knowledge of salt marsh ecology evolved.

Although salt marshes are found up the Atlantic coast as far its Nova Scotia, they do not reach their most luxuriant growth in individual plant size or area until the land merges more gradually with the sea from the mid-Atlantic coastal plain south. In addition, the rock-ribbed rivers of Canada and New England are parsimonious with mineral overburdens in contrast to the silty rivers of the Carolinas and Georgia. And ever since erosion-prone farming practices were introduced by European colonists in the seventeenth century, agriculture's losses of topsoil have been the littoral zone's gain in marshes.

Two plants of one genus dominate the salt marsh. As silts are washed from uplands and carried down to the estuaries, they begin to settle where the downstream currents are counteracted by incoming tides. As silt banks build, they become potential seedbeds for a variety of brackish-loving organisms including oysters and the pioneering form of *Spartina* known as *alterniflora*.

Spartina will germinate in seawater after being submerged for many weeks, but the sweeter the water, the less time it takes for the germination process to begin. This is why the most vigorous marshes lie in or close to brackish-water estuaries like those in the Chesapeake or the marshes of Glynn. This is also why upstream damming and the diversion of sweet water can cause the decline of downstream marshes as has occurred along parts of the Texas coast.

Seeds dropped farthest up an estuary and, hence, in a preferred location for marsh expansion are quick to germinate before drifting off an some ebbing tide to more saline environments. Once a seed misses its chance to propagate in the estuary that spawned it, or when a seed is dropped by a plant growing on the backside of a barrier island already far removed from estuarine influences, it becomes an oceanic space probe in which all metabolic processes are delayed with the evolutionary hope that the seed may eventually lodge in the muds of some previously unvegetated sandbar or flat.

An established marsh's vigor depends less on its seeds than on its rootstocks. *Spartina alterniflora* dies back each winter, leaving only a coarse stubble. However, each spring—unless a dry winter intervenes — emerald grass grows up, sometimes four feet high, from the old rhizomes. The lushness of this growth is dependent on injections of rainwater or estuarine mixing, and a dry winter can lead to stunted growth, even from well-established rhizomes, the following summer.

Similarly, an oil spill can suffocate a salt marsh's potential to renew itself in the spring by coating the rhizomes with tars or saturating the peat with chemicals having the effect of herbicides. However, unless an impervious crust forms over the rootstock, most salt marshes appear to recover from most forms of oil contamination within a year or two, even though all the subtle relationships between other plants and animals living within the *Spartina* matrix may not be reestablished for many years or even decades afterward.

The development of salt marshes parallels the millennial rise of the sea. Old barrier islands are washed away and tidal lagoons are drowned, but new marshes continue to emerge as fresh deposits of minerals are made off river mouths. There is an eternal standoff between the sea and the grass. Some years, the sea makes greater headway than the marsh — perhaps helped by the excavations of man and muskrat as well as by coastal subsidence due to tectonic plate movement. Other years and more often during the past several centuries, the marsh creeps out into the sea.

The fact that the marsh can rise as fast or slightly faster than the sea is due to the sod substrate created by the latticework root system of *S. alterniflora*. As each year's growth dies back, new plants find life in the peat of former years, and millimeter by precious millimeter, the marsh builds upon itself until it is no longer flooded twice a day by tidal waters and *Spartina patens* takes over the task of marsh consolidation.

S. patens — known as salt hay grass in New England, salt meadow hay in the mid-Atlantic, and marsh hay cordgrass in the South — is programmed to prevent the marsh from rising more than one foot above mean high water. It does this through the biologically clever expedient of creating such a dense and permanent mat of itself that nothing but its own kind ever has a chance to germinate in those areas where *S. patens* is most lush. However, where unusually high tides deposit mats of old *Spartina* cane on top of a marsh hay meadow, *S. patens* runs the risk of having itself overshadowed by a host of plants ready and eager to invade the detritus-enriched and elevated sod.

First, there is black needlerush, with spiky leaf tips and coarse rhizomes which form dense mats resistant both to erosion and to challenge from *S. patens* once it has been supplanted by needlerush in the marsh. In drier or sandy areas of an upland marsh, saltwort or glasswort often assumes dominance. Many long-time coastal dwellers are happy about this, for they pickle and preserve the succulent terminal branches of saltwort and say the flavor is comparable to watermelon rind. And in the days before the sea goose called brant learned to feed in upland fields, the nutrient-rich *Salicornia* was an important late winter food for these birds after local supplies of eelgrass and sea lettuce were all consumed.

Sea oxeye is a yellow flowering plant found in dense colonies along the upper fringe of almost every salt marsh from Virginia to Florida and, wonderfully enough, in Bermuda. Although dark brown, burrlike seed heads appear in late autumn, the most common method of propagation is by way of underground rhizomes that result in dense colonies which compete, wherever an additional millimeter of elevation allows them, with *Spartinas patens*.

Still, the most substantial threat to *S. patens'* accommodation with the sea is the saltbush community dominated by marsh elder and groundsel. Although most people assume these similar-looking plants are the same, they are readily distinguished by the fact that marsh elder's toothed and thicker leaves are oppositely arranged on their stems, while groundsel's thinner, more rounded (but still slightly toothed) leaves are alternately arranged. These salt-tolerant shrubs are found on the fringes of every salt marsh and intrude into *S. patens'* sphere of influence by trapping great mats of flotsam and jetsam on their branches during extreme high tides which then settle and shade out the lower-growing *S. patens.*

Of course, these typical steps in plant succession are disrupted wherever man goes with his draglines and backhoes. The concern is not that man alters the environment. After all, nature does that continually. But while nature always acts within the logic of its own imperatives, man simply doesn't know very much about what he is doing. He *thinks* he is dredging a marina or creating landfill for a housing development, but he invariably does the littoral equivalent of opening Pandora's box. Because man is a single-minded animal absorbed by immediate pleasures and profits, he rarely considers the dozens of chain-related consequences generated by even a single morning's work.

The question is not whether the U.S. Army Corps of Engineers should dredge, but only what to do with the endless tons of often highly contaminated spoils. The cost of dredging doubles for every half mile you must move the spoil from a dredge site, and most coastal cities long ago filled up every possibly cost-effective site within and without their corporate limits.

Savannah is plagued by silting that prevents ships beyond increasingly shallow drafts from moving upstream to off-load. Dredging is done periodically, but the former scouring effect of the Savannah River has been greatly diminished by upstream dams creating impoundments that straddle the Georgia — South Carolina border. Another dam that will eliminate a major portion of the free-flowing watershed that still exists between Augusta and the sea is on the engineering drawing board, and despite occasional political and fiscal setbacks, the Russell Dam seems fated to be built. It may provide some more largemouth bass habitat but it will do nothing but aggravate Savannah's increasingly tenuous commercial relationship with the sea.

Although man knows better, time and again he lets economic expediency overrule his common sense. In addition to the horrors that dumping toxic wastes and raw sewage wreaks on local water quality, such dumping inevitably contributes to shoaling when the many solids in each unfiltered discharge settle to the bottom. Yet for a long time Savannah dumped her municipal and industrial wastes directly into the river. The struggle between environmentalists and the business community culminated in 1972 when, being confronted by a December 31 court-ordered deadline, the American Cyanamid Corporation announced that it would no longer dump two thousand tons of sulfuric acid and heavy-metal traces every twenty-four hours into the Savannah River. Furthermore, it was abandoning plans to dump the wastes offshore in the Gulf Stream. Instead, American Cyanamid would create additional jobs and profits by using the wastes to manufacture dry wall for the housing market. After such a powerful adversary became their ally, environmentalists found that improvement of local water quality became a steady, although occasionally set-back, activity. Today Savannah and the marshes of Chatham County are no more polluted than Brunswick and the marshes of Glynn. That statement may sound cynical, but in comparison with what the situation was only twenty-five years ago, genuine progress has been made.

Nature has an apt symbol for man's foolhardy finagling with marine marshes and their water quality. It is a gigantic non-native grass found almost everywhere Americans have disturbed or contaminated coastal wetlands. From Jamaica Bay, New York —where mountains of garbage cover vast acreages of once-fertile fields of *Spartina* — to Glynn County, Georgia — where causeways across the marsh disrupt ancient patterns of water flow — reed grass or *Phragmites* flourishes where few other plants can survive.

Phragmites grows up to twelve feet high. This coarse exotic is often mistaken by people unfamiliar with wholesome marshes as characteristic of any marsh because *Phragmites* is characteristic of areas where marshes used to be. In the late fall, *Phragmites* develops feathery seed heads which are collected by coastal visitors and carried home to fill vases to decorate holiday sideboards. Such aesthetic gestures guarantee the spread of this subtle intruder into still more disturbed ecosystems.

This highly adaptable plant mirrors man's own adaptability, and its aggressive rhizomes enable it to spread rapidly once its feathery seeds have given it a toehold. Eventually it excludes all vegetative competition. *Phragmites* has adapted to both fresh-water and tidal environments and, thanks to well-intentioned tourists, it is now found throughout the world. It provides no food for wildlife, but in some areas it provides impenetrable shelter for colonies of rats, which forage out onto the nearby garbage mounds or littered roadways.

Man has used *Phragmites* to stabilize spoil banks, to provide windbreaks (difficult to eradicate once you decide to plant the area with something else), and in Eastern Europe, some people still make paper from its fibers. Finally, since it is such a super assimilator of all available nutrients in poor or salty soils, sanitation engineers are trying to learn whether filtering waste water through *Phragmites* stands will offer cheaper, but as thorough, secondary treatment as sewage plants.

Fortunately, once you leave roads, dikes, and spoil sites behind as you wander out over the marsh, you leave behind this emblem of man's degradation. It is then that you encounter the salt marsh's own symbol, the clapper rail.

> As the marsh-hen secretly builds on the watery
>   sod,
> Behold I will build me a nest on the greatness
>   of God;
> I will fly in the greatness of God as the
>   marsh-hen flies
> In the freedom that fills all the space 'twixt the
>   marsh and the skies.

Several members of the Family Rallidae are found as transients in the marshes of Glynn. The Virginia rail, sora rail, and the American coot are frequent migrant visitors. And the black and yellow rails may be far more common in Georgia marshes than their secretive ways permit local birders to know. These marshes are, also, well within the breeding and wintering range of both the common gallinule and the purple gallinule. However, none of these birds is as common to all the coastal marshes running from New England to Mexico as the marsh hen, alias clapper rail, alias *Rallus longirostris*.

My favorite moment in the marsh is just before the peak of high tide. During the spring and fall equinoxes, particularly if there is a steady northeast wind, water completely inundates the marsh and sometimes covers coastal roads so that cars appear to be running over the surface of an enlarged bay. When the tide finally turns in furious retreat to the sea, the marsh hens skulking in the roadside reeds herald the change with raucous laughter as though they themselves had turned the tide.

The marsh hen is a clown. Waiting in my duck punt for the sudden sight of waterfowl hovering overhead, I've become so engrossed with the fussy antics of an ablutionary clapper that ducks have come and gone without my notice. Once, in a flooded blind, a marsh hen and I played peekaboo, with the bird peering at me from the roof in a curious upside-down fashion and me trying to sneak my hand up to grab the bird's downcurved bill before it could pull away. The game went on for half an hour, and I never did catch the rail — or shoot a duck.

The call of the red-winged blackbird may define spring along the fringes of the upland marsh as the muttering of waterfowl defines autumn in the tidal guts and creeks. However, in most every season, the changing tides, the dawns and dusks, are signaled by the clamor of the clapper rail.

Marsh hens eat a variety of insects, fish, and crustacea, but the most important food in its diet is one of three species of fiddler crabs, *Uca minax*, *U. pugilator*, and *U. pugnax*. Two of its three specific names suggest a pugnacious temperament for this crab, and certainly the oversized cheliped or claw of the male gives them a formidable appearance. Furthermore, because the fiddler is predominately diurnal, casual human observers see what appears to be a good deal of fighting in the crab colonies. However, this apparent combat has more to do with love than war.

Uca minax, known as the mud fiddler, is the largest fiddler and is found farthest up estuaries where its tolerance for low salinities enables it to survive where other crabs cannot. *U. pugilator*, the china-back fiddler, displays a cream-colored shell interrupted by purple patterns. It inhabits sandy areas and is found running over the dunes some distance from the sea. *U. pugnax* is the marsh fiddler, and the smallest and most abundant of the trio. It is normally a dark brown color, which makes these sun-loving creatures inconspicuous against the marsh mud they inhabit.

Fiddlers hibernate during cold weather, which means more than five months in northern latitudes and, perhaps, three months in Georgia. However, a spell of warm weather in February is likely to bring them forth trotting in droves across a bar or the males hypnotically waving their major chelipeds by their burrows.

Light intensity and tides dictate the rhythms of fiddler existence. As soon as lengthening days assure the male fiddler that spring will not renege on its promise of lasting warmth, the crab repairs his burrow, which consists of two chambers at either end of an underground passageway. Spoil is packed into pellets and carried to the surface by using two or three legs on one side of his body as a cradle. The pellets are deposited to one side of the burrow's entrance and sometimes used to fashion a cone or hood as added protection from both the sun's desiccating radiation at low tide or as an extra millimeter of flood control at high tide. The china-back fiddler can create no such sophisticated constructions in sand, so it solves its home-maintenance problem by building burrows well above the high-tide line and often where it can receive some shade from the western sun by a convenient ridge or dune.

Of the two behaviors commonly seen in fiddler crabs — droving and cheliped waving — only the latter has an obvious explanation. As to why the crabs periodically move about in sizable hordes, the theory that these are migratory or dispersal marches, or that they represent feeding binges, is not supported by details within the activity itself. Here is an instanse in which a thoughtful observer could make a significant contribution to our understanding of a major component of the marsh ecosystem.

By contrast, there is no mystery about waving displays. They are used by male crabs to advertise their presence to other fiddlers. The waving is a warning to other males to keep away. At the same time, it allures reproductively active females. From dawn to dusk during all low tides, male fiddlers spend almost every moment waving their oversized chelipeds. Only after the tide reaches the halfway mark will the male crabs take time out to eat or repair their burrows. Otherwise, like conductors of silent symphonies, fiddlers scattered all along the muddy berm wave their massive batons.

When a female crab strolls into one of these amphitheaters, the tempo of claw waving becomes frantic. From a Brahms third symphonic movement, the orchestra suddenly switches to a Beethoven symphonic fourth. The nearest male dashes out to meet the female with his major cheliped held high. He attempts to herd her toward his burrow, and as she flirtatiously darts away, both crabs suddenly find they are in the territory of another male, who may rush out to lock claws with the interloping male. As the two males scuffle in a ritualized struggle designed to get the invader back onto his territory with a minimum of damage to the adversaries, the female may wander onto the territory of still another male, who finally succeeds in forcing the female into his burrow. Quickly he follows, plugs the entrance, and blocks any of her attempts to leave until she lays eggs in the far chamber. At that point, the male may emerge to feed, for he intuitively knows that once the female has laid eggs, she will stay in his burrow to incubate them.

When the eggs are ready to hatch, the female carries them in her apron, a chitinous integument beneath the belly carapace, out of the burrow and to the water's edge, where the brood is released as planktonic larvae. This is no random dispersal of young. The larvae are always released on a neap tide during the first or third quarters of the moon, when the tidal range and, consequently, water movement are at a minimum. This timing ensures that during the first few days of their development, when the larvae are most vulnerable, they will not be subjected to the additional hazard of being swept far from their natal shore.

Yet the larvae are not entirely passive passengers of the tidal flux. They swim to the surface on incoming tides to take advantage of the greater flow of water in the upper layers so they can remain close to future potential landing sites. Contrariwise, when the tide begins to ebb, the larvae sink toward the bottom to be out of the mainstream of outflowing water. After twenty-one days, the fiddler larvae have metamorphosed into adults and are ready to come ashore on a higher-than-usual spring tide which occurs on the new or full moon.

Within the simple cycles of existence in the marsh, procreation is nature's most compelling synonym for life itself. When the sun sets on the waving chelipeds of male *Uca* so that females can no longer see their come-hither movements, the males tap their feet, drum their chelipeds, or stridulate their body parts the way crickets "sing" in the dark to attract females throughout the night.

Each female crab must breed once a month during the warmer months of her brief life for her species to perpetuate itself. Thus, although such fundamental activities as feeding and burrowing are triggered by the sun, procreation is triggered by the moon's effect on the sea. The tide, not sunlight is what gives life to the fiddler crab.

> *How still the plains of the waters be!*
> *The tide is in his ecstasy.*
> *The tide is at his highest height:*
> *And it is night.*

The marshes at night murmur with sound. The ticking of yellow rail and the snapping of shrimp are heard against the subtle background rustle of water rising through the reeds. Periodically a plop says "muskrat," or a frantic splash describes an otter closing on fish, or a clapper rail so intent on extracting a fiddler crab from his burrow that the rail fails to notice the sibilant wings of a short-eared owl coursing over the flooding grass.

> *But who will reveal to our waking ken*
> *The forms that swim and the shapes that creep*
> *Under the waters of sleep?*

Thanks to enterprising fisheries biologists, we know a great deal more than Sidney Lanier could have imagined about the forms that swim and the shapes that creep within the marvelous marshes of Glynn. Although the littoral diversity seems typical of all the coast from Cape Hatteras to central Florida, an amazing variety of summer juveniles including grouper and angelfishes reminds the seiner of tropical waters farther south, much as winter visitors like tautog and weakfish recall the chilly waters of New England.

However, there are larger visitors to the marshes of Glynn that would have awed Lanier had he known of their existence "below when the tide comes in." Each May and June, tarpon, some of which weigh more than 150 pounds, and blacktip sharks, some more than seven feet long, move north along the beaches and into the bays behind the barrier islands to feed on the croaker and sea trout they find there in abundance. These fish are gypsies, and because you see a leaping, spiraling blacktip or a rolling, armor-scaled tarpon reflecting the late afternoon sun in a tidal channel one day does not mean they will be there the next.

Equally nomadic and far more awesome are the huge lemon sharks that pursue their ancient prey, stingrays, well into the marshes of Glynn. Some of the great predators are eleven feet long and weigh many hundreds of pounds, yet they can be found on the flooding tides at night in drains where men cull oysters in ankle-deep water by day.

Lemon sharks are Carcharhiniformes, which comprise the largest order of sharks, totaling 8 families, 47 genera, and approximately 199 species. The lemon is a member of the requiem shark family, which includes numerous "man-eaters" such as the bull, bronze whaler, ocean whitetip, and tiger; the lemon shark itself has been credited with several attacks.

The horror of being eaten by a shark is compounded in most people's minds by the alleged primitiveness of sharks in general. While it is no less fatal to be eaten by a bear or tiger, such a prospect is not so terrible in our imaginations, perhaps, because we share the land and warm blood with bears and tigers. We may feel sufficient courage to try talking one of these terrestrial predators out of attacking us or even, in extremis, we may counterattack the mammal. However, a shark has no cerebrum, and it is not intimidated by the mystery of the human voice nor by defensive-aggressive displays that, indeed, may only trigger the shark's feeding urge when it sees what it interprets to be an awkwardly swimming — hence, injured — marine animal.

The lemon shark is supremely well adapted to survive and flourish within the littoral zone, that area of the sea where man is most frequently found. It is no more primitive for its lack of a cerebrum than we are for not being able to outswim such creatures. In fact, sharks and man share a significant but rare predatory attribute: We are both able to feed on creatures larger than ourselves.

However, man maintains an ideal of instantaneous death which we call "humane," and much of our horror of sharks is based on our knowledge that not only do some species regularly attack large and warm-blooded prey, but that they cannot kill this larger prey humanely. In fact, the ideal of the tiny cookie-cutter shark is never to kill its prey at all! The cookie-cutter merely bites chunks out of a whale or dolphin until the frantic animal escapes — and by escaping, ensures that there will be future meals for cookie-cutter sharks elsewhere in the ocean.

Thus, while the sea trout and bluefish found in the marshes of Glynn are limited to prey they can swallow at one fell swoop or, at most, chomp up in two or three quick bites, a lemon shark can prey on sea trout, bluefish, or especially stingrays many times larger than its mouth. Such prey is seized, shaken, and a piece torn out and swallowed. If the prey is still available, it is seized again and again until all has been eaten or the shark's appetite has been satisfied. When such habits are applied to a human swimmer, it soothes our imaginations not one whit to know that the shark is not acting out of malicious intent.

The lemon shark is not only the largest predator found in the marshes of Glynn, its tolerance for a broad range of salinities and temperatures makes it a hardy research species from which scientists hope to learn more about the physiology and behavior of sharks in general. Already researchers have discovered how lemon sharks can exist in warm tidal backwaters and other environments with a low-oxygen content. Like human fetuses and burrowing animals, the lemon shark's blood has a high affinity for oxygen. When a lemon shark senses that the stingray it is trailing is on the verge of entering water too shallow for the shark to follow, an abundance of red blood cells suddenly inundates the shark's bloodstream and 20 percent more of the shark's gill surface is exposed to water flowing through the creature's mouth to extract all the oxygen possible from the surrounding environment. The shark accelerates to striking speed, and by the time the first chunk of the ray's wing has been ripped from its body, the shark's blood is saturated with oxygen at a partial pressure 200 percent lower than in most fishes at any activity level.

Cruising lemon sharks patrol more than a mile of new territory every hour. They are strongly affected by sunlight, and at dawn and dusk they generally move toward it. Thus, as the sun sets, lemon sharks off Georgia beaches move inshore, through inlets, and, if under the spell of a flooding tide, well up into the marshes to feed. As the tide turns, the sharks move back to the deeper channels within the marsh and bays until the rising sun draws them offshore again.

Even more curious, a lemon shark's hunger seems to wax and wane within four-day cycles. Lemon sharks consume the equivalent of 3 percent of their body weight daily, but this is average consumption over the four-day periods. Every fourth night lemon sharks appear to be more aggressively hungry and will attack more prey than during other nights of the cycle. Thus, a 400-pound lemon shark is more likely to eat one 48-pound meal to hold him 96 hours than 12 pounds of flesh every night for four consecutive nights.

Every Georgia summer, a small and secretive number of recreational fishermen angle for the huge lemon sharks that move into the marshes at night. The fishing is considered most sporting if it is done from a stationary platform like a dock or launch ramp. Balloons are used to suspend the bait just off bottom so crabs and other scavengers can't chew up the fresh ray's wing before a cruising lemon shark discovers it.

Water-skiers also use the marsh channels for their recreation, and one afternoon several years ago, three boys and a girl were taking turns behind their speedboat when one of them spotted a balloon moving slowly in the current. They ran over to it, caught up the end of the broken line, and were excited to feel a live weight at the other end. However, when a shark's head broke the surface whose eyes were "an ax handle apart," they dropped the line and switched their waterskiing to Lake Sinclair 120 miles away and inland!

Unlike Sidney Lanier, they had never wondered "what swimmeth below when the tide comes in on the length and the breadth of the marvellous marshes of Glynn." Also unlike Lanier, they wanted to know nothing more about it!

Going Underwater

Waters right next to the shore are often turbid, especially at river mouths. But many seasides are worth underwater exploration; certainly reefs are. Here's the man who started it all.

MENFISH
by Captain J. Y. Cousteau with Frédéric Dumas

From their book The Silent World. *Cousteau and his merry band (Dumas and Philippe Tailliez) developed the demand valve that could deliver compressed air from a backpack of tanks to a diver, whatever his or her diving depth. It meant freedom to swim underwater to all depths with both hands free, freedom to explore the silent world. Cousteau has gone on to bigger things; he is underwater man personified. But "Menfish" is Cousteau at his earlier, simpler best, just beginning to get under and record the wonder of the deep.*

I missed a chance to meet the Captain in 1953. I was with a bunch of U.S. Navy divers doing some work in the Mediterranean, all of us using three-bottle Aqua-lungs, Cousteau's invention, when we heard the great man was in Marseilles. We tried to hook up with him, but alas, as usual, he was on the move.

⚓

ONE MORNING in June, 1943, I went to the railway station at Bandol on the French Riviera and received a wooden case expressed from Paris. In it was a new and promising device, the result of years of struggle and dreams, an automatic compressed-air diving lung conceived by Emile Gagnan and myself. I rushed it to Villa Barry where my diving comrades, Philippe Tailliez and Frédéric Dumas waited. No children ever opened a Christmas present with more excitement than ours when we unpacked the first "aqualung." If it worked, diving could be revolutionized.

We found an assembly of three moderate-sized cylinders of compressed air, linked to an air regulator the size of an alarm clock. From the regulator there extended two tubes, joining on a mouthpiece. With this equipment harnessed to the back, a watertight glass mask over the eyes and nose, and rubber foot fins, we intended to make unencumbered flights in the depths of the sea.

We hurried to a sheltered cove which would conceal our activity from curious bathers and Italian occupation troops. I checked the air pressure. The bottles contained air condensed to one hundred and fifty times atmospheric pressure. It was difficult to contain my excitement and discuss calmly the plan of the first dive. Dumas, the best goggle diver in France, would stay on shore keeping warm and rested, ready to dive to my aid, if necessary. My wife, Simone, would swim out on the surface with a snorkel breathing tube and watch me through her submerged mask. If she signaled anything had gone wrong, Dumas could dive to me in seconds. Didi, as he was known on the Riviera, could skin-dive to sixty feet.

My friends harnessed the three-cylinder block on my back with the regulator riding at the nape of my neck and the hoses looped over my head. I spat on the inside of my shatterproof glass mask and rinsed it in the surf, so that mist would not form inside. I molded the soft rubber flanges of the mask tightly over forehead and cheekbones. I fitted the mouthpiece under my lips and gripped the nodules between my teeth. A vent the size of a paper clip was to pass my inhalations and exhalations beneath the sea. Staggering under the fifty-pound apparatus, I walked with a Charlie Chaplin waddle into the sea.

The diving lung was designed to be slightly buoyant. I reclined in the chilly water to estimate my compliance with Archimedes' principle that a solid body immersed in liquid is buoyed up by a force equal to the weight of the liquid displaced. Dumas justified me with Archimedes by attaching seven pounds of lead to my belt. I sank gently to the sand. I breathed sweet effortless air. There was a faint whistle when I inhaled and a light rippling sound of bubbles when I breathed out. The regulator was adjusting pressure precisely to my needs.

I looked into the sea with the same sense of trespass that I have felt on every dive. A modest canyon opened below full of dark green weeds, black sea urchins and small flower-like white algae. Fingerlings browsed in the scene. The sand sloped down into a clear blue infinity. The sun struck so brightly I had to squint. My arms hanging at my sides, I kicked the fins languidly and traveled down, gaining speed, watching the beach reeling past. I stopped kicking and the momentum carried me on a fabulous glide. When I stopped, I slowly emptied my lungs and held my breath. The diminished volume of my body decreased the lifting force of water, and I sank dreamily down. I inhaled a great chestful and retained it. I rose toward the surface.

My human lungs had a new role to play, that of a sensitive ballasting system. I took normal breaths in a slow rhythm, bowed my head and swam smoothly down to thirty feet. I felt no increasing water pressure, which at that depth is twice that of the surface. The aqualung automatically fed me increased compressed air to meet the new pressure layer. Through the fragile human lung linings this counter-pressure was being transmitted to the bloodstream and instantly spread throughout the incompressible body. My brain received no subjective news of the pressure. I was at ease, except for a pain in the middle ear and sinus cavities. I swallowed as one does in a landing airplane to open my eustachian tubes and healed the pain. (I did not wear earplugs, a dangerous practice when underwater. Earplugs would have trapped a pocket of air between them and the eardrums. Pressure building up in the eustachian tubes would have forced my eardrums outward, eventually to the bursting point.)

I reached the bottom in a state of transport. A school of silvery sars (goat bream), round and flat as saucers, swam in a rocky chaos. I looked up and saw the surface shining like a defective mirror. In the center of the looking glass was the trim silhouette of Simone, reduced to a doll. I waved. The doll waved at me.

I became fascinated with my exhalations. The bubbles swelled on the way up through lighter pressure layers, but were peculiarly flattened like mushroom caps by their eager push against the medium. I conceived the importance bubbles were to have for us in the dives to come. As long as air boiled on the surface all was well below. If the bubbles disappeared there would be anxiety, emergency measures, despair. They roared out of the regulator and kept me company. I felt less alone.

I swam across the rocks and compared myself favorably with the stars. To swim fishlike, horizontally, was the logical method in a medium eight hundred times denser than air. To halt and hang attached to nothing, no lines or air pipe to the surface, was a dream. At night I had often had visions of flying by extending my arms as wings. Now I flew without wings. (Since that first aqualung flight, I have never had a dream of flying).

I thought of the helmet diver arriving where I was on his ponderous boots and struggling to walk a few yards, obsessed with his umbilici and his head imprisoned in copper. On skin dives I had seen him leaning dangerously forward to make a step, clamped in heavier pressure at the ankles than the head, a cripple in an alien land. From this day forward we would swim across miles of country no man had known, free and level, with our flesh feeling what the fish scales know.

I experimented with all possible maneuvers of the aqualung — loops, somersaults and barrel rolls. I stood upside down on one finger and burst out laughing, a shrill distorted laugh. Nothing I did altered the automatic rhythm of air. Delivered from gravity and buoyancy I flew around in space.

I could attain almost two knots' speed, without using my arms. I soared vertically and passed my own bubbles. I went down to sixty feet. We had been there many times without breathing aids, but we did not know what happened below that boundary. How far could we go with this strange device?

Fifteen minutes had passed since I left the little cove. The regulator lisped in a steady cadence in the ten-fathom layer and I could spend an hour there on my air supply. I determined to stay as long as I could stand the chill. Here were tantalizing crevices we had been obliged to pass fleetingly before. I swam inch by inch into a dark narrow tunnel, scraping my chest on the floor and ringing the air tanks on the ceiling. In such situations a man is of two minds. One urges him on toward mystery and the other reminds him that he is a creature with good sense that can keep him alive, if he will use it. I bounced against the ceiling. I'd used one-third of my air and was getting lighter. My brain complained that this foolishness might sever my air hoses. I turned over and hung on my back.

The roof of the cave was thronged with lobsters. They stood there like great flies on a ceiling. Their heads and antennae were pointed toward the cave entrance. I breathed lesser lungfuls to keep my chest from touching them. Above water was occupied, ill-fed France. I thought of the hundreds of calories a diver loses in cold water. I selected a pair of one-pound lobsters and carefully plucked them from the roof, without touching their stinging spines. I carried them toward the surface.

Simone had been floating, watching my bubbles wherever I went. She swam down toward me. I handed her the lobsters and went down again as she surfaced. She came up under a rock which bore a torpid Provençal citizen with a fishing pole. He saw a blonde girl emerge from the combers with lobsters wriggling in her hands. She said, "Could you please watch these for me?" and put them on the rock. The fisherman dropped his pole.

Simone made five more surface dives to take lobsters from me and carry them to the rock. I surfaced in the cove, out of the fisherman's sight. Simone claimed her lobster swarm. She said, "Keep one for yourself, *monsieur*. They are very easy to catch if you do as I did."

Lunching on the treasures of the dive, Tailliez and Dumas questioned me on every detail. We reveled in plans for the aqualung. Tailliez pencilled the tablecloth and annnounced that each yard of depth we claimed in the sea would open to mankind three hundred thousand cubic kilometers of living space. Tailliez, Dumas and I had come a long way together. We had been eight years in the sea as goggle divers. Our new key to the hidden world promised wonders. We recalled the beginning. . . .

Our first tool was the underwater goggle, a device that was known centuries ago in Polynesia and Japan, was used by sixteen-century Mediterranean coral divers, and has been rediscovered about every decade in the last fifty years. The naked human eye, which is almost blind under water, can see clearly through watertight spectacles.

One Sunday morning in 1936 at Le Mourillon, near Toulon, I waded into the Mediterranean and looked into it through Fernez goggles. I was a regular Navy gunner, a good swimmer interested only in perfecting my crawl style. The sea was merely a salty obstacle that burned my eyes. I was astounded by what I saw in the shallow shingle at Le Mourillon, rocks covered with green, brown and silver forests of algae and fishes unknown to me, swimming in crystalline water. Standing up to breathe I saw a trolley car, people, electric-light poles. I put my eyes under again and civilization vanished with one last bow. I was in a jungle never seen by those who floated on the opaque roof.

Sometimes we are lucky enough to know that our lives have been changed, to discard the old, embrace the new, and run headlong down an immutable course. It happened to me at Le Mourillon on that summer's day, when my eyes were opened on the sea.

Soon I listened hungrily to gossip about heroes of the Mediterranean, with their Fernez goggles, Le Corlieu foot fins, and barbarous weapons to slay fish beneath the waves. At Sanary the incredible Le Moigne immersed himself in the ocean and killed fish with a slingshot!

There also was a fabulous creature named Frédéric Dumas, son of a physics professor, who speared fish with a curtain rod. These men were crossing the frontier of two hostile worlds.

Two years of goggle dives passed before I met Dumas. He told me how it had begun with him. "One day in the summer of 1938 I am out on the rocks when I see a real manfish, much further on in evolution than me. He never lifts his head to breathe, and after a surface dive water spouts out of a tube he has in his mouth. I am amazed to see rubber fins on his feet. I sit admiring his agility and wait until he gets cold and has to come in. His name is Lieutenant de Vaisseau Philippe Tailliez. His undersea gun works on the same theory as mine. Tailliez's goggles are bigger than mine. He tells me where to get goggles and fins and how to make a breathing pipe from a garden hose. We make a date for a hunting party. This day is a big episode in my undersea life."

The day was important for each of us. It brought Tailliez, Dumas and me into a diving team. I already knew Tailliez.

Undersea hunting raged, with arbalests, spears, spring guns, cartridge-propelled arrows, and the elegant technique of the American writer, Guy Gilpatric, who impaled fish with fencing lunges. The fad resulted in almost emptying the littoral of fish and arousing the commercial fishermen to bitter anger. They claimed we drove away fish, damaged nets, looted their seines, and caused mistrals with our snorkels.

One day, however, when Dumas was diving he noticed a picturesque individual watching him from a large power boat, a formidable man stripped to the waist. He exhibited a gallery of torsoid tattoos consisting of dancing girls and famous generals such as Maréchal Lyautey and Papa Joffre. Didi winced as the individual hailed him, for he recognized Carbonne, the dreaded Marseilles gangster, whose idol was Al Capone.

Carbonne summond Didi to his ladder and handed him aboard. He asked him what he was doing. "Oh, just diving," Didi said, warily.

"I am always coming out here to take a peaceful rest from the city," said Carbonne. "I like what you are doing. I wish you to conduct all of your activities from my ship."

Didi's patron heard about the fishermen's hatred of divers. It incensed him and, cruising among the fishing boats with his hairy arm flung over Didi's shoulder, he bawled out, "Hey, you fellows — don't forget this is *my friend*!"

We twitted Didi about his gangster, but noted that the fishermen no longer molested him. They diverted their protests to the government, which passed a law severely regulating underwater hunting. Air-breathing apparatus and cartridge-propelled harpoons were forbidden. Divers were required to take out hunting licenses and join a recognized spear-fishing club. But from Menton to Marseilles the shore had emptied of larger fauna. Another remarkable thing was noticed. The big pelagic fish had learned how to stay out of range of weapons. They would insolently keep five feet away from a slingshot, exactly beyond its range. A rubber-propelled harpoon gun, which could shoot eight feet, found the fish a little over eight feet away. They stayed fifteen feet from the biggest harpoon guns. For ages man had been the most harmless animal under water. When he suddenly learned underwater combat, the fish promptly adopted safety tactics.

In the goggle-diving era Dumas made a lighthearted bet at Le Brusq that he could spear two hundred and twenty pounds of fish in two hours. He made five dives within the time limit, to depths of forty-five to sixty feet. On each dive he speared and fought a mammoth fish in the short period he could hold his breath. He brought up four groupers and an eighty-pound liche (palomata or leerfish). Their total weight was two hundred and eighty pounds.

One of our favorite memories is of a fighting liche which probably weighed two hundred pounds. Didi speared him and we went down in relays to fight him. Twice we managed to drag him to the surface in our arms. The big fellow seemed to like air as much as we did. He gained strength as we wore out, and at last the monarch of liches escaped.

We were young and sometimes we went beyond the limits of common sense. Once Tailliez was diving alone in December at Carqueiranne, with his dog Soika guarding his clothes. The water was 52° Fahrenheit. Philippe was trying to spear some big sea bass but had to break off the chase when he could no longer stand the cold. He found himself several hundred yards from the deserted shore. The return swim was a harrowing, benumbed struggle. He dragged himself out on a rock and fainted. A bitter wind swept him. He had small chance of surviving such an exposure. The wolfhound, moved by an extraordinary instinct, covered him with its body and breathed hot air on his face. Tailliez awoke with near-paralyzed hands and feet and stumbled to a shelter.

Our first researches in diving physiology were attempts to learn about cold. Water is a better heat conductor than air and has an extreme capacity for draining off calories. Bodily heat lost in sea bathing is enormous, placing a grave strain on the central heating plant of the body. The body must above all keep its central temperature constant. Exposed to cold the body makes a ruthless strategic retreat, first abandoning the skin to cold and then the subcutaneous layer, by means of vasoconstriction of the superficial blood vessels — gooseflesh. If the cold continues to draw off heat, the body will surrender the hands and feet to conserve the vital center. When the inner temperature drops, life is in danger.

We learned that bathers who wrapped in blankets were doing exactly the wrong thing. A covering does not restore heat, it merely requires the central heating plant to burn up more calories to flush warmth into the outer layer. The process is accompanied by severe nervous reactions. By the same token hot drinks and alcohol are useless in restoring surface temperature. We sometimes take a drink of brandy after a hard dive, rather for its depressant effect than with any expectation of gaining warmth from it. We learned that the best way to restore heat is the most obvious one, to get into a very hot bath or stand between two fires on the beach.

We discovered a surprising fact about the practice of coating oneself with grease for cold swims. Grease does not stick to the skin. It washes away, leaving a mere film of oil, which, far from protecting the swimmer, slightly increases the loss of caloric heat. Grease would be acceptable insulation, however, if it could be injected under the skin to simulate the splendid blubber underwear of the whale.

To protect myself from cold I spent days tailoring and vulcanizing rubberized garments. In the first one, I looked something like Don Quixote. I made another which could be slightly inflated to provide more insulation, but there was only one depth in which the suit was equilibrated, and I spent most of the time fighting against being hauled up or down. Another weakness of this dress was that the air would rush to the feet, leaving me in a stationary, head-down position. Finally, in 1946, we evolved the constant-volume dress we use now in cold water. It is inflated by the diver's nasal exhalations, blown out under the edges of an inner mask. Air escape valves at the head, wrist and ankles keep the diver stable in any depth or bodily position. Marcel Ichac, the explorer, found it effective in dives under Greenland ice floes on the recent Paul-Émile Victor Arctic expedition. Dumas has designed a "mid-season" dress, a feather-light foam rubber jerkin which protects for twenty minutes in cold water and leaves the diver all his agility.

Vanity colored our early skin dives. We plumed ourselves at the thought that we latecomers could attain the working depths of pearl and sponge divers who had made their first plunges as infants. In 1939 on Djerba Island, off Tunisia, I witnessed and confirmed with a sounding line a remarkable dive by a sixty-year-old Arab sponge diver. Without breathing apparatus he reached one hundred and thirty feet, in an immersion time of two and one-half minutes.

The ordeals of such dives are only for the exceptional man. As the naked diver sounds through increasing pressure layers, the air in his lungs is physically shrunk. Human lungs are balloons in a flexible cage, which is literally squeezed in under pressure. At a hundred feet down the air in the balloon occupies one-fourth the space it does at the surface. Further down the ribs reach a position of inflexibility and may crack and collapse.

However, the working depth of sponge divers is usually not more than the three-atmosphere stratum, sixty-six feet, where their rib cages are reduced to one-third normal size. We learned to go that deep without apparatus. We made sixty-foot dives of two-minute durations, aided by several pounds of belt weights. Under twenty-five feet the weights became heavier in proportion to the compression of the rib cage, so that there was a certain uneasiness about meeting with accidents while weighted to the bottom.

Dumas's skin-diving technique consisted of floating face underwater and breathing through a snorkel tube. When he spotted some attraction below, he would execute a maneuver called the *coup de reins*, literally "stroke of the loins," the technique the whale uses to sound. For a floating man, it consists of bending from the waist and pointing the head and torso down. Then the legs are thrown up in the air with a powerful snap and the diver plummets straight down. Lightning dives require well-trained, wide-open eustachian tubes to deal with the rapidly mounting pressure.

When we had attained the zone of sponge divers we had no particular sense of satisfaction, because the sea concealed enigmas that we could only glimpse in lightning dives. We wanted breathing equipment, not so much to go deeper, but to stay longer, simply to live a while in the new world. We tried Commandant Le Prieur's independent diving gear, a cylinder of compressed air slung across the chest and releasing a continuous flow into a face mask. The diver manually valved the air to meet pressure and cut down waste. We had our first grand moments of leisure in the sea with Le Prieur's lung. But the continuous discharge of air allowed only short submersions.

The gunsmith of my cruiser, the *Suffren*, built an oxygen-rebreathing apparatus I designed. He transformed a gas-mask canister of soda lime, a small oxygen bottle, and a length of motorbike inner tube into a lung that repurified exhalations by filtering out the carbon dioxide in the soda lime. It was self-contained, one could swim with it, and it was silent. Swimming twenty-five feet down with the oxygen apparatus was the most serene thrill I have had in the water. Silent and alone in trancelike land, one was accepted by the sea. My euphoria was all too short.

Having been told that oxygen was safe down to forty-five feet, I asked two sailors from the *Suffren* to man a dinghy above me, while I dived to the boundary of oxygen. I went down with a ceremonious illusion. I was accepted in the sea jungle and would pay it the compliment of putting aside my anthropoid ways, clamp my legs together and swim down with the spinal undulations of a porpoise. Tailliez had demonstrated that a man could swim on the surface without using arms or legs. I borrowed the characteristics of a fish, notwithstanding certain impediments such as my anatomy and a ten-pound lead pipe twisted around my belt.

I undulated through the amazingly clear water. Ninety feet away I saw an aristocratic group of silver and gold gilt-heads wearing their scarlet gill patches like British brigadiers. I wiggled toward them and got very close without alarming them. My fish personality was fairly successful, but I remembered that I could swim a great deal faster by crudely kicking my fins. I started chasing a fish and cornered him off in his cave. He bristled his dorsal fins and rolled his eyes uneasily. He made a brave decision and sprang at me, escaping by inches. Below I saw a big blue dentex (bream) with a bitter mouth and hostile eyes. He was hanging about forty-five feet down. I descended and the fish backed away, keeping a good distance.

Then my lips began to tremble uncontrollably. My eyelids fluttered.

My spine was bent backward like a bow.

With a violent gesture I tore off the belt weight and lost consciousness.

The sailors saw my body reach the surface and quickly hauled me into the boat.

I had pains in neck and muscles for weeks. I thought my soda lime must have been impure. I spent the winter on the *Suffren* building an improved oxygen lung, one that would not induce convulsions. In the summer I went back to the same place off Porquerolles and went down forty-five feet with the new lung. I convulsed so suddenly that I do not remember jettisoning my belt weight. I came very near drowning. It was the end of my interest in oxygen.

In the summer of 1939 I made a speech at a dinner party, explaining why war could not come for at least ten years. Four days later I was aboard cruiser, speeding west under secret orders; the next day at Oran we heard the declaration of war. At our ship line lay a division of Royal Navy torpedo boats, one of which was disabled by a heavy steel cable fouled in her screw. There were no navy divers at Oran. I volunteered to make a skin dive to survey the situation.

Even the sight of the screw did not cool my ardor: The thick wire was wound six times around the shaft and several times around the blades. I called on five good skin divers from my ship, and we dived repeatedly to hack away the cable. After hours of work clearing the propeller, we crawled back on our ship, barely able to stand. The torpedo boat sailed out with its division, and as it passed, the crew turned out in a line at the rail and gave three cheers for the crazy Frenchmen. That day I learned that heavy exertion under water was madness. It was absolutely necessary to have breathing apparatus to do such jobs.

Later in the war while I was working for Naval Intelligence in Marseilles against the occupying powers, my commander insisted that I continue diving experiments when my duties permitted. Diving helped camouflage the secret work. I tested the Fernez diving apparatus, which consisted of an air pipe from a surface pump. The pipe was carried across the diver's face to a duck-beak valve which released a constant flow of pumped air. The diver tapped the flow with a mouthpiece, sucking the air he needed. It was the simplest diving gear ever designed. It tethered a man to the surface and unnecessarily wasted half the air, but at least it did not use treacherous oxygen.

I was enjoying the full breaths of the Fernez pump one day at forty feet when I felt a strange shock in my lungs. The rumble of exhaust bubbles stopped. Instantly I closed my glottis, sealing the remaining air in my lungs. I hauled on the air pipe and it came down without resistance. The pipe had broken near the surface. I swam to the boat. Later I realized the danger I had faced. If I hadn't instinctively shut the air valve in my throat the broken pipe would have fed me thin surface air and the water would have collapsed my lungs in the frightful "squeeze."

In testing devices in which one's life is at stake, such accidents induce zeal for improvement. We were working on defenses against broken pipes one day with Dumas seventy-five feet down, breathing from the Fernez pipe. I was in the tender, watching the pipe, when I saw it rupture. Dumas was trapped in pressure three times greater than the surface. I grabbed the pipe before it sank and reeled it in frantically, ill with suspense. I could feel heavy tugs from below. Then Dumas appeared, red-faced and choking, his eyes bulging. But he was alive. He, too, had locked his glottis in time and had then climbed the pipe hand over hand. We worked on the gear until it operated more reliably, but the pump could take us no further. It fastened us on a leash and we wanted freedom.

We were dreaming about a self-contained compressed-air lung. Instead of Le Prieur's hand valve, I wanted an automatic device that would release air to the diver without his thinking about it, something like the demand system used in the oxygen masks of high-altitude fliers. I went to Paris to find an engineer who would know what I was talking about. I had the luck to meet Émile Gagnan, an expert on industrial-gas equipment for a huge international corporation. It was December, 1942, when I outlined my demands to Émile. He nodded encouragingly and interrupted. "Something like this?" he asked and handed me a small bakelite mechanism. "It is a demand valve I have been working on to feed cooking gas automatically into the motors of automobiles." At the time there was no petrol for automobiles and all sorts of projects were under way for utilizing the fumes of burning charcoal and natural gas. "The problem is somewhat the same as yours," said Émile.

In a few weeks we finished our first automatic regulator. Émile and I selected a lonely stretch of the river Marne for a test dive. He stood on the bank while I waded in over my head. The regulator furnished plenty of air without effort on my part. But the air rushed wastefully out of the exhaust pipe in the fashion of the Fernez gear. I tried standing on my head. The air supply almost ceased. I couldn't breathe. I tried swimming horizontally, and the air flowed in a perfectly controlled rhythm. But how were we going to dive if we couldn't operate vertically?

Chilled and disappointed, we drove home, analyzing the regulator's reason for such tricks. Here it was, a miracle of design, the first stage efficiently reducing one hundred and fifty atmospheres to six atmospheres, and the second control stage rationing that to breathing density and volume. Before we reached Paris we had the answer.

When I was standing up in the water the level of the exhaust was higher than the intake and that six-inch difference in pressure allowed the air to overflow. When I stood on my head, the exhaust was six inches lower, suppressing the air flow. When I swam horizontally, the exhaust and intake were in the same pressure level and the regulator worked perfectly. We arrived at the simple solution of placing the exhaust as close as possible to the intake so that the pressure variations could not disrupt the flow. The improvement worked perfectly in a tank test in Paris.

Author, Author
(An Interlude)

Writers pursuing other goals or covering other subjects will often make casual references to the seaside on their way to fry bigger fish. Here are four examples from recent literature, selected and included here just for the hell of it.

RABBIT IS RICH
by John Updike

This is the third of the four-book cycle of Rabbit books, about growing up in eastern Pennsylvania, first a pretty fair high school basketball player, later a linotype operator, an automobile dealer, and then in retirement. Here Rabbit, (Harry Angstrom), his wife, and two other couples are flying to the Caribbean from Philadelphia for sun, drinking, golf, and a little wife swapping. The plane's flight path takes them across southern New Jersey.

FREE! Macadam falls away beneath the wheels, a tawny old fort can be glimpsed as they lift off the runway beneath the rounded riveted edge of one great wing, the gas tanks of South Philadelphia are reduced to a set of white checkers. The wheels thump, retracted, and cruel photons glitter on the aluminum motionless beside the window. The swift ascent of the plane makes their blood weighty; Janice's hand sweats in his. She had wanted him to have the window seat, so she wouldn't have to look. There is marsh below, withered and veined with salt water. Harry marvels at the industrial buildings beyond the Delaware: flat gravel roofs vast as parking lots and parking lots all inlaid with glittering automobile roofs like bathroom floors tiled with jewels. And in junkyards of cars the effect is almost as brilliant. The NO SMOKING sign goes off. Behind the Angstroms the voices of the Murketts and the Harrisons begin to chatter. They all had a drink at an airport bar, though the hour was eleven in the morning. Harry has flown before, but to Texas with the Army and dealers' conferences in Cleveland and Albany: never aloft on vacation like this, due east into the sun. How quickly, how silently, the 747 eats up the toy miles below! Sun glare travels with them across lakes as momentarily as across a mirror. The winter has been eerily mild thus far, to spite the Ayatollah; on golf courses the greens show as living discs and ovals amid the white beans of the traps and on the fairways he can spot moving specks, men playing. Composition tennis courts are dominoes from this height, drive-in movies have the shape of a fan, baseball diamonds seem a species of tattered money. Cars move very slowly and with an odd perfection, as if the roads hold tracks. The houses of the Camden area scatter, relenting to disclose a plowed field or an estate with its prickly mansion and eye of a swimming pool tucked in the midst of woods; and then within another minute, still climbing, Harry is above the black-red carpet of the Jersey Pines, scored with yellow roads and patches of scraping but much of it still unmarred, veins of paler unleafed trees following the slope of land and flow of water among the darker evergreens, the tints of competition on earth made clear to the eye so hugely lifted. Janice lets go of his hand and gives signs of having swallowed her terror.

"What do you see?" she asks.

"The Shore."

It is true, in another silent stride the engines had inched them to the edge of the ocean of trees and placed underneath them a sandy strip, separated from the mainland by a band of flashing water and filled to a precarious fullness with linear summer cities, etched there by builders who could not see, as Harry can, how easily the great shining shoulder of the ocean could shrug and immerse and erase all traces of men. Where the sea impinges on the white sand a frill of surf slowly waves, a lacy snake pinned in place. Then this flight heads over the Atlantic at an altitude from which no whitecaps can be detected in the bluish hemisphere below, and immensity becomes nothingness. The plane, its earnest droning without and its party mutter and tinkle within, becomes all of the world there is.

NIXON IN MIAMI
by Norman Mailer

From his book Miami and the Siege of Chicago. *Subtitled "An Informal History of the Republican and Democratic Conventions of 1968," the book starts in Miami Beach, August 3, as the Republicans gather. Mailer sets the scene with his impression of the shore, the beach, and the earth beneath the streets.*

⚓

MIAMI BEACH

THEY SNIPPED THE RIBBON in 1915, they popped the cork, Miami Beach was born. A modest burg they called a city, nine-tenths jungle. An island. It ran along a coastal barrier the other side of Biscayne Bay from young Miami — in 1868 when Henry Lum, a California 'forty-niner, first glimpsed the island from a schooner, you may be certain it was jungle, coconut palms on the sand, mangrove swamp and palmetto thicket ten feet off the beach. But by 1915, they were working the vein. John S. Collins, a New Jersey nurseryman (after whom Collins Avenue is kindly named) brought in bean fields and avocado groves; a gent named Fisher, Carl G., a Hoosier — he invented Prestolite, a millionaire — bought up acres from Collins, brought in a work-load of machinery, men, even two elephants, and jungle was cleared, swamps were filled, small residential islands were made out of baybottom mud, dredged, then relocated, somewhat larger natural islands adjacent to the barrier island found themselves improved, streets were paved, sidewalks put in with other amenities — by 1968, one hundred years after Lum first glommed the beach, large areas of the original coastal strip were covered over altogether with macadam, white condominium, white luxury hotel and white stucco

159

flea-bag. Over hundreds, then thousands of acres, white sidewalks, streets and white buildings covered the earth where the
jungle had been. Is it so dissimilar from covering your poor pu-
bic air with adhesive tape for fifty years? The vegetal memories
of that excised jungle haunted Miami Beach in a steam-pot of
miasmas. Ghosts of expunged flora, the never-born groaning in
vegetative chancery beneath the asphalt came up with a tropical
curse, an equatorial leaden wet sweat of air which rose from the
earth itself, rose right up through the baked asphalt and into
the heated air which entered the lungs like a hand slipping into
a rubber glove.

The temperature was not that insane. It hung around 87 day
after day, at night it went down to 82, back to the same 87 in
the A.M. — the claims of the News Bureau for Miami Beach
promised that in 1967 temperature exceeded 90° only four
times. (Which the Island of Manhattan could never begin to
say.) But of course Miami Beach did not have to go that high,
for its humidity was up to 87 as well — it was, on any and every
day of the Republican Convention of 1968, one of the hottest
cities in the world. The reporter was no expert on tropical heats
— he had had, he would admit, the island of Luzon for a summer in World War II; and basic training in the pine woods of
Fort Bragg, North Carolina, in August; he had put in a week at
Las Vegas during July — temperatures to 110; he had crossed
the Mojave Desert once by day; he was familiar with the New
York subway in the rush hour on the hottest day of the year.
These were awesome immersions — one did not have to hit the
Congo to know what it was like in a hothouse in hell — but that
87° in Miami Beach day after day held up in competition against
other sulphuric encounters. Traveling for five miles up the
broken-down, forever in-a-state-of-alteration and repair of
Collins Avenue, crawling through 5 P.M. Miami Beach traffic in
the pure miserable fortune of catching an old taxi without air
conditioning, dressed in shirt and tie and jacket — formal and
implicitly demanded uniform of political journalists — the sen-
sation of breathing, then living, was not unlike being obliged to

make love to a 300-pound woman who has decided to get on top. Got it? You could not dominate a thing. That uprooted jungle had to be screaming beneath.

NOME
by Joe McGinniss

From his book Going to Extremes. *McGinniss has caught an Alaska that most other books miss. Here is not so much the beauty, the wildlife, and the open spaces, but rather the terrible struggles of the state to come to grips with the 20th century, the oil, and the boomers who threaten the already by-the-thread existence of the natives. McGinniss has gone on to write true books about murders and murderers. One can hope that he gets back to meaningful stuff. McGinniss's trip starts in Seattle, where he boards the ferry for Haines (the boat trip is a story of its own). At Haines, he catches a ride to Anchorage. From there, he sets out on forays in all directions.*

⚓

NOME

I WENT TO NOME for New Year's Eve. It was another of the Alaskan towns to which there wasn't any road. To get there from Anchorage you had to fly first to Fairbanks and then through Kotzebue. The plane went only three days a week in the winter, and Nome was at the end of the line. It was built right on the beach, on Alaska's bleak and treeless western coast — subject to floods; battered by storms, which blew unchecked across the Bering Sea, and raked, almost constantly, by biting winds. The few whites who lived there saw themselves as keepers of the flame: the last of the unbridled romantics, in whose hearts and minds the gold rush lingered on.

In the summer of 1900, at the peak of the gold rush, there had been thirty thousand people in Nome. People like Rex Beach, the novelist; Tex Rickard, who later built Madison Square Garden; Tommy Burns, a future heavyweight boxing champion of the world; Doc Kearns, who became Jack Dempsey's manager; Wilson Mizner, the playwright, screenwriter, and developer of Florida real estate; and Wyatt Earp, who was fined fifty dollars that summer for assaulting a policeman on Front Street.

The town had been named by mistake: a nineteenth-century mapmaker, misreading an old naval chart, had interpreted the notation "? Name" — a query as to whether a particular point of land had a name — as "C. Nome," or Cape Nome, and he so marked the point near which the town of Nome was later founded.

There had been, however, no mistake about the gold. It was there, in great quantity, in the creek beds that led down to the coast. The first discoveries were made in the summer of 1899, just as the Dawson strikes, the biggest of the Klondike gold rush, were petering out. In May 1899 there had been only two hundred people in the vicinity of what soon would be Nome, but by late summer there were two thousand. By winter, there was an established town on the site, with twenty saloons, sixteen lawyers, twelve general-merchandise stores, eleven doctors, six restaurants, six lodging houses, six bakeries, five laundries, four wholesale liquor stores, four hotels, four bathhouses, three secondhand stores, three watchmakers, three packers, three fruit, confectionery, and cigar stores, two paper hangers, two photographers, two tinsmiths, two sign painters, two meat markets, two dentists, plus a brewer, a boat shop, a bookstore, and a massage parlor.

There was a general atmosphere of tolerance about the town. Five prostitutes were confined to a makeshift jail on the second floor of the city hall when they refused to pay an assessment of $17.50 levied against them by municipal court, but it was reported that "they enjoyed themselves, singing French and American songs lustily, and making the dogs howl." The most severe hardship imposed by winter isolation was that the price of beer rose to one dollar a bottle over the bar.

The social highlight of Nome's first winter was, unquestionably, the arrival of Ed Jesson with newspapers from San

Francisco and Seattle. Jesson traveled from Dawson City by *bicycle*: an eight-hundred-mile journey that took him more than a month, as he tried to keep his wheels in the narrow tracks made by dog sleds. The Indians at Fort Yukon had never seen anything like it: "Geasus Christ", one of them said, "white man he set down, walk like hell." When Jesson arrived, the dance hall was taken over for a public reading of the newspapers, which continued through the night, punctuated by outbursts of cheering as news of victories in the Spanish-American War was announced, and by many toasts drunk to Admiral Dewey and the battleship *Oregon*, and by the repeated tossing of hats in the air. More relevant to Nome's future, however, were stories of the thousands of people already flocking to the Seattle docks, clamoring for space aboard the first north-bound boats of the spring.

The first wave brought ten thousand people to Nome. They dumped their belongings on the beach and went quickly inland to search for gold. Except for those who were so disillusioned that they returned immediately to their ships when they found that the beaches of Nome consisted of sand, and not of gold dust, as they had been led to believe. One man was reported to have jumped ashore, grabbed some of the sand in his fingers, and shouted, "I knew it was all a hoax." He then returned to his ship, remarking that he was "glad to get out of the damned country."

For those who stayed there was, in a few cases, astonishing wealth, but for all there was turbulence, danger, and unprecedented opportunities for debauchery. The town, said Doc Kearns, smelled like beer, whiskey, unwashed bodies, and cheap perfume. An aroma complemented, not infrequently, by gunpowder. A new doctor arrived and recorded that the first sound he heard as he stepped ashore was that of a gunshot. Fired by a gambler at the Northern Saloon — Tex Rickard's bar — as a means of expressing displeasure at a cut of the cards. A prospector named Will Ballou turned up for three days and reported that each day there was a killing. He said, "We had a dead man for breakfast every morning."

One new arrival penned this description of the scene:

We reached Nome, that human maelstrom, at night. We could see from afar the twinkling of the lights and their reflections dancing in the waters of the sea. We proceeded through the main street, and if ever pandemonium raged, it raged there. The streets fairly swarmed with a heterogeneous mass of people. Drunken gamblers grovelled in the dust; women, shameless, scarlet women, clad in garments of velvet, silks, laces, of exceedingly grotesque character but universally *décolleté*, revelled as recklessly as any of their tipsy companions. From the rough dance halls the scraping of a fiddle rose above the noisy clattering of heavy boots that sounded like a chariot race in an empty garret. Dust settled around about us like a heavy fog. We waded through rivers of it before we reached our hotel. There were thirty thousand inhabitants in Nome at that time, of nondescript character. Cultured, intelligent men hobnobbed with the uncultured and ignorant. The one touch of nature that made them all akin was the greed for gold.

It was the kind of town where Jimmy the Goat won $14,000 in a no-limit faro game at the Hub Saloon and, when someone started shooting in protest, so many new players were attracted by the sound that the game had to be shifted to the more commodious Northern Saloon in order to accommodate them.

By August 1900 there were more than a hundred saloons in Nome and it sometimes seemed as if the whole population of the town was inside them all at once, that no one was out looking for gold. There were marked cards and loaded dice and, three days in a row, a dissatisfied customer tried to set fire to Dick Dawson's Second Class Saloon. The social scene was further enlivened by the arrival of Miss Short and Dirty — one of the Far North's most renowned prostitutes.

Wilson Mizner, who years later would describe his days in Hollywood as "a trip through a sewer in a glass-bottomed boat," was known, in Nome in the summer of 1900, simply as the Yellow Kid — a nickname which implied no lack of courage, but which had to do rather with the technique Mizner had developed, while working as a saloon cashier, of pouring a bit of syrup in his hair in order that, as he weighed out gold dust from a miner's poke, he would be able to brush a hand through his hair and cause a few particles to remain.

Jack Hines was there in the summer of 1900, too. Nome's Merry Minstrel he was called, a man with a fine tenor voice. The following year, a Russian count named Podhorski absconded with Hines's young wife and Hines tracked him from Alaska to New York City and back to Nevada before shooting him three times through the heart. While testifying in his own defense, Hines sang some sad love songs for the jury, which was so moved that it voted quickly for acquittal.

Even Swiftwater Bill Gates came to Nome. He was a prospector, gambler, and entrepreneur who once, in Dawson City, infatuated with a show girl named Gussie Lamore, and aware of Gussie's passion for fresh eggs, had purchased, for $2,800 in gold dust, every fresh egg in Dawson City, and had then informed Miss Lamore that her only means of satisfying her craving in the morning would be to satisfy several of Swiftwater Bill's through the night.

As a not necessarily disapproving young minister who arrived in the summer of 1900 phrased it: "You see more, live more, in twenty-four hours in Nome than in a cycle of Cathay."

EAST BY SOUTHEAST
by William Least Heat Moon

From his book Blue Highways. *Least Heat Moon bought a used van, named it Ghost Dancing, jumped into its remodeled interior, and drove around the United States to experience the back roads and their citizenry.*

He starts in Columbia, Missouri, heading east by southeast. In this selection, Least Heat Moon guides Ghost Dancing across North Carolina toward the coast.

⚓

OUT OF GREENVILLE, on route 32 just northeast of the road to Pinetown, gulls dropped in behind the Farmalls and poked over the upturned soil for bugs, and the east wind carried in the smell of the sea. People here call the dark earth "the blacklands. " Scraping, scalping, bulldozers were clearing fields for tobacco and pushing the pines into big tumuli; as the trees burned, the seawind blew smoke from the balefires down along the highway like groundfog. Trees burned so tobacco could grow so tobacco could burn. But where great conifers still stood, they cast three-hundred-foot shadows through the morning, and the cool air smelled of balsam.

In Plymouth I saw a sign at a gas station: DIESEL FUEL AND OYSTERS IN SEASON. A man, his eyes a camouflage of green and brown speckles, white hair to the wind, filled the tank and said, "How's this weather for ye?"

"Fine today. But it's been rough."

"Hard weather makes good timber. How's that Missouri weather?"

"Hard."

"Yessir," one word, "that's why your Harry Truman was good timber. Toughern oak. No trees out your way is there?"

"Lots of trees. Especially oaks. Red, white, bur, blackjack."

"Flat though, ain't It?"

"Lots of hills. *This* is flat land."

"Whistle me Dixie! This county don't get up in the air no higher than a boy can throw a mud turtle. But it's God's Country. And a good town. Woulda been a better town but the Yankees shot it all to hell. Union gunboats got it, sir. Hard to believe now gunboats out in the Roanoke. Fierce river fightin'. They had to make coffins out of pews from Grace Church. Buried men in their own pew. That's no joke to us."

As he wrote up the credit slip, I said, "Looks like they're taking out timberlands for tobacco fields."

"Govnor comes out and shoots you personally if you say against tobacco in this state. I smoked thirty-odd years. Did my duty and got a right to talk. Truth is you cain't buy a real, true cigarette anymores. That's why they name them that way — tryin' to convince you what ain't there. Real. True. Nothin' to it. They cut them long, they cut them skinny, they paint them red and green and stuff them with menthol and camphor and eucalyptus. What the hell, they's makin' toys. I'll lay you one of them bright-leaf boys up in Winston-Salem is drawin' up a cigarette you gotta plug in the wall. Nosir. your timber's comin' down to make toys."

"You don't smoke now?"

"Why smoke what's no taste to it? Same as them light beers and whiskies: no flavor. Americans have just got afraid to taste anything. You ask me, sir, it started with oleo. Or maybe the popalation got scared by them mouse spearmints wheres they give a mouse a needle-shot of a substance ever day until he dies a cancer. Nosir, my advice is to live your life."

"That's solid advice."

"And harder to do than you think. Take me. I retired and ended up settin' and worryin' about myself, about my health. Then I bought this station to get away from myself. My own worst enemy. Don't need the money comes in — it's the people comin' in I need. But I been remarkin' recently, people don't listen liken they used to."

"I've noticed that." I was down the road when I realized his tumble of notions had distracted me from the oysters. There would be more.

The face of the tidewater peninsula lying between Albemarle Sound and the Pamlico River showed clear now: cypress trees cooling their giant butts in clean swamp water black from the tannin in their roots, the road running straight and level and bounded on each side by watery "borrow ditches" that furnished soil to build the roadway. Ditches, road, trees — all at right angles. The swamp growth was too thick to paddle a greased canoe through, and, although leafless, the dense limbs left the swamp without sun.

Then, precipitately, the vegetable walls stopped, and the wide Alligator River estuary opened to sky and wind. Whitecaps broke out of the strange burgundy water. As I drove the long bridge over the inlet, a herring gull, a glare of feathers, put a wingtip a few feet to the left of Ghost Dancing, and, wings steady, accompanied me across.

Dare County, named after the first white child (says tradition) born in America, is a curious county with four times as much water as land and only two highways and four towns — a pair on the mainland and a pair on Roanoke Island. Most of mainland Dare is a spongy place, a bog that until recently discouraged developers. But now, about the county, men with caliper hands and parallelogram brains were taking the measure of the salt marsh and trying to "reclaim" it — a misleading word since this tidewater has always belonged to the sea.

A second long bridge crossed Croatan Sound to Roanoke Island, a low rise a little larger than Manhattan and lying just inside one of the most unusual geographic features in the country: the Outer Banks. A skinny chain of sand, the Banks stretch for nearly two hundred miles along the North Carolina coast. On Roanoke Island, there is no enduring symbol for the first "permanent" English settlement in America like the rock at Plymouth, Massachusetts. In place of a symbol, Roanoke has mystery. Here Virginia Dare was born only to vanish from history without a trace nine days later. The woods, a thick mat of shrubs and trees, looked in places as it must have when the Dares, members of Raleigh's third Roanoke expedition, came ashore. It may be that the absence of such a ready symbol as Plymouth Rock has helped keep Roanoke from the destruction of this time.

The highway wound into the dark trees again as it traversed the very place where the English colonies disappeared, the last group leaving behind America's most famous mystery word — *Croatoan* — carved in a stockade timber. Roanoke Island gave a shadowy sense of an older time that Plymouth Rock, surrounded, dwarfed, and protected in stone and steel, has lost. A man told me, "Out on Roanoke, you can feel the beginning."

At the bottom of Queen Elizabeth Avenue, the main street of Manteo, North Carolina, where it comes down to the sound, stood a Brobdingnagian statue, ten feet of a single cypress trunk cut into a sixteenth-century English courtier. A woodpecker, with uncanny accuracy, had drilled a hole in Sir Walter Raleigh's pantalooned posterior, and now there were predictable jokes in Manteo about the hole and Sir Walter's woodpecker.

Manteo is the seat of Dare County and one of the few courthouse towns, as the Carolinians call them, on an island in the Atlantic Ocean. Not so remote as Key West, or so big as Newport, Rhode Island, or so famous as Nantucket, or so elitist as Edgartown on Martha's Vineyard, Manteo was a pleasant place: smaller, humbler, quieter. The docks once lining the harbor had dwindled to three, and the seashell-paved streets were now macadam like everywhere else. The red-brick, turn-of-the-century courthouse opened to the waterfront where formerly a fleet of mail, freight, passenger, and fishing boats tied up. Now the sport-fishing craft in red, blue, and yellow, each sprouting long whip antennas that gave them the look of water bugs, rocked in the little marina. Even still, Manteo looked as if it belonged with its face in the Atlantic winds.

At Raleigh's immense wooden boots, a man worked quickly in

the bright, cold wind as he brushed preservative over the base of the statue. He was one of the town commissioners working to refurbish the old wharfside of Manteo. Between two big oil tanks abandoned by the owners, the town had built a park reaching into the basin off Roanoke Sound.

He spoke with the old London accent of the Banks that some people believe to be the speech of the Elizabethans. "We may be able to use one of the tanks in our new sewage system," he said. "If not, down they'll come. This statue is the focal point for rehabilitating Queen Elizabeth Street. New bridges did in most of the work boats, but it's the bridges that bring out tourists now. We've got six million dollars of federal funds coming here over the next two years. When we finish, you won't recognize Manteo."

Across the sound at Nag's Head, a new highrise broke the flat horizon of the Banks where once only small, low buildings stood. "I hope you're not going to put highrises here too," I said.

"That's a Ramada Inn."

"Overwhelms everything out there — no harmony at all between it and the land. Architecture without regard for place or history. They've been Jersey Shored, if you ask me."

"The sea never forgets where it's been, and it's been over that land many times. We haven't had a major hurricane in nearly twenty years, whereas we used to have a hard blow every few years. New people don't know that. They come in and see open beach and figure they've found open land. But the Banks aren't ordinary islands, and that's why they've been left alone. People didn't used to build much they couldn't afford to see washed away, because sooner or later most things out there get washed away. I know — I've lived there. It's always been a rough place. Land pirates, sea pirates. Blackbeard was killed down at Ocracoke where my family comes from. One of my ancestors was on the Arabian ship that wrecked and spilled the Banks ponies that used to run wild."

"They don't now?"

"Fenced in by the Park Service. They overpopulated and started cropping beach grass so close as to kill it. Pawed holes in the sand to get fresh water and caused erosion—the number-one problem on the Banks. People get up in arms about the fencing, but the ponies aren't natural to the island. Of course, grass isn't either. Or men. Indians used to hunt the Banks, but I don't think they lived there. They're barrier islands. Some of that land's moving south as much as twenty feet a year. It's a natural process, the way the sea washes sand over the islands from the coast side and drops it on the sound side. But the Corps of Engineers and Park Service have built jetties and grassed dunes so sand doesn't get washed over now. They've tried to stop a natural process, and so you get erosion on the east and no build-up on the west."

"That's the corps: redesigning and stabilizing nature."

"Today we've got bridges over land and roads ending up in the water. Been millions of dollars spent trying to pin down the Banks. You talk about the Ramada. A motel at Wrightsville Beach is built where an inlet used to be. They have to pump sand back in to keep the building standing. An architect has to understand our natural balance of the change that keeps things —in the long run—almost unchanged. It's not stability, it's balance. Living on the Banks, you learn the difference real quick."

"Sounds like somebody wants to keep something not his to keep."

"Ninety percent of the U.S. coast is privately owned. It isn't easy to give up your land—even to the ocean."

Fishing for Fun and Profit

Fishes (and other marine creatures) are among the few remaining wild things that humans pursue for food. Just about everything else gets to market from the farm. The angling literature is as old as the sport itself, but "popular" commercial fishing writing is a more recent development (some of it records history, for the days of untrammeled commercial fishing are probably over). The line between sport and commercial fishing is blurred; bringing to mind a joke— Question: What's the difference between sport and commercial fishing?. Answer: The sport takes pictures of his catch before he sells it.

IN BONAC: CLAMMERS AND SCALLOPERS, and CHANGES
by Peter Matthiessen

From his book, Men's Lives. *This is about the surfmen and baymen of the South Fork of Long Island, New York, and about a way of life that is threatened and may be dying. It is about old families who have for many decades harvested from the bays and the rich sea on Long Island's Atlantic Ocean side. They are threatened by land development which has polluted shellfish beds and by the changing times which have outlawed their pursuit of fish that sport anglers now want to claim for their own.*

Matthiessen is on the side of tradition. He sees a way of life disappearing, and he doesn't like it. The title of the book comes from the Sir Walter Scott lines: "It's not fish ye're buying, it's men's lives."

⚓

IN 1684 the East Hampton Town Trustees sent sixteen men to Meantecut to help the Indians open the tidal creek from the bay into Montauk Great Pond, apparently to revive its oyster beds with more salt water. Big local oysters, often a foot long, were a basic food of both Indians and settlers, and because — unlike fish — they could survive the sea voyage to market in New England and New York, oysters, like clams, were harvested for export to New England as well as for extensive local use.

In the 1700s an immense oyster bed was located to the west, off Blue Point, on the Great South Bay, attracting an ever-increasing group of men "who depended for their subsistence upon the products of the waters of the bay. They were called baymen. For nine months the baymen lived on the profits derived from the oyster beds, and depended upon the other three for clamming and fishing. They were poor for the most part, but independent." Working from small catboats, sloops, and the flat-bottomed sharp-prowed work skiff called the sharpie, the baymen harvested these beds with tongs, and by the early nineteenth century had all but exhausted the Blue Point field. But oyster packing houses in Patchogue continued to buy oysters taken elsewhere on Great South Bay, which were shipped in kegs to New York's Fulton Fish Market. In the 1860s, when oyster tongs were replaced by the dredge, the last beds were already overfished, and soon the independent baymen were put out of business by large companies that planted oysters on prepared grounds and saw to it that the use of dredges was outlawed elsewhere.

On the South Fork, where the salt ponds and harbors were once crusted with wild oysters, this fishery had been domesticated, too. In 1831 Isaac Van Scoy of Northwest received permission from the East Hampton Town Trustees to plant an oyster bed in Northwest Creek, and by century's end large oyster operations based in Greenport were laying beds in Peconic and Gardiners bays; the "Gardiners Bay salt" challenged the Blue Point as a celebrated oyster in the city markets. By 1900, the last wild oysters were old lone "coon-foots" on rocky bottoms avoided by the scallopers and clammers. All that remained of this great public fishery was the name "baymen," which had spread eastward with the refugee fishing families from Great South Bay. The heretofore independent baymen were reduced to dredging jingle shell cultch for the privately owned oyster beds, and even today, the few oysters taken by the baymen are mostly sold as seed stock to the corporations.

One of the best oyster grounds, in the whole township was Accabonac Creek, a few miles northeast of East Hampton village. In the early fifties, when I first came there to live, the Springs, or Bonac, was mostly farmland owned by Bennetts, Talmages, and Millers, sloping down across the tidewater to Bonac Creek; at the head of the creek was a community building and a gas pump and general store. Originally the main source for salt hay for the settlers' stock, Bonac Creek was a peaceful and very pretty place of meadowland and cedar fields and a quiet lead of water, widening out eastward past Tick Island to the sand spit at Louse Point and Gardeners Bay.

This backwater had changed very little in the long slow decades since the turn of the century, when the Wood family arrived here from the Great South Bay, one of the first fishing families (they are still coming) to be driven eastward by the destruction of the fisheries farther west. "They were clam and oystermen, they had sloops, and they went clammin in the ocean, and flounder fishin, eelin," says Jarvis Wood, born in the Springs in 1908, and they were baymen (although Jarvie says that this name did not come into general use out here until recent decades). "My grandfather, he fished all the time, he was a fisherman all his life. And my father was a fisherman, only thing he ever done. So naturally I started, I come fishin, too."

At the creek head (still called Pussy's Pond after an old Miss Pussy Parsons) the Parsons oyster house, used for opening scallops "after the oysters run out," later became Smith's general store, where storytelling took place every Sunday evening. In the twenties, dances were held there once a week. The two churches were Episcopal and Presbyterian, divorce and unwed couples were still scandalous, and old people without furnaces or relatives went to the poorhouse thirty or forty miles "up-Island" (Jarvie's father-in-law was Overseer of the Poor). For many years his mother took in laundry for the summer people in East Hampton, which had turned from a farming-fishing town to a resort by the turn of the century.

"Nobody was in a real rush to do anything, they didn't need all this money, all this stuff to *go* to, all they wanted was to make a livin. Everybody was fishin or farmers; s'all there was. Either go fishin or farmin, and a lot of the farmers went fishin. In the summertime, when they had their crops in, they'd go down clammin; in the wintertime, when their crops are gone, they go scallopin, oysterin. Everybody got along, y'know, they had taters in the cellar, maybe a barrel of pork, something like that; no one went hungry.

"In them days, fishin wasn't so easy as it is today. Today you got trucks and motors, you got everything to do all your work with; them days, you done all your work with your hands. If you wanted to go somewhere you took a pair of oars and you rowed your boat; you didn't just steer a boat, go down where you wanted to fish! But flounders, used to be so many in the bay, if you set a fyke out you couldn't even get 'em in, there was too much in the fyke. Then all of a sudden they disappeared, couldn't get no flounders, everybody went out of business. Then they come back again, though there ain't as many as there used to be cause of the draggers."

As a small boy, Jarvie lived at Lazy Point in Napeague, where his family were clammers and dug skimmers for the cod trawls in the ocean; he remembers that eels were collected in a barrel until some "backer" (tobacco) was tossed in to stun the slippery creatures before attempting to "skun 'em out." (Some baymen put ashes on their hands for "sloimin," others use burlap bags to grasp the eel, which is fixed by the head on a nail stuck through a wall; the throat is then cut through the bone, and a slit made down the length of the belly, after which the head and skin are stripped away.) For a time he worked on "Old Man Schellinger's" farm, one of many in the neighborhood that raised chickens and corn and wheat. But Jarvie quit high school after a year to become a fisherman.

"If we wanted eels or clams or fish, we always got'em fresh, cause there was no problems gettin stuff to eat. In the wintertime we used to shoot ducks. Them days people didn't kill themselves like they do t'day, cause there was no problems. Whatever you want'd to catch, there was plenty of it. You go out and catch a couple bushel clams, if you was ambitious three bushel; man had a big family, he had to work harder. Any time you didn't have nothin to do, you'd go out clammin."

Quahogs, or hard clams (in market terms — in ascending size —littlenecks, cherrystones, and chowders) have been a Long Island subsistence food since prehistoric times. The Indians used the purple and white interior for wampum, and the strong valves served very well as hoe blades. Even today the hard clam is the most dependable of all the fisheries, between seasons, in winter, and when times are poor. (Soft clams, or steamers — known to the commercial men as piss clams because of the jets of water they emit in times of stress — are dug from soft mud flats with a clam hook, like a short forked hoe, or "grinded" in shallow water by an outboard propeller that spins the clams up to the surface. Like the long clam (surf clam or skimmer) — the big clam cast up on the ocean beach in storms and used as ashtrays in the summer cottages that began to turn up on the dunes in the 1880s — soft clams were considered unworthy of human consumption in the early days, and were mainly harvested for cod bait, hog and poultry food, or fertilizer. The common blue mussel and the whelk, or winkle, once so sought after for wampum, were ignored. Today steamers, winkles, and mussels are much in demand, and the fried clam served in summer restaurants is usually the lowly skimmer.)

Hard clams are mostly taken with a scratch rake fitted out with an iron basket. A longer and larger rake with back strap and crossbar pull handle, called the bull rake, is often used by the commercial men in deeper water. In winter the bayman may resort to long-poled double-basket rakes in the form of pincers, worked from a small boat and known as tongs. Whatever the implement, even when hard clams were common, the average bayman rarely took more than five bushels on a tide (although Bill Lester, in his days on Montauk Lake, took six or seven). Now the clams have been overharvested. The three-bushel limit is hard to achieve, and its value varies: chowder clams may be worth just five dollars a bushel, whereas cherrystones — five for a penny at the turn of the century — may sell for fifty dollars a bushel, sometimes more. Especially on rocky bottoms (and also in winter, when the sand is hard and dense, and the clams are deeper) clams are much more work for a lot less money than the free-swimming scallops, which in most years support a very profitable local fishery.

In the Depression, as Captain Nathan Lester told the *Island*

News in 1933, it was "pretty hard to make a decent living fishing." Like many baymen, Jarvie Wood tried work at regular jobs, returning to fishing about 1940. In the early fifties, when I lived in the Springs, he had opened a small store near his Neck Path house, on the road to Amagansett, but in 1964 he sold the store and returned to fishing once again. "Was makin some good money, too," he told me twenty years later. "But I said to my wife, 'What we ever goin to do with all that money? Get to be old, y'know, ain't nothin much you want to do anyway.' She didn't want to sell but she agreed to it, just to go along with me."

In the early fifties the Springs was still back in the woods, and rents were very inexpensive. My friend John Cole lived in the old Parsons house, across from the old school and Pete Scott lived in a small cottage on the salt marsh. (During World War II, on visits to East Hampton, I had become friends with John's family, and sometimes, as a friend of Pete Scott's brother, I had stayed in the Scott cottage, called the Box, a very old house near "Home Sweet Home" on East Hampton's Main Street.) With my wife and infant son, I found a cottage on Fireplace Road just west of the horse and cattle farm of George Sid Miller. In those days there were few writers in the region, and apart from the Coles and Scotts, most of the people that we saw were painters. Francile and Sherry Lord, Lee and Jackson Pollock, Charlotte and Jim Brooks were neighbors as well as friends, and many other painters lived not far away, with more still coming. To the local people, all of us were "people from away," the forerunners of many still to come. (As Milt Miller says, "I always thought of all outsiders as foreigners — still do, I guess.")

The fall of 1953 was my first season clamming and scalloping in Three Mile and Northwest Harbors. My fishing partner was John Cole (who like myself was unsuited to urban work and had sought a leaner way of life outdoors) and our scallop boat was a nineteen-foot double-ended Quebec codfish boat with a short mast and a one-cylinder engine (hence her name, *Vop-*

Vop) which, in size and sound, if not in her appearance, must have reminded the old-timers of the first Jersey boats launched through the surf. Rigged out with culling board and scallop dredges, the *Vop* was moored in a small anchorage just north of Emerson Taber's lobster dock in Three Mile Harbor — the Town Commercial Dock site, given to East Hampton by the Gardiner family back in the thirties. On the still warm Indian summer clays of mid-September, no dredges or culling board were necessary; we drifted the broad harbor flats south of the long neck called Sammis Beach, pouring a little bunker oil upwind to smooth and clear the surface of the water and using the rim of long-poled dip nets to tap the edges of somnolent scallops in their sand nests in the eelgrass, causing them to somersault backward into the mesh.

The delicious inshore pecten, or bay scallop, was regarded with suspicion by the early settlers. Scallop shells abound in the Indian middens, but the creature's lurid interior design, set off by a mantle of phosphorescent turquoise, was apparently not approved by local Puritans, especially when plainer shellfish were so plentiful. Even a cat, it was related, might discover that its tail had fallen off after eating a scallop. This peculiar species was a free swimmer, not easily confined to domestic beds; unlike more stick-in-the-mud mollusks, it was able and ready to rise up from the bottom and jet through the water by opening and shutting its valves, and might gallivant "down bay" for a considerable distance before this errant impulse had subsided.

But if the settlers were conservative, they were also practical. Local opinion of the scallop changed in the middle of the nineteenth century — or so it is said — when an enterprising fisherman from Connecticut did very well with a cargo of scallops from Peconic Bay, inspiring a beached whaleman of Sag Harbor to develop a small market for this seafood in New York City. With the appropriation of the oyster industry by private interests, the desperate baymen flocked to the new fishery, and by 1873, five thousand bushels were taken in one season from Peconic. Old discarded oyster dredges worked well with scallops, which would flip upward in a backward somersault into the wide mouth of the oncoming dredge, and almost any small craft, rowed or sailed, would suit the purpose. By the turn of the century, two hundred small boats were engaged in scalloping.

In those days, eelgrass was widespread in Gardiners Bay, and the scallops so thick, according to Jarvie Wood, that a sloop could bail a boatload in a half day. In 1928 the eelgrass died off in a mysterious plague, and the bay scallop (and also the small coastal goose known as the brant) all but died with it. For some reason, the soft clam vanished, too. Eelgrass, scallops, and soft clams returned to the harbors in the early thirties, but the grass has yet to take hold again out in the bay. Decades later, juvenile scallops still appear as thick as ever on Jarvie's trap stakes, but without the shelter of the grass, most seem to wash ashore or are otherwise lost.

Already in the thirties it was realized that there might be a limit to scallop numbers, which fluctuated a good deal from year to year, and in 1934 the town set a daily limit of five bushels. At present a daily limit of ten bushels per licensed bayman, fifteen per boat, is still in force in East Hampton Town waters.

Not all baymen haul seine or lift gill nets and traps; these days, because "the clams are down," there are probably a few who do not clam. But almost every able-bodied bayman will go scalloping, at least in the early weeks of a good season, when the daily limit may be harvested in two hours' work. In most years the scallop is the major resource of the bayman, who pursues it from the soft days of Indian summer until the hard windy days of early spring, when the adult scallops begin to die. Usually his income is increased by his own family; his wife may sort scallops on the culling board, and many women in the fishing community are expert openers, or shuckers, separating the firm white "eye" (the adductor muscle that closes the two scallop-edged valves) from the colorful but unacceptable mantle and guts.

Most commercial men use the traditional fourteen-foot sharpie, which is the bayman's all-purpose skiff (the so-called trap sharpie, used for lifting traps, is longer and wider). Until the mid-sixties, when the use of power was permitted, the scalloper anchored, drifted downwind perhaps two hundred feet, then hauled, or kedged, back up the running line, dragging a dredge and sometimes two behind. The scallop dredge, thirty inches across and weighing more than twenty pounds, is the same "Greenport sloop dredge" used at the turn of the century. Pronounced "drudge" (as in "hung new twoine on thim drudges, did ye?"), it may scrape up over fifty pounds of eelgrass, mud, water, rock, and shell that must be heaved onto a culling board before the scallops can be sorted.

Unlike more sedentary bivalves, the scallop lives only about eighteen months, and scallop seasons vary considerably, depending on weather conditions at the time of spawning as well as survival of the small "bug" scallops over their first winter. In 1953 the bugs had prospered, and in the first weeks of September the scallops were so thick that, using dip nets, we harvested our boat limit in a few hours' pleasant work. Loading the crunching burlap sacks into John's old greenish truck, we would cart them across Abraham's Path (named for that Abraham Schellinger who built the first wharf out at Northwest in 1700) through the warm September woods of pitch pine and scrub oak to the scallop openers in Amagansett.

• • •

With windy weather, as Indian summer turned to fall, the scallops became scarce in shallow water. We turned to heavy labor with the dredges, dumping the wet loads of eelgrass and codium, or Sputnik weed, onto the culling board. The load was never twice the same. The elegant scallops, snapping their shells, were occasionally accompanied by an unwary flounder, together with an indiscriminate assortment of crabs, horsefoots, sand worms, glass shrimp, sea horses, sponges, whelks, stones, bottles, sneakers, dead shells, and — not uncommonly — small clump of wild oysters.

Later that autumn, when the scallops thinned out inside the harbors, we went prospecting for virgin scallop beds as far away as Napeague, Montauk Lake, and Gardiners Island, putting in at Promised Land for our supplies. One day of late October, as we scalloped off the western shore of Gardiners Island, a cold front came in toward midday, with a stiff wind out of the northwest. Though heavily crusted with quarterdecks, or boat shells, the scallops on this rocky bottom were plentiful, and we were hurrying to complete our twenty-bushel boat limit and head home when the one-cylinder motor on my old boat conked out and would not revive. Hoisting the *Vop*'s parched gaff-rigged sail, we beat upwind toward the mainland.

Already a hard gale was blowing; despite her deep keel, the boat was banging into white-capped waves. Halfway across the channel the pine mast broke off at the deck, and mast, boom, and canvas crashed upon our heads. Not saying much, we sorted out the mess as the wind carried us back toward Gardiners Island. (Years ago, an old-timer named Puff Dominy broke down off Lion Head Rock and drifted back east to Gardiners on this same course. Told to throw over the anchor, his retarded crewman cried, "No twing! No twing!" Impatient and uncomprehending, Puff hollered, "Let 'er go, goddamn it, 'twing' or no 'twing'!" Thrown overboard with no "string" attached, Puff's anchor disappeared forever, but "twing or no twing" has survived in local lore.)

Nearing the island, we threw over an anchor, but by the time the grapnel finally took hold, the *Vop* was scarcely two hundred yards offshore in Bostwick Bay, buffeted by wind and seas in the growing weather. It was midafternoon of a swift day of late autumn, and a cold sun was sinking fast, with no boat in sight, nothing but whitecaps and wind-blown gulls and long black ragged strings of cormorant beating across the wind toward the southwest. Not only was the boat wide open, but the hatch covers of the fish holds forming her deck were only three inches lower than the gunwales, which provided no shelter from the wind. On this north end of Gardiners Island, never inhabited, lay the last primeval forest of white oak on all Long Island; the view from the sea was as wild as it was three centuries before when the Algonkian people known as Montauks escorted Lion Gardiner to his New World home.

In 1676, by the Dongan Patent, Gardiners Island — roughly seven by three miles, or about 3,300 acres — had been deemed a manor, and it is, in fact, the last of the old English manors to remain in the same New World family to the present day. In the 1690s, Captain William Kidd, a minister's son and retired sea captain pressed into service as a privateer by a syndicate that included the English governor of Massachusetts, was arrested in Boston and sent to England. There he was hanged for disputed reasons, among them, it is said, the protection of the reputations of those who had benefitted from his voyages, including the hard-living "Lord John" Gardiner, son of the incumbent Lord of the Manor, David Lion Gardiner, who had first welcomed Kidd to Gardiners Island. Captain Kidd's only known treasure of gold dust, gold coin, jewelry and the like, retrieved from the pond behind the beach in Cherry Harbor off which we had been scalloping when the boat broke down, was turned over to the authorities by Lord John, who escaped unpunished. In 1728 the manor was commandeered for three days by real pirates, causing the family to look for safer lodgings in East Hampton Village. Since then, Gardiners Island has been occupied intermittently by the Gardiner family, which has often leased it to other people.

In the 1950s the island was still inhabited by an estimated five hundred pairs of ospreys, by far the largest colony of these striking fish hawks in North America and perhaps the world. High cliffs to the eastward (a source of clay for the early settlers) slope gradually to low fields in the west, with broad lowlands, salt marsh, ponds, and sand spits, north and south. Where we were anchored was the windward shore of the northern sand spit, in Bostwick ("Bostic" to the fishermen) Bay, where a bad August storm of 1879 had overturned a lobster boat out of New London, drowning two crewmen. Another storm in 1892 parted this sand spit, creating an islet out at the north point where a lighthouse had been built in 1855; the shoddily constructed building, weakened by storms, collapsed two years later, and the light was abandoned. During the Spanish-American War, a round structure called Fort Tyler was built upon this shored-up islet, part of a whole string of forts on Plum, Gull, and Fishers Islands designed to protect Long Island Sound from unfriendly gunboats. Since its abandonment in 1924, Fort Tyler has been much diminished by erosion and bombing practice, and is usually referred to as "the ruin."

Twilight had come, and a sharp autumn cold. To the north the old fort, in dark and gloomy silhouette on a cold sunset, rode like a ship in the running silver tide against the lightless islands and the far black line of the New England hills where the last light faded in the sky. Our young wives would not worry about us until after nightfall, so no help could be expected until next day.

Eight miles to the northeast lay Fishers Island, the eastern-most point of Suffolk County, where I had spent most of my first fifteen summers; five miles to the southwest lay Three Mile Harbor in East Hampton, where I visited first in 1942. Now it was 1953, I was in my mid-twenties, and had moved perma-nently to the South Fork. Thus I had lived in Suffolk County all my life, on or about the edges of these waters; this wild and lonely place where our small boat washed up and down on the high chop lay at the very heart of my home country.

On this cold rough October evening, hunched knee to knee in cramped anchor cuddy, we ate raw scallops from the upright burlap bags that hunched like refugees on deck, and listened to the waves slap on the hull; if the anchor dragged during the night, our small wood boat would wash ashore on Gardiners Island. It was already gunning season, and we wanted no night dealings with Charlie Raynor, the caretaker and dangerous en-emy of enterprising young gunners such as ourselves who would sneak ashore at the south end while out coot shooting around Cartwright Shoals and be reasonably sure of snagging a few pheasants along the airstrip. Raynor's reputation as a man who would shoot first and talk afterward saved him a lot of trouble on the job. Especially in the hunting season, he made no distinctions between castaways and trespassers, and anyway he lived too far off to be of help.

At daylight the cold wind from the northwest had not diminished, and there were no signs of boats or sail. All Gardiners Bay was tossed in a white chop, crossed by the strings of cormorants, the hurrying scoters and solitary loons, the wind-tilted gulls, hard wings reflecting a wild light that pierced the metallic clouds.

Toward midmorning a Coast Guard plane came over; when we waved our arms, the plane went away, and still there were no boats on the rough horizons.

In early afternoon a black fishing boat appeared. Its hardy skipper was Fanny Gardiner Collins of Three Mile Harbor, a member of the island clan and avid fisherwoman who knew much more about Gardiners Island and its waters than her wealthy kinsmen. Fanny took us in tow and hauled us back to Three Mile Harbor.

In November, when the scallops became scarce, I helped out now and then on a small haul-seine rig led by Jimmy Reutershan, who came from a local "up-street" family of nonfishermen, and had John Cole and Pete Scott as his steady crew. The rig consisted of Jimmy's Land Rover, small dory, and small seine, and it stuck pretty close to a stretch of beach near the old Georgica Coast Guard Station. On those bright cold autumn days, with sharp sand blowing, the silver ocean, sparkling and clear, seemed empty; we were beginners, and we made one dry haul after another, standing around the limp and forlorn bag as if puzzling out an oracle. On one such morning Jimmy drew an ancient black banana from the seat box on the Land Rover and offered it upright, with his wry tough smile, to his weary crew. "Have a banana," Jimmy said, "lightly flecked with brown."

For the next four years I was traveling to remote corners of the Americas, from Alaska and the Yukon to Tierra del Fuego, and I rarely visited the South Fork. The *Vop-Vop* had already gone to a charity summer camp on Three Mile Harbor, and I sold a half-interest in the *Merlin* to my brother Carey, who was now a marine biologist on Martha's Vineyard. In the late fifties I took the *Merlin* to the Vineyard, where Carey showed me his boat-casting spots on the ocean shoals south of Chappaquiddick. Here striped bass and blues, on the right tide, could be taken with almost every cast into the breaking seas. Like many Massachusetts sportsmen, he was taking big bass in such numbers that he sold commercially what he could not use.

One day on the way to No Mans Land, looking for swordfish, we came upon a dead humpback whale under Gay Head. The huge black body lay awash in the heavy swells, which rode ashore and boomed under the cliffs, the echo riding back in the soft mist. That summer I had a phone call from a charter boat-man who sailed out of Provincetown. Knowing of my interest in whales, he told me that orcas, or killer whales, had appeared on Stellwagen Bank, between Cape Race and Boston, together with finbacks, humpbacks, and pilot whales. I left next morning for Provincetown, and found all four species on the surface in a slick August calm.

Then in the summer of 1960 I visited for a while at a friend's house in Sagaponack, an old farming community in the potato fields between Wainscott and Bridgehampton, in Southampton Town. From these farm communities, a road led over the scrub oak moraine to Sag Harbor (originally Sagaponack Harbor) where the South Shore farmers had once kept their boats. In the old days, these fields were "dressed" after the Indian fashion with the tons of menhaden seined out of the bays. As the American Midwest became planted in wheat, the local wheat crop was replaced by diversified crops of potatoes, strawberries, and cabbage, and potatoes emerged as the main crop when, in the first part of this century, a number of Polish clans arrived to join the founding families.

"Sagaponack" is another form of "Accabonac," an Indian word for an edible tuber that was gathered in both places.Like all of the earliest settlements, it was still organized in the European way, with the house lots within shouting distance up and down Sagg Main Street as a protection against Indians, wolves, and pirates, and the unbroken fields stretching east to the next farm village at Wainscott. Westward lay Sagaponac Pond, in country so opened up by farming that the bone white steeples in Bridgehampton could be seen against dark hills of the high moraine off to the north. This little-known farm hamlet south of the highway had one of the last "little red school-houses" in the Northeast, and a small spare general store owned by Lee Hildreth, who was also postmaster and gas pump operator. The schoolhouse and store, together with an excellent summer boarding house run by Mrs. Sczepankowski on the family farm (the first summer people in the Hamptons found lodgings in farm homesteads such as these) comprised the whole of downtown Sagaponack. All but a few of the old houses belonged to Toppings and Hildreths, Whites and Fosters, who had been here for many generations; one piece of Topping land between the cemetery and the sea was the oldest piece of land in the United States farmed continuously by the same white family.

No houses were available in Sagaponack, and that fall I lived in a small cabin in the Springs by the Green River cemetery where Pollock had been buried four years before. Toward the end of that year, I was offered a fine property in Sagaponack, part of a tract, still called Smith Corner, inhabited originally by that Richard (Bull) Smith who founded Smithtown after his eviction from Southampton. In 1960 the sudden rise in local land values had not started, and the whole property — six acres, a large decrepit house, an outlying stable and small cottage — cost much less than just one of those overgrown acres would be worth today. The value of the property increased three times in the very first year that I owned it; since then, the selling off of the South Fork has become so frenzied that children of many local families, and the fishermen especially, can no longer afford to live where they were born.

By the early sixties almost all of my old friends were gone. John Cole had settled down in Maine, Pete Scott had died in a car accident in California, and tough "Jimmy Root" would die a few years later of a flawed heart, not long after he had built his house on my former land on Stony Hill in Amagansett. ("Jimmy was a *scientific* fisherman," Milt Miller once observed, "experimental, always looking into different ways of making and hanging nets. Trial and error, mostly error, but since then I have seen different people using his ideas.") Jackson Pollock was dead, and so was Herb Latshaw of the Three Mile Harbor Boatyard, one of my gunning partners on those wintry days stringing for coot at Cedar Point; the only friend from the old days I saw regularly was the painter Sherry Lord, who moved from the Springs to Sagaponack a few years after I did.

When my neighbors realized that, come the autumn, I would still be there behind my hedge, I was accepted. My friend Bud Topping got me into the local gun club, and sometimes I filled in on the beach with the farmers' haul-seine crew led by Bob Tillotson, whose brother Frank had been Ted Lester's original partner in Montauk Seafood. Another crewman — the potato farmer in striped coveralls who would later bring that salmon into my yard — was a namesake and descendant of the John White who appears in the town records within a few years of the first settlement in 1640. Most of these men's ancestors had been farmer-fishermen, and they were still attached to the fishing tradition. Although the farmers were beset by the erosion of poor crop years, heavy inheritance taxes, and the increasing pressure of a summer resort economy, most of the old farm families had held onto their land, which had suddenly become immensely valuable.

The full-time fishermen, struggling to survive, had none of their land left to fall back on. An exception to the rule was Cap'n Ted, who seemed tired, yet more enterprising than ever. On the upper level of Montauk Seafood, near Charlie Lester's old vegetable stand, the fish store run by Jenny Lester and her daughters was doing fine, and so was Lester's Liquors, opposite Brent Bennett's Store, which was now owned and operated by Walter Bennett. But I saw Ted rarely and never saw the other fishermen at all; I lived ten miles away to westward, and was traveling all over the world. I bought a small wood bass boat for the bays, and went clamming and scalloping for my own use and satisfaction out of Sag Harbor; in the fall there was surfcasting for bass and bluefish, as far east as Montauk Light and as far west as Shinnecock Inlet. One winter day with my young daughter Sara, I found a whale skull that emerged from beneath the dunes after a storm. Perhaps this creature had been a drift whale, like that dead humpback rising and falling in the sea under Gay Head, or perhaps it was killed from a small boat by the farmer-fishermen of other days.

In 1958 the Army Corps of Engineers, at the instigation of a rich and influential summer resident who desired to shore up his dune house at Georgica at the public expense, had begun the construction of a series of ocean groins, or jetties, up to 750 feet long, to stabilize the unstable ocean beach. The vast enterprise failed to take into account the very strong set, or current, alongshore, and the sea carved huge scallops in the beach between these rock piles, which had no more place on the open Atlantic coast than that doomed fish pier that broke up at Napeague in 1881. Captain Frank Lester called the engineers "damned fools," and all those with experience of the ocean beach agreed that the jetties had seriously worsened the great damage caused by the line storm of March 1961, with its violent northeasterly gales. The storm picked off some houses built on sand that had no business on the high dunes in the first place, and temporarily laid bare stretches of peat, scored by cart tracks and ox prints of colonial times, that had long since been covered over by the sands. The high dunes at Sagaponack where Bud Topping had a big green summer tent were washed away, and Southampton Town replaced the dunes with a large parking lot, trash cans, and toilets, together with a big poster picture of the politician who wished to take credit for all this progress.

With the sudden rise in value of the land, the peaceful atmosphere of the South Fork began to change. The change developed like faraway massed clouds in the northern sky, the first iron weather of winter storm. Sagaponack was now the closest public beach to Sag Harbor, and traffic down its main street increased quickly. Within a few years the old Hildreth store expanded its services to accommodate the swelling tide of tourists, and the old village's quiet days were over. A new rash of real estate speculators, entreating other newcomers to "share our heritage," discovered Sagaponack, where the smaller local farms, unable to compete with the huge agribusiness in the West, or survive the growing tax on land inheritance, had begun to die. Even that oldest family farm in the United States was sold off by the squabbling heirs, with most of the money, it was said, gone to the lawyers.

The wells and water table had been polluted by chemical pesticides and fertilizers that leached into the earth and were washed by rain into the creeks, where the stunned fish were scavenged by the ospreys. The DDT absorbed by the microorganisms and plankton, and concentrating in the fish tissues on which they fed, weakened the osprey eggs, which broke when incubated. The great fish hawks were once so common here that twenty-five or thirty at a time could be counted over Fort Pond Bay; by the early sixties the huge primitive nests on Gardiners and Cartwright Shoal stood empty. Within the decade, the osprey was so rare that I would call my children out to look when one passed over, for fear that this sighting might be the last. The blue crabs that used to run in streams out of every salt pond when the gut was opened to the sea, and the fiddler crabs, once so thick in the spartina grass of the tidal wetlands that the flow of claw-snapping brown creatures could be channeled into tubs for use as bait, were killed off by DDT in the aerial sprays. Filling, bulkheading, and pollution of the wetlands were eliminating marine life spawning grounds and the last resorts of the wild duck, and even the long strings of sea duck had been much diminished by massive oil spills in the coastal waters. The remnant flocks were harassed by speedboat shooters who cared more about noise than boats and birds, who chased the flocks as they labored off the water and did not bother to pick up what they blasted down.

For a few years I resumed coot shooting at Cedar Point with Alvin and Bud Topping, Cliff Foster, and Ed Hildreth, but as rapidly as the fast plastic boats increased, the birds declined. A few years later, despite some memorable shoots at Sagaponack Pond, I gave up all gunning for good. Occasionally in fall I drove over to Northwest, past white pine woods and hoary orchards and the old fields of the early settlers with their fallen wells and shadowy foundations, to the Alewive Brook landing where our sharpies were once launched for Cedar Point. Here I harvested scallops washed ashore in a northwest blow or forked up a truckload of bleached eel-grass for the garden from the windrows on the quiet stretch of shore known as Kirk's Beach. In winter I went clamming from this shore, stopping every little while to blow on my red hands and watch the strings of coot and old squaw beating north over the chop toward Cedar Point.

One fair October afternoon I was surfcasting in autumn solitude at Mecox, where the gut had just been opened to the sea. The ocean was sparkling and mild, in a mild sun. A thud on my line was the first sign of what turned out to be a school of medium bass, and I had three fine stripers on the beach when Bobby Lester's Southampton seine crew came along and set around me. Bobby was Cap'n Frank's third son; I knew him by the resemblance to his brothers, the pale blue eyes in the hawk-nosed ruddy face. The trailer was backed down at high speed into the wash, the man at the truck wheel hit the brakes, and the big dory shot straight off its rollers through the surf and kept on going. This was the first dory I ever saw that was powered by an outboard motor, which was kept clear of the net in a well toward the bow. The old cotton nets, once six hundred fathoms long, had been replaced by nylon nets three times that length; instead of turning east a hundred yards out, this dory, larger than any I remembered, was going way offshore back of the bar.

On other days I saw the rigs from Amagansett, but except for Bill Lester's steady crew — I recognized his son Billy Lester, and the long-faced Havens boys, and Dom-Dom Grace — few of the faces seemed familiar; I felt like a stranger, and I kept my distance. The dark bulk of beach trucks in the pearly mist was reassuring, it was good to know that the haul-seiners were still there, yet my heart was struck each time I saw them by a pang of loss. I missed those fishing years much more than I cared to admit. I enjoyed my work and was making a good living, and I came and went, as independent as any fisherman, yet book royalties and magazine fees had no reality when compared to a day's pay earned out of doors. I missed the dawn light and the sunrise, the suspense of every haul, the calloused hands; I missed the smell and feel of boats and I missed the water. Also I missed the rough humor and old stories of such great events as the time that Lindy Havens and another fisherman, the late Edward (Peebo) Raynor, who lived out back of Cap'n Posey's house, got their car stuck while jacking deer in the Hither Hills. Having bent his shotgun barrel trying to lever out the car, "Hell, *that* don't mean nnnottttin!" Peebo said. He hacksawed it off short and kept right on going.

In 1966 I sailed on a commercial Cayman schooner on a green turtle fishing voyage to the Miskito Cays off Nicaragua, and in 1969 I was writer-diver on an oceanic expedition to the Indian Ocean and Australia that obtained the first undersea film (*Blue Water, White Death*) of the great white shark. But here at home, having just ten miles west of Amagansett, I had lost track of "all thim Poseys." One early spring I bailed a truckload of minnows trapped in Sagg Pond dreen to spread upon my vegetable garden, and another year I bought his whitebait seine from Bobby Tillotson, thinking to fish it by myself down on Sagg Pond; the seine lies untouched on the shed rafters with my old clam tongs, harpoon, and outriggers, and some balsawood black duck decoys from my gunning days. My scallop dredges had been "barried" some years ago and never returned, the big tuna rod that had bested that flying porgy was missing, too, and so was the old fighting chair that we mounted for the epic voyage of the Shinnecock chiefs to Rosie's Hole, off the New England shore.

Promised Land had closed down in 1968, and the big bunker steamers and swift seine boats, working the menhaden schools off the ocean beach, passed by no longer. Long-range factory stern trawlers from Europe and Japan, often visible on the ocean skyline, were fishing the continental shelf, increasing pressure on the open ocean species even as the fish themselves declined. Overfished by the long-liners (a long line is a trawl, up to sixteen miles long, set in deep water, usually along the deep sea canyons), the bluefin tuna so abundant in the fifties had been drastically depleted, necessitating strict quotas, and long-lined swordfish seemed certain to follow. Meanwhile, the expanding dragger fleet worked much closer to shore, roiling the water brown inside the bar.

Weakfish and kingfish, fluke and bottle fish had vanished, whereas striped bass and bluefish were abundant; despite the doom cries of the sportsmen, the numbers of striped bass had continued to grow. In 1968 Bill Lester's crew made the biggest haul ever recorded on the South Fork, and bass landings in 1973 were the highest ever. The next year the striped bass began a long decline, but demand for these fish kept the price so high that the diminishing fishery maintained its value. Nevertheless, the seine crews dwindled, one by one. Beach ordinances (as well as the bass decline) forced Bobby Lester off the beach, down in Southampton; as Bob Tillotson grew older and the bass harder to find, the farmers' haul-seine crew in Sagaponack disbanded, too. Frank Lester, injured, had long since retired, Bill Lester's strong crew had broken up, and although he fished intermittently until 1970, Cap'n Ted had sold his rig some years before.

"They are all gone now, the Indians and the whalers, the

Indian whalers, the part-Indians, the part-whalers, the farmer-fishermen...the narrow insular men and women who lived and bred for two and a half centuries in a backwater-corner of the United States, yet sometimes knew Canton or the Sandwich Islands better than they knew New York," wrote Captain Josh Edwards's great-grandson in 1978. There was truth in this, but the statement seemed premature; a few still knew about the old traditions.

One day in December 1964, Stuart Vorpahl, Jr., codfishing with Dominic Grace seven miles offshore near the Mecox sea buoy, felt swells begin to rise beneath the dory and headed for shore. (This was Captain Clint Edward's old dory in which Milt Miller had been so sick fifty years before. "She was cedar with hackmatack wood knees, from Nova Scotia," Stuart says. "All I had to do was put a new stem into her; the old one was nail-sick from two hundred Posey nails. That old girl's there back of the fish market yet today.") It was snowing hard by the time they neared the coast, the winter day was already growing dark, and Stuart could not make out the landing road or see the truck that he would need to haul the dory out of the surf where he came ashore; if he landed farther down the beach, he might lose the dory. Therefore he was happy to see headlights, shining out to sea from the landing at Beach Lane. The lights were a beacon from Elisha Osborn, an old fisherman-farmer of the Wainscott whaling clan. Like many old surfmen, Cap'n Lisha had the habit of driving down and gazing at the ocean. Coming upon Stuart's truck and trailer, he had known at once that a cod fisherman might be in trouble, trying to regain the shore on a darkening day.

STRIPER
by John N. Cole

Cole grew up on Long Island chasing bass and other game, moved to Maine, where he worked on newspapers in Bath, Brunswick, and Kennebunk, then helped found (with Peter Cole) the Maine Times, *a lively and beautifully designed weekly tabloid paper. He took time off to build an environmentally correct house (subject of his book* From the Ground Up*) and since has devoted his time to writing and being a curmudgeon.*

IN THE STRIPER'S BEGINNING was the glacier.

It came, a great, ponderous ice plain, one hundred thousand years ago. Moving south from what is now Labrador, the vast sheet slid as slowly as the centuries. Like a hatch cover closing, it obliterated lakes, rivers, forests and all the earth as far south as the mouth of the Hudson River.

In the tumult of its melting and recession 15,000 years ago, the glacier gouged new seas, cut new waterways, mixed the brine of the Atlantic with the pure fresh waters of inland lakes and rivers. From this massive, disordered and traumatic crumbling of natural barriers, the striped bass evolved: a freshwater creature who found a new environment in the channels the glaciers had gouged to the salt sea.

That heritage has shaped the striper's behavior. Since its violent genesis, the creature has never lost its affinity for the purity of its beginnings. Stripers are seldom, if ever, seen more than three miles off the coast; they swim up rivers with the ease of their distant forebears; they select the fresh waters of their ancient ancestors for their most critical rite — reproduction and the preservation of the species.

It was this compulsion that first brought the fish to man. Before Christ was born, East Coast Indian tribes could find the striper spawning in shallow rivers flowing by spring campgrounds. There are records in shell heaps and other archaeological detritus that indicate the waterway tribes knew of the creature; and early in the seventeenth century, with the coming of the European explorers to the New World's Atlantic coast, written documentation of the striper's abundance is duly recorded by the captains, historians and journal keepers who took detailed notes on whatever novel species were discovered, particularly if they appeared to be of value.

The fish is a sort of white salmon, which is of very good flavor and quite as large; it has white scales; the heads are so full of fat that in some there are two or three spoonfuls, so that there is good eating for one who is fond of picking heads. It seems the fish makes the Indians lascivious, for it is often observed that those who have caught any when they have gone fishing have given them, on their return, to their women, who look for them anxiously. [Isaak De Rasieres, a Dutch commercial agent on the Hudson River, 1623.]

The Basse is an excellent Fish, both fresh & salte, one hundred wherof salted (at market) have yielded five pounds (sterling). They are so large, the head of one will give a good eater a dinner, & for daintinesse of diet they excell the Marybones of Beefe. There are such multitudes that I have seene stopped in the river close adjoining to my house with a sands at one tyde so many as will loade a ship of 100 tonnes. I myselfe at the turning of the tyde have seene such multitudes passe out of a pounde that it seemed to me that one mighte go over their backs drishod. [Capt. John Smith, off the New England coast, 1614.]

The basse is one of the best fishes in the Country, and though men are soon wearied with other fish, yet are they never with basse. It is a delicate, fine, flat, fast fish.... sweet and good, pleasant to the pallat and wholesome to the stomach.... When they use to tide in an out of the rivers and creeks the English at the top of high water do crosse the creek with long seanes or bass nets which stop the fish; and the water ebbing from them, they are left on dry ground, sometimes two or three thousand at set, which are salted up against winter, or distributed to such as have present occasion either to spend them in their homes or use them for their grounds. [*William Wood*, New England Prospect, 1634.]

The maize growers and squash planters of seventeenth century New England were allowed to continue using striped bass as fertilizer for "their grounds" for just five years after 1634. Recognizing the commercial and food value of the fish, the General Court of the Massachusetts Bay Colony issued an order in 1639 which prohibited that practice.

Thirty years later, the patriarchs of Plymouth Colony decreed that funds from the sale of striped bass be used to construct the first public schools in North America. Thus, more than a century before the United States declared its independence the presence of the striped bass had become a bright and significant thread in the American tapestry. So admired was the creature from the very earliest days that in 1879 a sprightly and ingenious public servant named Harry W. Mason spent ten days in June on the Navesink River in New Jersey trying to collect a significant number of striped bass fry for his boss Livingston Stone, the United States Commissioner of Fish and Fisheries.

It was Commissioner Stone's purpose to respond to a plea from his state counterpart in California, S. R. Throckmorton, chairman of that state's fish commission. Throckmorton had discovered the striper on a trip east; he urged Stone to try to transplant some to the West Coast, and Stone dispatched Mason to the Navesink.

"On reaching Red Bank," writes Mason in a subsequent report to his chief, "I found none of the arrangements which we had directed to be made had been attended to; the two men — I cannot say fishermen — had but a faint notion of what was wanted, and had provided themselves with an eel seine wholly insufficient for my use."

Overcoming these nineteenth century bureaucratic barriers with a dogged zeal, Mason got his two "men" to haul a bass seine every high tide around the clock (midnight included) for a week. He and his unwilling crew went to the upper reaches of the river, and... "also spent Saturday morning exploring the mysteries of mud and water in every ditch and brook that empties into or communicates with the Navesink River above Red Bank." He continues:

The hauling was continued Wednesday, but as I had sixty small bass, 3 1/2 to 4 1/2 inches long, and thirty medium-sized bass, 6 to 8 inches long, I thought best to be sure of keeping some of them alive, at least, and so staid myself with the fish on the shore for the first time, the men going out alone with an empty tank and a thermometer. As might have been expected, they made a large haul of 139, mostly small, and lost all but twelve before getting back to the wharf. This rather disheartened them, but after considerable argument they were persuaded to try again Thursday, and very fortunately in the first haul we took seventy-five small bass and six large, and succeeded in bringing every one safe to the tank. The tanks were thoroughly washed and filled with water, half from the river, high tide, and half from a spring with sea salt added.

Thursday noon took the train from Red Bank, the tanks being expressed to Grand Central depot, charge, $15. A large truck and three men from Adams Express Company met the train from Jersey City, and at five o'clock the tanks arrived at Grand Central, and on examination only one dead bass was found.

Finding the baggage car was run through Chicago without change I made arrangements to have the tanks taken in that car, discharged the boy I had brought from Red Bank to help, and congratulated myself that I had one hundred and thirty-three small bass and thirty-four medium-sized bass alive and in good condition. The trip to Albany was uneventful, and with the delivery of the fish I gladly relieved myself of the responsibility that had weighed rather too heavily for comfort upon me during the ten days of my service.

The difficulty in obtaining the bass, requiring the services of from four to eight men day and night for a week made the expense of my experiments more than it would have been under more favorable circumstances (as a week later in time), but I did not dare relinquish in the least particular lest I should lose all the fish I had, and leaving the account to speak for its own necessity I respectfully submit this report of my ten days at Red Bank.

Mason may have worried about the reception given to his expense account, but he shouldn't have. In terms of public monies invested, his ten days at Red Bank and the care he bestowed on his small charges can surely rank as one of the most rewarding projects the U.S. Government ever executed. Of the original Mason group, one hundred seven stripers survived the transcontinental rail journey and were released in the Carquinez Straits near San Francisco. Twenty years later, the West Coast commercial catch of the progeny of Mason's travelers topped one million pounds of striped bass a year. Today, after passage of West Coast laws which prohibit netting, the bass ranges from San Diego County to Vancouver.

The creature that originally surged through the tumult of the glacier's wake to adapt to the East Coast salt sea had successfully survived the man-made tumult of a three-thousand-mile train trip in 1879, and adapted to Pacific waters as well. This is evidently a creature committed to survival.

And well equipped for it too. The striper is strong, muscular, hardy, and — in a marvelous evolutionary metamorphosis — better able than any other fish to cope with the thumping chaos of breaking surf. Hard headed, its gill plates covered with bony protection (plus a set of cutting gills), and blessed with a tail that can be extended laterally to become almost as broad as the broadest part of its body, the striper sports at the foaming fringes of the sea as a mountain goat leaps from peak to peak, or a gibbon swings from branch to branch high above a jungle floor.

Whenever the southeast wind has cleared the south-facing Atlantic beaches of the northeast — especially those in Massachusetts and on Long Island — bass can be seen in the very curve of a cresting wave. Driving smaller bait fish into the white water where the minnows become confused and unable to maintain equilibrium in the surge, the striper feeds easily in the scattering panic, maneuvering gracefully in water so shallow that the fish's bronze shoulders gleam above the pale foam. The striper never loses its composure in its high-risk environment. Often, when a wave's backwash leaves it almost high and dry, the fish will lie calmly on its side in the slight depression between two sand ridges, waiting in the two inches of sea water for the next incoming wave to bring it enough watery space to swim in.

The sight of a four-foot fish weighing close to fifty pounds, on its side in the shallow wash of the Atlantic, startles and amazes most observers. What few of them are likely to realize is the depth of the creature's experience. Bass that size are at least twenty years old, more likely twenty-five. The fish live relatively long lives, even when that longevity is measured on a human scale. Stripers weighing more than one hundred pounds — and catch records over the years are dotted with such giants — are between forty and fifty years old.

On both east and west coasts, the great striper populations spend much of these long lives on their migratory journeys. Vast numbers of the fish follow coastal geography in and out of estuaries, up and down rivers and streams, through natural and manmade tidal channels and canals, around the rims of bays and harbors, and, with conquering vitality, through the swells, riptides, undertows, foaming breakers and surging seas of that most violent place where ocean and land come together.

That meeting line, if every convolution of its granite and sand could be straightened, would cover tens of thousands of miles. The striper is a presence along every one of them, from the St. John River in easternmost Maine to Florida's bather-burdened Atlantic beaches. The striper concentrations, however — the teeming schools which had Captain John Smith believing he could walk "drishod" on their backs — range from the Chesapeake Bay's southern gateway at Cape Charles to the northernmost harbors of Massachusetts at Plum Island and Newburyport. It is between these points that most of the bass move each spring and fall, originating in the Chesapeake each April when the fish move north to return again in December for a somnolent winter in the bay's deeper reaches.

It is a journey that moves them past the great industrial sprawls of the most heavily populated, the richest, the most developed and electrified coastal corridor anywhere on the globe. Past Norfolk, Richmond, Washington, Baltimore, Wilmington, Philadelphia, Trenton, Newark, New York, Bridgeport, New Haven, Providence, Boston and Lynn they go — past more than fifty million humans working in more than ten thousand factories, living in more than twenty-five million housing units, and persuaded that the American Dream is woven from threads of mass production, mass consumption and mass waste, persuaded that the pursuit of happiness demands a compulsive dedication to weekend recreation, and millions believing there are good reasons why fishing is the nation's number one leisure time activity. Many of these spend the work week in factory, store or office, restaurant, supermarket or car wash so they can afford to purchase the rods and reels and lines and boats and boots that will enable them to better catch the striped bass — a creature embattled by the very lunge to industrialism which makes leisure possible for the legions of blue-collar and white-collar and mink-collar humans who have made the striper their favorite fish because it dependably stays within reach, keeps to a seasonal schedule and possesses such a driving life force that it has been caught in city sewers by Manhattan fishermen who lower lines through manhole gratings knowing before they do that they will never be able to retrieve the fish they hook from the fouled, piped waters that run where brooks once ran when stripers swam past the tents of the Algonquin Indians.

No one is certain of all the reasons for the annual journey north from the Chesapeake and back. While the striper population of the Hudson River also migrates, most fisheries biologists, and observers of the river such as author Robert H. Boyle estimate the proportion that migrate from the Hudson at somewhere between ten and twenty percent, and those do not travel with the great sweep of their Chesapeake brethren. The former move only from the river mouth to either Long Island Sound or Montauk Point via the ocean route. If the wintering stripers in the Chesapeake were sealed in that bay by nets at Cape Charles and across the Chesapeake and Delaware Canal, the megalopolistic millions would be denied their favorite sport.

Is it the tides of the creature's evolution that pull it on its voyage? Surely, in addition to its search for food, those currents of past eons must be part of the reason. Like travelers from another country searching for their birthplace in a distant nation, the stripers could be trying to retrace that first journey that began with the glacier's elemental convulsions. The erratic history of the creature's scientific nomenclature is evidence that some ichthyologists share this thesis. Originally christened *Roccus lineatus* (Latin doggerel for the coastal rocks the fish prefers and for the lines, or stripes, that mark it) the bass had its name changed in the 1930s to *Roccus saxatilis* (a redundancy that means rocks found among the rocks) when it was learned that *Roccus lineatus* was a name previously bestowed on a Mediterranean fish that was no relation. Then in 1967, after what has been labeled "considerable research," the striper became *Morone saxatilis* in the wake of pronouncements by the British Museum that the genus *Morone* more accurately indicated the striper's ties to the freshwater perch — the evolutionary progenitor who, with the help of the Ice Age, was probably the genetic parent of the fish that now swims the Atlantic coast twice a year in its search for a homeland that lies buried beneath megatons of glacial till, or under lakes the striper would have to cross mountains to reach.

The price in its numbers the adult striper has paid for its migratory compulsion is a price beyond counting. Who can guess how many thousands of stripers were trapped and speared by hunters of the Atlantic Indian tribes, eager to ease the winter's yearning for fresh meat with the flesh of this large creature that finned slowly through salt marsh channels, or rolled in the shallows of narrow rivers, intent only on its spawning rituals?

Who can ever measure the numbers that were taken by the English and the Dutch and the Spanish and the Italian fleets that made landfall in the New World only to find those harbors writhing with the silver-sided splashings of stripers chasing herring or shrimp? And will there ever be any counting of the stripers stop netted in tidal coves, their gleaming carcasses soiled on the mud flats of their final thrashing after the ebb had left them by the thousands for colonial farmers to hoist to handbarrows for their trip to the cornfields and their burial there?

And, as the nation grew, who ever tallied the bass taken by a growing commercial fishing effort that utilized hand lines, trot lines, line trawls, gill nets, stake nets, drift nets, runaround nets, seine nets, fyke nets, pound nets, trawl nets, scoop nets, trammel nets, and bag nets specially made to be slid under a river's winter ice to trap the bass as they crowded in giant schools near the bottom where the specific salinity and the water temperature were just at the brink of survival limits, nearly cold enough to crystallize the creatures' blood?

And who has ever conceived of a system that would tabulate the depredations of two centuries of recreational, sport, and meat fishing by individuals using hand lines fashioned from packing string or silk, rods from hickory branches or Calcutta cane; fishing from fifty-foot motor cruisers or wading in the surf; casting Atom plugs, bucktails, tin squid, cedar jigs, live eels, plastic worms, Mooselook wobblers; or trolling umbrella rigs, Japanese feathers and Rebel minnows; or drifting live eels, menhaden, mackerel or a soft-shelled crab tied to the hook with elastic thread?

No, there is no way the fare charged the striper for its annual trips can ever be computed. Every fish taken becomes a river of fish, then a cataract of billions, cascading over the centuries in a torrent of silver shapes that roars its testimony to nature's awesome abundance.

In their annual verification of that abundance, mature stripers still leave the rivers around the Chesapeake every spring after they have spawned. Thinned and weakened by the vigor and intensity of their spawning, the fish ease down the rivers, borne as much by the current as by the listless movement of their tails. After the April nights when the rivers gleam with the fecundity of these fish, the stripers depart the Nanticoke, the Choptank, the Wicomico, the Chester, the Pocomoke, the Wye, the Corsica, the Sassafras and fourteen more Chesapeake rivers that are still striper nurseries. On their way, the spent fish are taken by the river's drift netters, but once by those and in the open bay, they are relatively free of harassment by fishermen.

Starved during their spawning, the fish feed as they travel, gathering numbers as they move, segregating into schools according to size and age, establishing the behavior patterns that will set the schools on a compass course — first south to the bay's gateway at Cape Charles, then north along the barrier beaches of Maryland, past the oil refineries and chemical plants of Delaware and New Jersey, then across Sandy Hook and the Hudson delta in the shadow of the Statue of Liberty, and then past Brooklyn, Coney Island, Fire Island and on along the edge of the open Atlantic to the beaches of eastern Long Island and the oceanic migratory crossroads at Montauk Point where the

Atlantic meets Long Island Sound and Block Island Sound and where twenty or more species of food fish and game fish gather during the year on their migratory travels. Of these comings and goings, none is more certain, more regular than the arrival of the striped bass in May.

Movement ripples through Long Island's temperate spring on land and in the air as well as under the sea. Furred, hibernating creatures of the woods emerge from their dens; geese, warblers, wildfowl, shorebirds and the red-winged blackbird flock to the marshes and thickets of this sandy, scrub oak plain. This wind-scoured island has somehow withstood enough of the pressures of the city's millions to still provide East End ponds where Canada geese can rest on their flight from Carolina to Labrador, or where the golden plover can swing down for a safe pause on their three-thousand-mile trans-national trip from South America.

Yet each year a bit less eastern Long Island marsh remains; each year one more pond has been drained. Only the Atlantic survives and holds its territory essentially inviolate, and even that is invaded by behemoth barges carrying the offal of the city so it can be dumped in the ocean. But if Long Island's fish of May are deterred by that dumping, it is a sea change not yet understood or acknowledged by humankind. There are still too many fish for that.

There are great spring floods of fish, undersea rivers that over-flow their banks. First the herring, the alewives, bluebacks, and bunkers, the dense fluttering pods of their millions darkening the waters like oval clouds of blue dye, their nervous, fragile tails stippling the sea's surface like a squally breeze, the sound of their placid progress hissing gently like the wake of a sailing ship.

And after the herring come the dogfish, toothless cousins to the shark — summer dog and spiny dog, gray replicas of shark shapes, but in such numbers that if ever they should sprout the teeth and meanness of sharks there would soon be no other fish in the sea. They glide by Long Island's eastern beaches in

May, the bellies of the females stretched with their cargoes of pups, the infant dogfish born complete, dropped swimming by the dozen from their mothers' wombs with a day's supply of food suspended in the yolk at their umbilici—a day, that's all, to learn to hunt, catch and eat.

Under the dogs move skates and rays, flying over the sea bottom on the undulating wings that give such grace to these creatures of whipping tails and ugly, grimacing features set in the pale alabaster of their unseen undersides. And with the rays and skates, nuzzling the same sea floor, are the sea robins, sand crabs, lady crabs, blue crabs, spider crabs, angler fish, scup, sea bass, tautog, ling, sturgeon, and starfish—all of these and more setting the sea in motion with the sustained movements of their May migration.

The inshore Atlantic, the half-mile of breaking, rolling, surging sea between the outer sandbar fashioned by the largest swells and the inner, barrier beach where the land begins, here in this single ribbon of brine, the scale of life becomes overwhelming in the Long Island spring. From the quiet windless dawns to the evenings ruffled by the afternoon's southwest winds, the corridor teems. Small bait fish—the silver-sided spearing and the sardine-sized herring—flash like a silver rain blown from under the sea. Terrified by the approach of an infant dogfish, or panicked by a scup's rush, the dense schools of these finger-length mites take to the air as if they could find safety where they can not breathe.

When the bait schools shatter the surface and spray upwards in the sun they make a sound like the tearing of a cotton sheet. If the feeding fish are persistent, terns and gulls gather screaming in the sky. Then, as the hapless minnows leap from the yawning mouths below, they jump into the scissoring beaks above. But it takes a feeding frenzy to alert entire flocks of birds. More often, the silver showers of bait break here, there, the length of the beach in occasional and random patterns little noted by either bird or human, yet which are overall a daily and nightly part of the spring sea's particular pattern.

It is only when the stripers and the other school fish move that the birds are likely to gather. First come the small bass, then the middle-weights, and finally, the ponderous patriarchs and matriarchs, the thirty, forty, fifty, and sixty pound fish who wait until May is almost gone before they slide past Shinnecock and the Hamptons. With them come the weakfish, bluefish and some of the larger sharks — makos, threshers and hammerheads.

There is an order to the procession. Places are made for all, even the dense and apparently aimless schools of blowfish, packing stupidly just behind the surf even though the conformation of their stubby frames and inadequate tails makes it difficult for them to survive the inshore surging. Somehow they do survive, even though breaking swells are often darkened by cargoes of hundreds of the small creatures tossed in disarray by their own misjudgments.

The bass make no such errors; nor do the blues and weakfish — the primary schooling, toothed, muscular feeders of the inshore territory. These are the mass killers of the silverside, the mullet, the herring, the shrimp, the tinker mackerel, the blueback and the bunker. When a school of three hundred or four hundred stripers receives its simultaneous feeding message from impulses not yet fully deciphered by humankind, the creatures detonate a group frenzy that shatters the water's surface with the violence of an erupting undersea geyser.

Everywhere the bait fish fly, as if some soundless, invisible tornado were sucking them up from beneath the sea. Broad bass tails smash the surface in white welts of foam; the turnings of the feeding fish start scores of swirling whirlpools, each a mark of the consummate energy a fish needs to reverse its course and swerve openmouthed through the very center of the mass of panic the bait fish school has become. Shredded bits of bunker, spearing or blueback drift to a surface made slick with the released oils of the tiny, dismembered fish. Sea birds scream of the carnage; their coarse signals carry for miles, attracting hundreds, sometimes thousands of their kin. Then the air above becomes part of the tumultuous mass—a sky filled with stripped feathers, the hysterical cry of anxious terns, the hoarser calls of the herring and blackback gulls, all diving, wheeling, hovering and heedless of any approach as they swallow the hapless bait fish whole whenever the prey are driven live from the sea, or pick with their bills at the flesh fragments that rise in the wake of the stripers' feeding rush.

The gluttony ends with the same unity it began. Another coded message stills the sated school, the birds become silent, scatter; just a few stay sitting on the surface, drifting markers on a patch of sea, mobile memorials to the oceanic moment when ten thousand tiny herring were devoured.

The striper school moves on, traveling east to Montauk, guided by the sound of the rolling surf, compelled to continue by voices calling across the Ice Age with urgings that have transcended every fear of net, spear, hook, and trap since the bass first embarked on their journey, before the Indians, before the colonists, before Harry Mason and before Manhattan's millions.

CHANNEL BASS
by Van Campen Heilner

From his book Salt Water Fishing. *Van Campen Heilner didn't have to worry about working for a living; he started fishing young and kept at it all over the world. He knew the great ones — Zane Grey, Michael Lerner, and Kip Farrington — and he went after the big fish, the tunas and marlin. But his first fishing was along the shore, and his warmest writing is reserved, I think, for fishing the surf. He was willing to spend time chasing down weakfish and fluke, and channel bass, which are the subject of this writing.* Salt Water Fishing *was one of Van Campen Heilner's most popular books, going through five printings between 1937 and 1940.*

⚓

I SUPPOSE THAT most of us have a first love, and without doubt this writer's is the channel bass. Perhaps because this fish was associated with my early youth or perhaps because he was the first large fish I ever caught, a 41-pounder by the way, the place he occupies in my heart is a near and dear one.

Memories of autumn days with the snipe trading down the beaches and the first flock of wild geese etched high against the sunset above the golden marshes, sea grass on the dunes bending, against the hiss of the first northwester, spring days with the miles of rolling breakers creaming in across the bar and the nesting terns and laughing gulls setting up their ceaseless clamor in behind the thoroughfare — these all mean but one thing to me, that lovable old coppery warrior of the tides, *Sciaenops ocellatus*, the channel bass.

From Barnegat Light to the Gulf of Mexico I have pursued him down the years with a relentlessness that has amounted to a mania. Other fish have I caught which proved gamier; other fish have I caught which were more spectacular, more deserving perhaps of their place in the sun, or sea; but none gives me a greater thrill or a greater desire to repeat sensations which each year seem as new and exciting as they seemed when first I experienced them.

He goes by many names. From Jersey to Florida he is the channel bass or red drum. But the name red drum should be discouraged because it only confuses him with his cousin, the black drum, an oafish fellow with a beard, a hump on his back, stripes like a convict and the fighting abilities of a sack of potatoes. From Florida south he is the redfish and as you wend your way around the Gulf Coast and approach Texas and Spanish America he becomes the red horse or *pez colorado.* But he's still the channel bass to me no matter under what name he masquerades.

The sportiest way to take him is by surf fishing. Surf fishing is to salt water angling what trout fishing is to fresh water. It is a one-man game from start to finish. You are the one and only factor. It is the same as still-hunting is to deer driving. Here you are and there he is. If he runs out all the line you can't pick up the oars or start the engine and follow him. No cushion of comfortable seat or chair supports your fundament, no thwarts against which to brace you feet, no companion to assist you or guide you. You must find your quarry yourself, you must rig and bait your hook yourself, you must become proficient in the art of casting so you may reach him, and you must bring him through a line of foaming breakers and surging tides until at last, whipped to a standstill, he lies gasping on the wet sands at your very feet. Then you must let him go because he deserves it.

Some bright morning in early summer you pack your duffle and rods and hie yourself to your favorite inlet. You have been mulling over that tackle all winter. Your rod is a two-piece split bamboo — maybe one piece — the tip is from 6' 6" to over 7'. It has a "spring butt" or straight one, 24" or longer. Maybe you've rewrapped it during the winter and given it three or four coats of varnish. You've certainly oiled and cleaned your 2/0 reel and filled it with new 12 thread line. You've sharpened your hooks which may run from 5/0 to 9/0, put on new leaders, cleaned your fish knife and sharpened it to a razor edge, re-riveted your rod belt, molded some new sinkers of your pet shape and weight, cleaned out your bait box and in this latter operation discovered the source of the terrible smell which bothered your wife in winter when she was sure that something had died somewhere in the house.

This season you have a couple of new gadgets. You've put a throat on the inside pocket of your beach bag with a drawstring, so the blowing sand can't get inside. You've made a disgorger out of a copper tube with a handle 18" long so you can get that hook out of the tummy of the bass without cutting your hands to pieces. And you have a finger gaff which is a big strong 10/0 hook drilled into a small barrel-shaped piece of wood so you can grasp it with your fingers. It only weighs a few ounces aad you can hang it in one of the buckle holes in your belt where it's easy to reach and weighs nothing.

At the fish house you've picked up a dozen fresh bunkers. They are nice and fat and fairly ooze oil. If you're beach camping or on your boat you have them already iced down, or you've made arrangements for someone to supply you with fresh ones every day.

At last you arrive at the inlet. You've judged it about right. The tide is some two hours down, the wind is onshore and while there isn't a heavy sea running, there's plenty of "fight" to the surf. You first make a survey to determine the most likely place. The formation has changed since you were here in the fall. Where is that beautiful pocket that lay just north of the point? It's gone and the beach there is as flat as a flounder. You walk on and pretty soon you find what you are looking for. A good cast from the beach lies a long bar over which the sea is breaking with diminishing intensity. It will be nearly dry at low water. Between it and the beach runs a long narrow slue, maybe half a mile long. Another hour or less and you'll be able to wade it. Thousands of broken clam shells strew the beach in all directions. You can see lots of small bait in the undertow. You drop your beach bag near the high-water mark, take out your sand spike and stand your rod up in it. You heave a big sigh. "This is the place!" you say. "If they're anywhere, they ought to be here!"

While you're waiting for the tide you cut some bait. You find a board and lay your mossbunker on it. First you scale him. Then you cut off his head and split him down the side, keeping the knife just this side of the backbone. Then the other side. Now you have two nice scaleless, boneless slabs of bunker. If he was a big one, cut these diagonally in half and you have four baits. It may be that you prefer to cut him in chunks from back to belly, but in any case cut just enough to fill your bait box, as fresh-cut bait is much better. Later, when the bunkers are a couple of days old, if you can't get any more you will have to wrap them on the hook with thread or they'll fall to pieces.

Now you're all set. If the water and weather are warm you'll discard boots and wade in. If it were late in the fall you'd probably be wearing boot-foot waders. Waders are better than boots, because sometimes the slues are deep. It's almost waist-deep in the slue and you climb out on the outer bar which is nearly dry. A short cast to wet your line, bait up, swing back and heave her out.

For a long time nothing happens. Then your heat skips a beat. Something moved in with your bait. You wait. There it is again! This time the line runs slowly out. You set the hook but instead of the expected rush, something flies to the surface and flaps the water furiously about. A skate! You reel in disgustedly and spend five minutes stabbing and sawing the grotesque nuisance into several pieces before you can recover your hook.

Cast again. What a peach of a cast! Your form was perfect! If some of your friends could have seen that one! Maybe you had better enter the tournament this summer. You are so busy congratulating yourself that before you know it your line is whizzing out in long steady surges that you know can mean but one thing. You clamp down your thumb and the fight is on!

Out he goes, then the tide catches him and he goes with it. You have him almost in and out he goes again. But each rush is shorter. In fifteen minutes you see him on the surface twenty feet away. He's swimming slowly but still headed out to sea. Tbe tide has changed now and the waves are getting larger. The bar is starting to cover. You bring him slowly to your feet and a receding wave leaves him flopping in a few inches of water. Luckily he's hooked in the mouth. You work the hook loose and with the next wave kick him back. About thirty-five pounds you guess. A good fighter.

It's getting pretty deep on the bar now and it's time you were leaving. You wade back across the slue and take up your station on the main beach. There's lots of movement in the surf now. 'Way to your left you see the gulls working over something that is breaking all over the surface. Blues! You're sorely tempted but you're after bigger game. Then you have a strong slashing strike and in a minute or two beach a beautiful weakfish, five pounder at least. Well, you'll take anything that comes. But you won't move from this spot, because — ah! that unmistakable pull! You'd know it anywhere, any time. He's running with it. Let him have it, let him have it...NOW!

Thus the mechanics of surf fishing for channel bass. But to me the fish are but incidental. The miles and miles of lonely beaches stretching from Montauk to the barrier islands of Texas. The dunes, shading from white to golden brown. The sedge grass blowing in the wind. The little "teeters" scurrying up the beach just ahead of the waves and right-about-facing just as quickly, to stab their long little bills in the moist sand behind the retreating surge. The confused clamor of hundreds of terns "working" over a school of blues. The wild fury of a "north-easter" pounding down on a deserted coast, with the whole beach under water and the flash of the distant lighthouse showing faint and blurred through the driving rain. Autumn, with the first crisp tang of a northwester, blue skies and blue surf and the first black ducks coming in at sunset to the marshes behind the inlet.

These are what I think of when I think of channel bass. And for myself I can think of nothing better.

SONG OF THE OLD TIMERS

Famous wherever surfmen gather.
Tune: "Watermelon Hanging On the Vine."

Oh, the weakfish am good
And the kingfish am great,
The striped bass am very, very fine;
But give me, oh, give me,
Oh, how I wish you would!
A channel bass a-hangin' on my line!

THE ART OF SURF FISHING
by Owen Hatteras

From Fish Stories, *a collection of pieces on marine topics (fishing and marine research) published by the American Littoral Society. Hatteras wrote this essay some 15 years ago. It summarizes his lifelong addiction to fishing from shore. Hatteras was a textile-factory owner in South Carolina, but found fishing and writing more satisfying (he was comfortably off and could afford a leisurely pace). Many of his early pieces (on other subjects) were published by H.L. Mencken, who claimed to have discovered him.*

⚓

MY FATHER TAUGHT me how to fish in the surf. One summer at the shore when idle time abounded, he gave me a short fishing rod, took me to the beach, and explained how a cast could be made seaward. There must have been a fish on my line soon after because that was around 1930, and I have been surf fishing ever since. The disease would not have caught on if the early experiences had been fishless.

Surf fishing has a number of advantages over other methods of fishing, the major one being that it is possible to go for very long periods of time without catching a fish. This is important because fishless time can be spent relaxing. There are other surf fishing advantages: it's cheap, it's lonely, it's healthy, and it wastes time. But most important, surf fishing, if done correctly, leaves time and energy for the more important aspect of angling anyway, which is to observe nature while thinking about fish.

In the northeast, surf fishing starts in May when the water is uncomfortably cold and fish are scarce. It hits its first peak in June when a week might produce two or three fish. Then come July and August, hot months with water almost too warm and most fish away. By September, the surf fisherman has accumulated at least four months of failure, and the reward arrives in the fall as both weather and fish conspire to cap the year with comfortable water, cool air, fewer people on the beaches, waterfowl migrating. and schools of fish feeding heavily before they move south. This makes it all worthwhile, and the happy surf person can enjoy it until a serious northeaster wipes everything out in November. That ends the season until the following May. Forty years of surf fishing (or tackling the suds as the magazines call it) qualify me to set down some tips about how to do it right. Thus, The Art of Surf Fishing.

The first rule is to travel light. This means rod and reel, tackle, bait or lures, and knife. Period. All this can be carried in the pockets of baggy shorts, or, if you prefer, a washable canvas army surplus bag over the shoulder. I wear shorts and, depending on the time of year, zero to seven shirts, sweaters, and jackets. No shoes. How can you walk in the sand and surf with shoes on? No boots or waders. If you need them it's too cold to fish. Besides, they usually leak and they chafe the inside of the left ankle. No gaff, no fish slugger, no sandspike, no whetstone, no bug spray, no tackle box, no pliers, no rod belt, no flashlight no folding chair, and no food or drink. A good fisherman is irritated; hunger and thirst help. Most of all, no beach buggy. Beaches and vehicles don't mix. Going fishing in a beach buggy is like running down wolves with a helicopter or taking a portable television set on a camping trip.

Now that you are traveling light, the question is. where do you travel? Simple...go where no one else is. The proper distance between two surf fisherman is no less than 75 yards and at least out of hearing range. If you are fishing alone and someone comes up next to you, move immediately, even if you are catching fish. Anyone who comes close to a surf fisherman and starts to cast should not be associated with; put distance between you.

Conversation with other surf people should be avoided. If you are fishing in the surf and someone walking along the beach stops and asks a question, usually, "Are you catching anything?" say, no. Here are some other conversation guides:

"How's it going?" Slow.

"Anything doing?" Nope.

"Where's a good place to fish?" Down there half a mile.

The point is to discourage entanglements and especially to discourage another fisherman from establishing a base of operation nearby. This is difficult if you have a fish on your line when the newcomer arrives at your side. In this situation, you have two alternatives. I favor the "ignore the fish" routine. This means standing with the rod in your hand, pretending there is no fish on the other end. If the tip throbs mightily and your unwelcome guest notices, explain that the waves are doing it or you happen to have for bait an extremely large, lively herring or mullet or whatever. I have carried on a conversation for 20 minutes while ignoring a decent striped bass on the other end of the line. The second alternative is to haul in the fish and leave the spot to the interloper.

Fishing time, like place, is important. The two best fishing times are sunup and sundown because this is when fish bite. Of the two, sunup is preferable because fewer people like to get up early than like to stay up late. It is likely to be cool before sunrise, but you can look forward to the sun's warmth. It is a good idea to avoid either a dead low or dead high tide right at sunup. And, never fish on a weekend.

Putting it all together, I go fishing most seriously and with the most promise of success on a Wednesday morning in September, with the tide halfway in, a week before a full moon on a beach where few people fish and where beach buggies are banned. There are probably only three such places in New Jersey and maybe only a few dozen in the northeast, but these are the places I seek out.

I go to fish, not to catch fish. Success is guaranteed if I get to the surf and stand alone for a few hours, casting lures or bait into a good looking sea with things happening around me. If I get a bite or even catch a fish, so much the better. If it is a good fish, I will have it for supper. If I don't want the fish I will tag and return it. If it is a very big fish I will surely return it whether I am hungry or not. I once killed a huge, surf-caught black drum. It weighed 75 pounds and I killed it and traded it for a dollar's worth of fishing tackle at a bait, tackle and seafood shop. It was full of worms and was thrown away and that's the last very big fish I have killed.

In the northeast surf in the fall, only two species are available and worth catching — bluefish and striped bass — and the latter are vastly overrated. They tend to bite indifferently, fight lethargically, and surrender easily. The saying goes, "Striped bass aren't much fun to catch but they sure are lousy to eat." This leaves bluefish and I prefer fishing for them with cut mullet in South Jersey in the fall more than any other kind of fishing.

Catching mullet for bait is easily as interesting as fishing itself. I use a small castnet. Schools of mullet come down the beach about 10 yards out. I go into a mullet stalk, walking into the water to intercept the school. The net is cast, the mullet trapped and brought ashore, and bait is taken care of. I once knew a gentleman in South Jersey who spent so many hours stalking mullet in the surf that he ended up looking like a great blue heron. The mullet are scaled and split into two or four greasy, fishy slabs. One such slab is applied to the hook, the line is cast, the wait begins, and things start to happen.

I choose to stand where the waves can wash gently over my feet, so the first thing that happens is that the ocean sends its messages of wetness and movement and a kind of vibration or sound. I wonder where the wave breaking over my ankles started. Was it from the Azores? Did it come from an eddy of the Gulf Stream near Iceland? What wind brought it? Waves usually wash up the beach at angles. They come, say, from the northeast and wash back down the beach to the southeast. Sand moves too on its journey with littoral drift. The sand behind my feet is cut away. Heels sink. I move my feet back a few inches, digging in. If no fish bite and I need not move laterally along the beach I am soon up to my ankle bones in sand. The sand is cooler deeper. If I could stand there through a whole tide would I sink from view? Maybe someone coming by a day later would see just a fishing rod sticking out of the sand.

Coastal birds are something else that happens during surf fishing. Shorebirds — peeps — drop at the edge of the wet beach and probe, then jump up as one and move down the beach, on their way to South America. With luck, one will fly right into my line, making it feel as if a fish is taking the bait. The bird isn't hurt and barely misses a wingbeat; it stays with the flock. If it is not too late in the fall, common and least terns scream and dive into the surf to snatch bait fish. Bigger, slower herring and blackback gulls glide down the beach farther offshore. Behind me, above the high-tide line, bunches of laughing gulls, their black heads now turned off-season grey stand facing the wind. They are tempted by the bait I have in my bag as they were earlier rewarded by the mullet heads and backbones I threw to them to catch in the air. If it is late in the fall, there might be strings of black waterfowl — scoters probably — dark lines a mile offshore just above the water. The strung-out flock undulates.

The play of oceanic wildlife is all around. Calico crabs and mole crabs scurry in and out of the sand near my feet. Amphipods snap and leap just above the tide line. Schools of bait fish pass by. Up in the dry sand are the burrows of ghost crabs, out of the day air but ready come nighttime to forage the driftline for food. It is difficult to be bored while surf fishing.

As the minutes and hours pass with no action on the wet end of the line, I am able to think back on past fish, proven and disproven theories, and general surf experiences. I recall that reading fishing columns in newspapers, the ones that tell what was caught the day before and predict the fishing for the next day, is an exercise in fantasy. To read these columns is to believe that large fish ("lunkers" in the trade) are so common that it is necessary to hide behind the dunes while baiting up, for fear the fish will come out of the surf and across the dry beach to attack. An angler will "high hook" with at least 50 fish, "topping out at" 42 pounds (that's not the total, that's one lunker). One will be able to fill up baskets with various species of fish. And one can read of anglers weighing in their catches at local bait and tackle shops, though the reason for exposing your catch (and thus your fishing spot) escapes me.

I am reminded of earlier days of surf fishing when we used linen line that had to be rinsed in fresh water and dried after each day's fishing and had to be wet before casting to avoid burnt thumbs and break offs. Mostly, I recall snarls, birds' nests, and backlashes which, in their regularity and ferocity, challenged any surf fisherman. I used nine-thread Cuttyhunk, 27-pound test. If you nursed it, it was good for two years.

There are "Things to Do When the Fish Aren't Biting." I enjoy disturbing seagulls. The basic beach gull likes to stand up just back of the beach berm. It is facing into the wind, relaxed, and watching me, especially to see if I drop my bait. If I turn to look, it shifts its feet and cocks its head. If I walk toward the gull, it waddles away. If I run halfheartedly, it flies a few feet and sets down again. If I run seriously, it takes off and makes a wide gentle circle downwind before settling onto the beach again. The best way to launch a large group of beach gulls is to run at them with arms spread, shouting "I want to be your friend." One is treated to a massive display of jump launching, defecating, squawking, flapping, wheeling, and gliding and an eventual landing down the beach.

Another thing to do when fishing is slow is to put down the rod, put on a face mask (add this to your canvas bag), and swim along the water's edge. I've done this many times and on occasion have been treated to startling displays. At Plum Island in Massachusetts, I once kicked up dozens of small skates which flew away from me out into the deep. On a Rhode Island beach, I swam out into chest-deep water and hand fed calico crabs bits of cut clam; they scrambled and fought each other and my fingers. And once in a calm slough in Maryland, I lay right in the waves's wash and watched juvenile spot fight the undertow to stay behind low sand rills, looking all the time for something to eat. It is often especially good to watch some active sea life first hand while nothing shows an interest in the baited hook, to confirm that indeed the ocean lives.

I spend idle moments figuring out why I am cold and how to ignore the discomfort. I have been in the water for two hours, legs alternatively wet and dry. The water is 68-degrees, the air is 55-degrees and it's windy. There are four solutions: (1) quit fishing, (2) shiver and let that warm me, (3) keep from shivering, or (4) wade out deeper until I am totally immersed in 68 degree water; this is warmer than 55 degree air and the evaporation problem is licked. My solution is a combination of the last three choices. None works, so I quit (see No. 1).

One thing that makes all fishing worthwhile is the possibility of the big-fish, the once-in-a-season-or-lifetime when some enormous sea creature takes the bait or goes on display. As I stand in the surf, I can recall half a dozen big fish events,

— At Cape Hatteras 20 years ago, I was fishing a handsome slough just north of what was then called the boiler, an old tugboat wreck. I was using large chunks of cut mullet, trying for fall channel bass. Big bass there will often pick up the bait, and take a direct approach to escape — straight out to sea. This happened and I gave line in surges until I was near the end; I waded into the surf and across the slough (with water up to my chest) out onto the farthest wave-washed bar which the fish had crossed ahead of me. After some minutes I got the fish in closer so that it came back across the bar into the slough. As it crossed in shallow water I saw that it was a very large shark, my size. Here I was facing the beach, the fish between me and land. "The hell with this," I thought, reeled in as much line as possible and broke the fish off.

— I hooked a fish in South Jersey that took me out some and then about a quarter mile south down the beach until I got it in the wash; a ray with wings six feet across, gasping in the breakers. I unhooked it and spent 10 minutes trying to break the suction made by its wings in the wet sand as I tried to haul it back into the sea. Finally I got it aimed the right way, gave it a lift with a piece of driftwood and it went back where it came from.

— While drifting in a canoe down the lower Suwannee River in Florida on an absolutely still night I was shaken out of a doze by a thumping splash close enough to put water in the boat. Only silence, then a barred owl throbbing a call. Was the splash a sturgeon? Whatever, a big thing.

— My brother and I shined the beam of a flashlight down into the moving water of Townsend Inlet, N. J., one summer night. A large brownish fish rose toward the surface, a fish mostly head, wide-spaced eyes, a wedge-like body and almost no tail. Maybe a large goosefish, but they are usually offshore and deep.

— Coming up the Sabine River in Texas on a tanker, our wake tossed up an eight-foot alligator gar, its side laid open and white. Our propeller must have struck the fish. It thrashed as if to sound but the tail didn't answer the head's instructions so it could only bob and struggle.

— At Island Beach State Park one evening a ranger told me to put on heavy equipment with wire or cable leaders because huge bluefish were tearing things up. I chuckled. used my regular gear and the bluefish tore it up.

The thoughts, then, while surf fishing are often of big fish and ones that got away, or simply came up nearby to show themselves. People who fish the sea think of big creatures that live down deep but visit the surface or the water's edge. The sea is so broad and deep that it must indeed harbor secret living things. Some believe that fish never stop growing and never get old. They just get bigger and slower but always growing. If that is true. why won't there sometime be a true giant of a bluefish (after all the record jumped almost five pounds a few years ago with one fish) or a striped bass larger than the fabled 125-pound fish that was trapped at Edenton, N.C.?

And what some stories those big fish could tell, for they have probably traveled the coast three dozen times, north in the spring and south as the waters chill in the fall. Or maybe they begin to travel less as they get older. Could they have found that some simpler migrations inshore and off will do the job? What amount of food do they need to fuel their bulk? They must be choosey feeders; if they had been careless they would not have survived. They are lucky to live in the sea where it is not possible for humans to know it all. New mammals don't get discovered much anymore. No one expects to see a 4000-pound grizzly bear. In fact, most of the grizzlies in North America have been seen by people, maybe even counted. Land holds few secrets and even fewer threats.

The surf line and the hard wet sand are good places to witness events of short life but lasting impression. How, for example, do shorebirds avoid being crushed by breaking waves? And how do they launch from the beach simultaneously? Once a shorebird walked between my legs while I was surf fishing. A friend of mine had a French poodle that waded out into the surf and brought back a sand shark. There was a surf fisherman who, in the hottest August weather, wore black boots and pants, and a black wool cardigan sweater and stood on the dry hot sand. He fished with a stiff split bamboo pole and used steamed mussels for bait and he caught lots of fish. Two people fish side by side. Same rigs, same bait, fishing the same distance from the water's edge. One catches six fish, the other none. Why? I see few women who surf fish. Is it cultural? Physical? Probably no one has ever bothered to invite them. Their fathers never taught them.

TIME AND TIDE
by Russell Chatham

From his book The Angler's Coast. *Chatham had moved to Montana by the time this book was published in 1976. That's a bad sign, for he got far from the West Coast, which he knew, fished, and wrote about (and painted) so well. Now he paints and is publisher of the Clark City Press.*

The copy on the book jacket calls it "The reflections of a flyfisherman on water he knows and loves. With illustrations by the author." It's not reassuring to see that the photo on the back of the jacket shows the author in the stern of a motorboat with a stout trolling rod plainly in view. No harm. Here Chatham writes about salmon and steelhead coming back from the sea.

⚓

TIME AND TIDE

SALMON AND STEELHEAD FORAGE widely on the open ocean in a dining room bound only by the continents, and this vastness implies perfectly the breadth of spirit these noble fish embody. To understand the salmon, it has been said, would be to crack the universe.

Unerringly, salmon come around their wheel to spawn and die at the place where they were born. So do steelhead, the great trout of the sea, though for them death is not always imminent. And while salmon are frequently taken inland in addition to providing the bulk of both the commercial and sport catch off the West Coast of North America, steelhead are rarely caught at sea.

Immediately before becoming riverbound both fish can be taken at their prime. Consider the cycle: one to five years of intense feeding solely to gain strength to survive the spawning journey. Clearly these fish are at their finest just prior to entering fresh water before using stored energy as they must when feeding ceases.

There are distinct stages in the lives of anadromous fish: river, transition, ocean, transition, river. The transitional periods are by far the shortest and it is the second of these that interests the angler.

As the migrants near shore their habitat gains a definition it didn't have at sea. In open water, trolling is the only practical way of fishing for salmon. But as the procreative urge draws the fish near his river or creek, the wader and rowboat fishermen have their day. Now, steelhead, too, become game for the angler and it is the only time in their saltwater life when this is so.

In a defined area fishing is more absorbing. For example, in offshore waters a thirty-pound salmon will make runs and dart about, perhaps even jump, but without any bottom or shore to relate himself to, he can usually be led close enough to be netted rather quickly. Assuming leader strength to be similar, that same thirty-pounder will give twice the battle in a tidal estuary because it is in the fish's nature to seek cover when it is available. You can be sure that if there is a brush pile nearby— as there so often is in a tidal reach—the salmon will try and get into it. Too, the fish will frantically avoid being led into shallow water.

Perhaps both species are slightly uneasy upon first entering confined water after years of living in an unlimited expanse. Somewhat cautious already then, when hooked it could be they are prepared to wage a more desperate battle. The fish is fighting for his life and never before has he had more reason to live.

I've fished the estuary of Paper Mill Creek and Tomales Bay into which it flows for almost a quarter of a century. During the first of those I was a spinning enthusiast but soon learned the greater joy of fly-fishing. More than that, I came to know above all it was the tide that spelled the difference between success and failure.

One year at Christmas there had been no rain for nearly three weeks. This left Paper Mill Creek itself extremely low and clear. No fish could move out of the estuary into it. It was time for the main run of steelhead to appear but I tried the usual holding places and neither caught nor saw any. It was obvious they hadn't gone through because you could see into all the holes upstream (where fishing is illegal) and there were only a few spent silvers.

The remaining possibility was that they were still in Tomales Bay. The odds against successfully searching such large water, especially with a fly rod, seemed so overwhelmingly high I put off trying and instead went duck hunting the next day, It was a fortuitous move, for quite by accident I found the fish.

There was a two-foot minus low tide in midafternoon that completely dried out the mud flats near Inverness. I'd thought to stalk some pintails which were sitting on a mud spit when suddenly I saw a fish's wake in several inches of water. Moments later there was another that surged erratically over the flat. Thinking they were striped bass I got the binoculars and saw clearly that instead they were steelhead. The wakes were disappearing into a small basin I knew was about three feet deep. Of course! On the big minus tide, the basin was one of the few places in the upper bay with any water in it.

Next day I arrived with a fly rod about noon. The tide was still much too high but it was rushing out rapidly. Since I knew precisely where the basin was even on the flood, having fished it many times for stripers, I waded out in a burst of early enthusiasm and made a few casts preferring that to just sitting and waiting for the tide to drop. Right away, in a stroke of luck unequaled before or since, I had a fish on. Twenty minutes later a fine twelve-pound female steelhead lay exhausted at my feet.

For an hour after that too-easy triumph, I cast diligently but caught nothing, so I sat down to wait it out. Two hours later the flats in front of me had only three or four inches of water over them and that was when the first wake appeared. But I didn't catch a fish until after seeing half a dozen more. With the tide dropping, the current became confined to the tiny channel and ran stiffly through the basin. Positioned slightly upstream, I began to cast, quartering down with a light number-six line which sank very slowly. On the third or fourth swing a fish took and tail-walked twenty yards to the far edge of the basin then ran back, half out of water. In a few minutes it had been caught and released. Fishing was extraordinary until dark. The fishing diary I used to keep reads, "...Dec. 28...15 steelhead hooked...11 landed...6 to 12 lbs."

Conditions lasted five more days. At the end of that time the minus tides were not severe enough to force the fish into the pocket and the lows were too late at night to be of any use. Besides, the fish moved to a different spot but that's another story. I was glad no one ever spotted me because a single unscrupulous fisherman could have literally wiped out the run. Altogether the log book shows fifty-seven fish on the beach all released but one — the first I caught that day on the high tide. Three I caught twice and two were foul-hooked due to the confined area. The single critical factor contributing to this good fishing, aside from the fact that the fish were there, was the tide. The spot was no good on anything less than a 1.5 minus because it took that little water to force the steelhead to bunch up in the basin.

A few miles north of San Francisco Muir Creek flows out of the famed Redwood National Park to join the Pacific. It is a tiny stream and like so many others, fish can enter it only after a substantial rain. In October silvers gather off its mouth and must occasionally wait until late December to spawn. Often they are joined in the surf by steelhead. Many years ago there was a dry winter and while both fish waited along the beach they could be seen leaping in the surf. I caught a number of them that fall in what was for me an unprecedented experience. Early on the fish were bright but by December most were dark and had formed the kype or hooked jaw associated with mature spawning fish. Salmon turn dark in relation to their state of maturity rather than because they've entered fresh water. Some of these appeared to be trying to spawn right on the beach, nosed against a spot where perhaps a trace of fresh water seeped through the sand.

In all tidewater fishing it is impossible to emphasize too strongly how critical the action of the tide is. As a rule the fresher the fish the better they seem to bite on the high water, particularly the top of the ebb. The larger runouts seem to activate fish also, at least in sloughs and estuaries where there is a riverlike flow.

An interesting point is that fresh silvers generally swim relatively near the surface. These are the ones that bite best on the high water. If these same fish are forced to lay for some time in tidewater before getting upstream, they seem to settle deeper as they would in a river pool and the older they get the farther down on the tide they bite.

Frank Allen took one such silver about fifteen years ago in Paper Mill's estuary. That fish weighed close to twenty-two pounds and at the time was clearly a world fly-casting record. Frank had wanted to release the fish because it was dark but the late Joe Paul persuaded him to keep it, saying it was surely a record. It was, but Frank was happy just to have caught it and never bothered to try for official recognition.

This pattern of new fish biting on the high water and older fish on the low is observable in many streams. On the Chetco River in Oregon old fish are most apt to be caught in the Morrison or Tide Rock Holes at the end of the outgoing tide. The fresh fish from Morrison on down to Snug Harbor seem to bite best on the high rise and high ebb.

During fall in California — Oregon, too, for that matter — all the short coastal streams are at their lowest. In creeks like Paper Mill little fresh water is present in the lagoons. The same could be said of rivers such as the Gualala, Garcia, Navarro and lower Eel below the Snag Hole. On several occasions I've caught silvers in the lagoon at Navarro on the high incoming tide when waves from the nearby ocean were rolling far up the river.

Once I had an excellent time just inside the bar of Red-wood Creek at Orick. A run of small king salmon called chubs had just entered the lagoon. When I saw them rolling I launched an eight-foot boat and, with only the gulls and crashing sea for company, caught a number of them.

One fall I caught silvers in Tomales Bay fly-casting from my pram. Actually I was out for stripers, but when the salmon kept jumping near the boat I tied on a comet and caught three in about two hours.

There has always been a "run" of salmon and steelhead in Bodega Bay. Ostensibly, the reason for it is that at one time nearby Salmon Creek emptied into Bodega at its north end. Even now some fresh water seeps in there. Some claim it is Salmon Creek water though the creek itself enters the sea a mile or so to the north. When its sandbar is closed, some fish find their way into Bodega, perhaps sensing the source of this seepage. Some exciting mornings have passed here when the fish were jumping within casting range. A floating line and smallish shrimp fly worked for me, especially on the high tide.

In Pescadero Creek, south of San Francisco, local anglers fish the high incoming tide when that stream is muddy from winter rains. For a few hours each day the rising water and heavy surge push the dirty water some distance back up the slough and casters fish the clear ocean water hoping to take bright steelhead fresh in from the sea.

The best day of steelhead fishing I ever had was in salt water at the junction of Paper Mill's estuary and Tomales Bay. It was near the end of February, so of course these were down-streamers — fish already spawned and on their way back to sea — but they proved to be vigorous quarry nevertheless.

I arrived about nine on a quiet overcast morning. The tide was halfway out and the water was clear. I fished carefully through the pool for an hour without luck. Somewhat discouraged I sat down to enjoy being alone on the beautiful moor. The tide had fallen a foot or so since I'd arrived and the current had slowed.

As I sat thinking of other things, a fish rolled in the center of the hole. I got up and made a hurried cast. Five strips into the retrieve the fish took, then jumped end for end several times before I could beach it, remove my fly and turn it loose. The steelhead would have weighed about six pounds and was in healthy condition. The bottom of its tail was just slightly abrased as in all spent steelhead and it still retained its silver color.

Soon I had another strike and again landed a six-pounder identical in appearance to the first. After releasing it I caught another. And another. At the peak of the bite, hits were coming regularly on every cast. Gradually the fish moved down toward the lower end of the pool so it took longer and longer casts to reach them. Finally, about three o'clock they were gone.

The tide turned and started to rise, but I couldn't get another strike. It was as though there'd never been any fish. Strangely, all during the time I was catching them there was never any surface indication that steelhead were present. The first fish that rolled was the only one all day.

To quote the log again, "Feb. 27...32 takes...23 fish landed...all 6 lbs." This last seems nothing short of remarkable for each fish was nearly identical to the next and even more, fought similarly. It was quite like catching the same fish again and again as in a film being reshown. And not once did the leader break. The same little black and orange fly stayed tied to the tippet throughout.

Before leaving I notched the thin trunk of one of the moor's few bushes twenty-three times and imbedded the fly below that. Ten years later the notches were no longer visible and the fly had rotted away, leaving a bare, rusted hook protruding enigmatically from the bush's stem. Today, no doubt, all that's left is the memory.

THE INSIDE PASSAGE TO ALASKA
by Joe Upton

From his book, Alaska Blues. *Upton was thirty (with thirteen years fishing experience) when he wrote this diary of a season of fishing in Alaska for salmon, hook and line and net. While the boats change and the salmon have good and bad years, every April it happens — boats leave the Puget Sound area for the trip north to work on the wind-swept waters of southeast Alaska.*

His newest book is Journeys Through the Inside Passage, *with lots more detail of trips up the coast from Seattle to Skagway. His works are published by Alaska Northwest Publishing Co., which publishes all sorts of good books about that territory.*

⚓

THE INSIDE PASSAGE TO ALASKA

THE WAY NORTH is through the sheltered waters of the Inside Passage. North of Cape Spencer, Alaska, and south of Cape Flattery, Washington, the North Pacific beats on a lonely and forbidding coast that has few harbors. Even large vessels travel with caution.

But between the two capes lie a thousand miles of sheltered waters, with many secure harbors. The tides are large, the currents swift, many dangers unmarked, and the weather is sometimes violent, but it's inside, and seldom are you more than a few hours from a good harbor. Without the Inside Passage, the fleets of smaller boats that travel to Alaska every year to fish never would have developed. With it, in the late spring and summer, even the smallest boat can travel to Alaska in relative safety and cross open water only twice in 600 miles.

For the first part of the trip north, the land changes rapidly. For a day you run past the towns and vacation-home settlements of Puget Sound and the Canadian Gulf Islands. Then you cross the Strait of Georgia, and soon the only settlements are logging and fishing communities. The shores become steeper and the hills higher and darker, often rising right up into the overcast from the water. The weather changes, and the warm springs and bright summers of the Puget Sound country give way to the gloomy and overcast summers of coastal British Columbia. Hardly more than a hundred miles north of the Canadian border, the coast road ends, cut off from the water by high mountains and deep inlets, and from here on you're pretty much on your own, with long distances between settlements, and boat and floatplane the only means of travel. The hills are so steep and the forests so thick that even walking on the shore is impossible in places.

The traditional steamer route is along the inside shore of Vancouver Island, across open water at Queen Charlotte Sound, and then back inside. The route then plunges deep into the interior through canyonlike channels, not venturing into open water again until crossing Dixon Entrance, the Alaska border.

South of Queen Charlotte Sound, there has been extensive logging in many places, especially on Vancouver Island. But to the north of the sound are some of the wildest and most remote areas of coastal British Columbia. It is easy to travel for days with only the sight of another boat or a light on a point to show that anyone has ever been there before. On all sides, deep and gloomy inlets wind far back into the hills to harbors and bays that sometimes must see years pass without a visitor.

On a bright day, running a boat up these channels — with a fair sky overhead and hill after hill slipping away astern — can be exhilarating. But on a stormy day, with low clouds pressing down on the water and nothing but dark walls rising on all sides, it can seem as if you're traveling without end through lost and empty country.

For the small boat, not in a hurry, there are many side channels and passages that offer even more shelter than the traditional routes, especially south of Queen Charlotte Sound. Many small vessels, instead of following the Vancouver Island shore through Discovery Passage and Seymour Narrows, prefer a more easterly route. This is by way of Malaspina Strait, Thulin Passage, Desolation Sound, Yuculta Rapids, Cordero Channel, Greene Point Rapids and on to Johnstone Strait through Sunderland Channel. It is a longer route, with rushing tides and places where you must wait for slack water, and it is a more intricate route, but there are good places to stop, and it shortens what can be a long and windy buck down Johnstone Strait.

North of Queen Charlotte Sound, nearly all vessels follow the steamer course, which lies far from the ocean and is well sheltered. The channels are for the most part straight, with bold shores and few places to anchor, but here and there in hidden coves are settlements and disused canneries with rotting floats where boats can lay.

Years ago, the coast was much more populated than today. Boats were slow and refrigeration uncertain, so the canneries were located wherever there was a heavy run of fish. Many of the larger inlets had little river valleys at their heads, with farming communities that had few outlets for their products; so people there lived more by barter than by cash. But then came refrigeration, and faster boats, and the many outlying canneries were consolidated into a few in the towns where labor was cheaper. The government ceded the big inlets to the logging companies and closed them to fishing. Now all that's left are the ruins of former settlements and stands of alders and hardwoods that grew up when the evergreens were cut down. In the fall you can run for hours along shores of dark evergreens, and then suddenly, in a little cove or bay, see a stand of alders, bright yellow and orange, the start of second growth telling of some settlement long since disappeared.

It is some 600 miles from Puget Sound to Alaska. A fast seiner running day and night without any stops can make it in two and a half days. The large boats often travel this way, but the small ones, often with only one or two people on board, usually just run during the day and hole up somewhere at night. The great tides pick up logs and drift from the beaches, and at night these make traveling hazardous. Running only in daylight hours, a small boat makes the trip in less than a week if the weather is good.

For some, the trip north in the spring can be a relaxing time. After weeks and perhaps months of hectic work on the boat, of seeing spring all around and not having time to enjoy it, the trip can be a real break before fishing starts. Running with friends, stopping early in the evening and going ashore, or perhaps even laying over a day and digging clams and oysters, or just poking around, is a good way to start a long season.

But more often it is the other way around. The last week ashore is just a blur of last-minute shopping and endless jobs to be done. When you finally get off, the boat's still a mess with stuff to be put away and a dozen jobs to be finished on the trip north. You're behind schedule, and the only way to get up there and make the opening of the season is to run 20 hours a day or more and hope that you don't hit anything at night.

And by the time many people head back in the fall, they just want to get home and don't really care too much about sightseeing. By then the weather has usually turned, and you have to travel when you can. After the first of September the days get rapidly shorter, and the fall gales build up offshore and sweep down the coast. Often they come back to back, one right after the other, and up and down the coast the anchorages fill up and the bottles and the cards come out, for then even the sheltered inside channels are impassable. It can be a long trip in the fall, perhaps laying up one day for every day that you run. Once a friend of ours was running in Grenville Channel when it blew up, the wind screaming down the narrow reaches. There was no place to go and the channel was too deep to anchor. He found a bight in the shore and tied his boat between two trees; the boat surged back and forth on the lines for two days.

The trip home from a season up north can mean running day after day without seeing another boat and lying in the evenings at deserted towns and canneries, perhaps having to roust out some sleepy caretaker to buy fuel. And it can mean getting blown in someplace for a couple of days somewhere along the line. After traveling for 8 or 10 days or more — and every day a fight with the weather — you come at last to two cities, Powell River and Campbell River, big mill towns. A day later you're home. Then Alaska seems very far away indeed.

I've made the trip many times, and seen the Inside Passage in most of its moods, fall and spring. But each time I travel it, north or south, I'm struck again by the lonely beauty of the coast.

THE FOURTH DAY
by Izaak Walton

From his book The Compleat Angler. *No reason to go on about Izaak Walton; one either reads him or not. The book is in the form of a dialogue between an experienced fishermen and someone new to the game. Today, we call the language and design quaint; it was, after all, written in 1653. Much of the biology is wrong, and today we don't pursue all of the fish he was interested in.*

Rather than a chunky excerpt from The Compleat Angler, *here are Izaak Walton's directions for cooking pike, back in the time before microwaves and cholesterol. Substitute your favorite fish and enjoy.*

⚓

THE FOURTH DAY

PISCATOR. The mighty Luce or Pike is taken to be the tyrant, as the Salmon is the king, of the fresh water. 'Tis not to be doubted, but that they are bred, some by generation, and some not; as namely, of a weed called pickerel-weed, unless learned Gesner be much mistaken, for he says, this weed and other glutinous matter, with the help of the sun's heat, in same particular months, and some ponds, apted for it by nature, do become Pikes. But, doubtless, divers Pikes are bred after this manner, or are brought into some ponds some such other ways as is past man's finding out, of which we have daily testimonies.

Sir Francis Bacon, in his *History of Life and Death*, observes the Pike to be the longest lived of any fresh-water fish; and yet he computes it to be not usually above forty years; and others think it to be not above ten years: and yet Gesner mentions a Pike taken in Swedeland, in the year 1449, with a ring about his neck, declaring he was put into that pond by Frederick the Second, more than two hundred years before he was last taken, as by the inscription in that ring, being Greek, was interpreted by the then Bishop of Worms. But of this no more; but that it is observed, the old or very great Pikes have in them more of state than goodness; the smaller or middle-sized Pikes being, by the most and choicest palates, observed to be the best meat: and, contrary, the Eel is observed to be the better for age and bigness.

All Pikes that live long prove chargeable to their keepers, because their life is maintained by the death of so many other fish, even those of their own kind; which has made him by some writers to be called the tyrant of the rivers, or the freshwater wolf, by reason of his bold, greedy, devouring, disposition; which is so keen, as Gesner relates, A man going to a pond, where it seems a Pike had devoured all the fish, to water his mule, had a Pike bit his mule by the lips; to which the Pike hung so fast, that the mule drew him out of the water; and by that accident, the owner of the mule angled out the Pike. And the same Gesner observes, that a maid in Poland had a Pike bite her by the foot, as she was washing clothes in a pond. And I have heard the like of a woman in Killing-worth pond, not far from Coventry. But I have been assured by my friend Mr. Segrave, of whom I spake to you formerly, that keeps tame Otters, that he hath known a Pike, in extreme hunger, fight with one of his Otters for a Carp that the Otter had caught, and was then bringing out of the water. I have told you who relate these things; and tell you they are persons of credit; and shall conclude this observation, by telling you, what a wise man has observed, "It is a hard thing to persuade the belly, because it has no ears."

But if these relations be disbelieved, it is too evident to be doubted, that a Pike will devour a fish of his own kind that shall be bigger than his belly or throat will receive, and swallow a part of him, and let the other part remain in his mouth till the swallowed part be digested, and then swallow that other part that was in his mouth, and so put it over by degrees; which is not unlike the Ox, and some other beasts taking their meat, not out of their mouth immediately into their belly, but first into some place betwixt, and then chew it, or digest it by degrees after, which is called chewing the cud. And, doubtless, Pikes will bite when they are not hungry, but, as some think, even for very anger, when a tempting bait comes near to them...

I am certain this direction how to roast him when he is caught is choicely good; for I have tried it, and it is somewhat the better for not being common. But with my direction you must take this caution, that your Pike must not be a small one, that is, it must be more than half a yard, and should be bigger.

"First, open your Pike at the gills, and if need be, cut also a little slit towards the belly. Out of these, take his guts; and keep his liver, which you are to shred very small, with thyme, sweet marjoram, and a little winter-savoury; to these put some pickled oysters, and some anchovies, two or three; both these last whole, for the anchovies will melt, and the oysters should not; to these, you must add also a pound of sweet butter, which you are to mix with the herbs that are shred, and let them all be well salted. If the Pike be more than a yard long, then you may put into these herbs more than a pound, or if he be less, then less butter will suffice: These, being thus mixt, with a blade or two of mace, must be put into the Pike's belly; and then his belly so sewed up as to keep all the butter in his belly if it be possible; if not, then as much of it as you possibly can. But take not off the scales. Then you are to thrust the spit through his mouth, out at his tail. And then take four or five or six split sticks, or very thin laths, and a convenient quantity of tape or filleting; these laths are to be tied round about the Pike's body, from his head to his tail, and the tape tied somewhat thick, to prevent his breaking or falling off from the spit. Let him be roasted very leisurely, and often basted with claret wine, and anchovies, and butter, mixt together; and also with what moisture falls from him into the pan. When you have roasted him sufficiently, you are to hold under him, when you unwind or cut the tape that ties him, such a dish as you purpose to eat him out of; and let him fall into it with the sauce that is roasted in his belly; and by this means the Pike will be kept unbroken and complete. Then, to the sauce which was within, and also that sauce in the pan, you are to add a fit quantity of the best butter, and to squeeze the juice of three or four oranges. Lastly, you may either put it into the Pike, with the oysters, two cloves of garlick, and take it whole out, when the Pike is cut off the spit; or, to give the sauce a haut goût, let the dish into which you let the Pike fall be rubbed with it: The using or not using of this garlick is left to your discretion. M. B.''

This dish of meat is too good for any but anglers, or very honest men; and I trust you will prove both, and therefore I have trusted you with this secret.

Creatures of
the Seaside

Now that you have read how to catch them and cook them, here are some writings about watching them. There are fishes here, and birds, and crabs. But mostly there are keen observers in evidence, seeing, learning, and passing the information along.

ARRIVAL
by John Hay

From his book The Run. *Hay was president of the Cape Cod Museum when he wrote this sensitive description of the annual ritual of herring (in this case alewife) migration from the Atlantic Ocean into Cape Cod Bay and up Stony Brook to still, freshwater ponds where the adults spawn in spring. While the parents run right back to sea, the youngsters spend more time in the ponds, before heading for the ocean. They will be back as adults in a few years to repeat the procedure.*

New Englanders take their herring runs seriously. Wardens guard the stream and measure the catch. Alewives are pickled or smoked, they become lobster bait, and their roe is eaten. At sea, they are forage for predators — bluefish, striped bass, and tunas. They seem to spend most of their lives being chased or swimming upstream to procreate. Here Hay sets the stage for their run.

⚓

ARRIVAL

A WEEK OR SO LATER, early in April, I finally saw my first alewife of the season. It had the brook to itself where I caught sight of it — a cloudy form running upcurrent — and when I went closer I could see it probing the rippling, beating waters, with all that fish articulation of separate fins together, fanning slightly, waving, threading, and steering, the fixed eyes staring on, its whole body weaving with the flow. It is a surprisingly large fish, seen for the first time in a narrow stream. Its length may be anywhere between ten and thirteen inches, and it has a heavy look for those who are used to sunfish and minnows.

An alewife was no novelty to me, but this one seemed to decide the year's direction. It started things out. I saw it for the first time, as child or genius does who finds some whole deep image in the air, or radiant clarity in the water. I had the feeling too that I was looking at a professional from an old water world, a new agent of old assurance, deserving profound respect. After all, it had been coming back here thousands of years before me, in the migrant history of its race, and by this time must have mastered its passage. And as a natural event, a part of the spring's development, it seemed to announce that bud scales on shrubs and trees would start to crack and fall away to let the inner shoots out that unfold as leaves and feed on the sun. It said that flies and wasps and spiders would come out of winter hiding and sleeping, that the song sparrows would begin to sing in the willows and viburnum bushes along the banks of Stony Brook.

There is something exciting and strange about the sudden appearance of new life in the spring, coming from another region, another climate. The terns or plovers that appear along the shore bring an unknown experience with them. They seem to start in or to assemble according to some tremendous demand which is in no way restricted to seasonal lags. They recur; they are recognizable; and yet they bring in endless tides and vivid journeys, being a part of that remarkable projection of nature in which a multitude of lives use their skill in navigation, their plumage, their scales, fins, and various senses, their particular drives toward fulfillment.

Migration is universal. That which prompts animals to emerge from their burrows, or to start moving over the ocean floor, to fly north, to swim into brackish or fresh water from salt, or even, like a ladybird beetle, to move a short distance from a forest floor to a meadow, must have a world-wide energy to it, with lines of communication that reach everywhere ahead and invite the human drive for knowledge. But in a strict sense there are two accepted definitions of migration for the animals. There is return migration, of which the alewives provide an example. Fish or birds in this category travel seasonally from one area to another, usually coming back to some home region after varying lapses of time. Otherwise, there is emigration, in which animals leave their home base but never come back again, lemmings and locusts being good examples. Both definitions, I should think, can prove that home stretches farther than we know.

The question of why the alewife migration takes place at all is not to be answered scientifically simply by using the words "instinct" or "sexual development," or by saying, "This is the way it has always been." The fish come inland to spawn, to lay their eggs, but even that phenomenon may be intricate enough.

To summarize it in a general way, the mature alewives migrate from salt to fresh water with annual punctuality. They are carrying out a reproductive cycle, caused by physiological changes in response to any number of factors in their environment. These may be the growing length of days, and the kind of light they receive, the temperature, the food they eat, and the currents in the sea. Having said that, I realize that what I have started I may be unable to finish.

The average onlooker waiting for the alewives to show up has, aside from the occasionally deceitful evidence of spring in his own senses, at least one simple clue to their migration. They start to come in when the fresh or brackish waters remain definitely warmer, if only by a few degrees at first, than the salt water into which they flow. This is our local, seasonal measurement, and with respect to the calendar, it seems to vary surprisingly little from year to year. The waters of March and early April are not quite warm enough — at least the big runs come later. Then why did that pioneer of an alewife, and the few others which probably came with it, arrive so soon? It is possible that they had migrated up Stony Brook before.

In the first place, alewives, as random in some respects as the rest of us, also tend to return to the place they started from. These early comers often appear to be larger than those that come after them, which suggests two things: first, that they are older and second, that they have spawned in that same run in a previous year.

Alewives, like other fish, seem to keep on growing, though there may be a maximum size reached in their fifth and sixth year. The only conclusive way to tell their age is by microscopic examination of their scales, which reflect each spawning year and its physical changes. Because the schools that follow these early fish are much more numerous, the survival factor is also suggested. Put simply, this means that the older a fish is the less chance it has to live. An alewife, or a sea herring, might theoretically grow to be nine or ten years old, but its chances of doing so in the omniverous world in which it lives are just about zero.

Work done by Keith Havey on alewives in Maine shows a minimum of alewives spawning at three years of age and the largest number in the four- or five-year-old range. No scales were found which reflected more than two spawnings. As to size, he gives a sampling of their length in inches which graduates up from 11.25 inches in the three-year-old fish to 11.80 in the four-year-olds, 12.35 in the five-year-olds, and 12.80 in the six. The female alewife, incidentally, is a little larger than the male.

The older fish may also be more practiced at finding their way. I am told that, with new fish ladders, observers have noticed the earliest arrivals seeking and passing through them more readily on the second year after construction than on the first, which leads to the belief that they have been through before. Age may improve the alewife in prowess, though it is a fish of crowds, and not one to strike out much on its own. The "homing instinct," still unfathomed, but about which I will try to say more later on, brings them back to their streams of origin with almost united force.

So my lone alewife marked the greatness it preceded, though it was early, in early and still undecided weather. At first the sleet, hail, flurries of wet snow came in profusion, stabbing between the sunshine, as though nature, before making its next terms known, was full of passionate unease. Then wings of warm rain would beat in over the Cape, to slash and curve and follow along trees and houses, through inland ponds, across the ridges and hollows, and the wind poured behind in great gusts, trying, it seemed, to shake a tight world loose. Underneath the struggling air many things waited for more chances in the sun, but under the stars, on foggy evenings or bright days, the singing of peepers in pools, ponds, or boggy land would swell and widen everywhere.

Then as the month kept advancing, that which came out began to stay, and to expand, in variety, flexibility, and strength. The wheels of the world seemed to turn more brightly. I felt a suggestion in each changing tree, in the loosening ground, the kinetic light and air, of new unfoldings, kaleidoscopic discoveries. The formality and power in the coming on of spring surprised me, as if it had never come before.

More winds began to blow from the southwest, the prevailing wind during late spring and summer. Yellow fingertips of bloom showed on the whip-long branches of the forsythias. The temperature edged toward the fifties, and there were deep new meetings between the moles and the worms. One day many tree swallows began to flit and dive low around the Herring Run. They skimmed along the surface of the water, then sailed up again. Their bellies were as white as a frog's or horned pout's, dark wings and tails trimly cut, backs almost a tropical blue in the light above the water, reflecting green at some angles, or a green-blue-purple the color of mackerel. Their flight dipped with the up and down flying insects they were chasing. When some insect, unseen to me, spiraled straight up along the banks, a swallow would leave its water gliding, twist suddenly, beating its wings, and almost spiral after.

That original source of energy, the sun, which men might still worship in good faith, was bringing out new facets to shine abroad. The web of life was stretching to its light. Birds, insects, plants, and fish were beginning to move to its changing measure; though if some days were warm with a budding, fringing, easing expectation, others were still raw, wet, and contracting, bringing winter back to flesh and fiber. We kept looking for the alewives. Cars would slow up at the Herring

Run. The drivers peered down to see the curving, dark forms of
a few fish holding up against the current. Then they drove on.
Or they got out, saw nothing, and went away in disappoint-
ment. But suddenly one moming toward the middle of April the
crowd of alewives had so increased as to cause an inescapable
excitement in the vicinity. The water was thick with fish, their
fins showing on the surface. It was almost as it had been a hundred years before when the whole population would cry out at
their coming, "The herring are running!"

BEAUTIFUL SWIMMER
by William W. Warner

From his book Beautiful Swimmers. *H. L. Mencken made a passing reference to Chesapeake Bay as a protein factory. Warner takes a whole book to describe one of the most prolific and pugnacious protein sources, the blue crab.*

This is not the only time Warner tackled a marine topic. His later book, Distant Waters, *tells of the big, offshore commercial fishing boats and how they could and did sweep the sea.* Beautiful Swimmers, *like the crab itself, is more poignant, as it contemplates this country's most-productive and most-pressured estuary and its bay people.*

⚓

THE ATLANTIC BLUE CRAB is known to scientists as *Callinectes sapidus* Rathbun. It is very well named. *Callinectes* is Greek for beautiful swimmer. *Sapidus*, of course, means tasty or savory in Latin. Rathbun is the late Dr. Mary J. Rathbun of the Smithsonian Institution, who first gave the crab its specific name.

Dr. Rathbun, known as Mary Jane to her Smithsonian colleagues, has often been called the dean of American carcinologists, as experts in crabs and other crustaceans are properly termed. Before her death in 1943, Mary Jane identified and described over 998 new species of crabs, an absolute record in the annals of carcinology. In only one case did she choose to honor culinary qualities. History has borne out the wisdom of her choice. No crab in the world has been as much caught or eagerly consumed as *sapidus*.

Whether or not *Callinectes* may justly be considered beautiful depends on whom you ask. Scientists tend to avoid aesthetic judgments. Many lay observers think the blue crab frightening or even ugly in appearance. They do not understand its popular name and often ask what is blue about a blue crab. The question betrays a basic ignorance of truly adult specimens. Most people see the species in the smaller back bays of the Atlantic coast; crabs never grow very large in these waters, since they are quite salty throughout and lack the brackish middle salinities that assure optimum growth in the Chesapeake and other large estuaries. The barrier beach islands and their back bays may provide our most dramatic seascapes, but they are not the place to see the pleasing hues of well-grown crabs. Large males have a deep lapis lazuli coloration along their arms, more on the undersides than on top, extending almost to the points of the claws. In full summer the walking and swimming legs of both sexes take on a lighter blue, which artists would probably call cerulean. Females, as we have said before, decorate their claws with a bright orange-red, which color is seen only at the extreme tips among males. Since females wave their claws in and out during courtship, it may be that this dimorphism is a sexually advantageous adaptation. If so, it is probably a very important one, since the blue crab is believed to be somewhat color blind.

Those who most appreciate *Callinectes'* beauty, I think, are crabbers and other people who handle crabs professionally. Some years ago in the month of October, I visited a clean and well-managed crab house in Bellhaven, North Carolina, a pleasant town on Pamlico Sound's Pungo River. In the company of the plant owner's wife I watched dock handlers load the cooking crates with good catches of prime sooks. As they should be at that of year, the sooks were fully hard and fat, although relatively recently moulted. Their abdomens were therefore pure white, with a lustrous alabaster quality. (Later in the intermoult period crab abdomens take on the glazed and slightly stained look of aging horses' teeth; often they are also spotted with "rust.") The carapaces or top shells were similarly clean. Thus, gazing down at the mass of three thousand or more crabs in each crate, we saw a rich and fragmented palette of olive greens, reds, varying shades of blue and marble white.

"Now, tell me, did ever you see such beautiful crabs?" the owner's wife asked, quite spontaneously.

"Prettiest crabs I seen all year," a black dockhand volunteered.

I had to agree. Anyone would.

Still, as is often said, beauty is in the eyes of the beholder. We can but little imagine the sheer terror which the sight of a blue crab must inspire in a fat little killifish or a slow-moving annelid worm. The crab's claw arms will be held out at the ready, waving slowly in the manner of a shadow boxer. Walking legs will be slightly, doubled, ready for tigerlike springs, and the outer maxillipeds — literally "jaw feet" or two small limbs in front of the crab's mouth — will flutter distractingly. The effect must be mesmeric, such as the praying mantis is said to possess over its insect victims. Perhaps not quite so hypnotic but of extreme importance to the crab in this situation are its eyes. Like most crustaceans, the blue crab has stalked eyes. When a crab is at peace with the world, they are but two little round beads. On the prowl, they are elevated and look like stubby horns. As with insects, the eyes are compound. This means that they possess thousands of facets — multiple lenses, if you prefer — which catch and register a mosaic of patterns. More importantly, simple laboratory tests seem to indicate that the stalked and compound eyes give the blue crab almost three hundred-and-sixty-degree vision. Those who with ungloved hand try to seize a crab with raised eyestalks from the rear will have this capability most forcefully impressed on them. If at all, the blue crab may have a forward blind spot at certain ranges in the small space directly between its eyes. Perhaps this accounts for the crab's preference for shifting lateral motion, from which it is easier to correct this deficiency, rather than rigid forward and back movement. Whatever the answer, a blue crab sees very well. Although colors may be blurred, the crab is extremely sensitive to shapes and motions. It has good range, too, at least for a crustacean. I have frequently tried standing still in a boat as far as fifteen feet from cornered individuals and then raising an arm quickly. Instantly the crabs respond, claws flicked up to the combat position.

Beauty, then, to some. Piercing eyes and a fearful symmetry, like William Blake's tiger, to others. But there are no such divided views on *Callinectes'* swimming ability. Specialists and lay observers alike agree that the blue crab has few peers in this respect. Some carcinologists believe that a few larger portunids or members of the swimming crab family — *Portunus pelagicus*, for example, which ranges from the eastern Mediterranean to Tahiti — might be better swimmers. But from what I have seen of the family album, I rather suspect that these crabs would fare best in distance events in any aquatic olympiad, while the Atlantic blue and some of its close relatives might take the sprints.

Certainly the blue crab is superbly designed for speed in the water. Its body is shallow, compressed and fusiform, or tapering at both ends. Although strong, its skeletal frame is very light, as anyone who picks up a cast-off shell readily appreciates. At the lateral extremities are wickedly tapered spines, the Pitot tubes, one might say, of the crab's supersonic airframe. (These spines grow very sharp in large crabs; good-sized specimens falling to a wooden deck occasionally impale themselves on them, quivering like the target knives of a sideshow artist.) This lateral adaptation is as it should be, of course, for an animal given to sideways travel.

Remarkable as this airframe body structure may be, it is the blue crab's propulsion units that are most responsible for its swimming success. These are the fifth or last pair of appendages, most commonly known as the swimming legs. Beginning at their fourth segments, the swimming legs become progressively thinner and flatter. The seventh or final segment is completely flat and rounded like a paddle, ideally shaped for rapid sculling. Equally remarkable is the articulation of the swimming legs. Even knowledgeable observers are surprised to learn that a blue crab can bend them above and behind its back until the paddles touch. They are unaware of this extreme flexibility, no doubt, because the occasions to observe it are rather rare. One such is to steal up on a pair of courting crabs. Prominent in the male blue crab's repertoire of courtship signals is one involving the swimming legs. A randy Jimmy will wave them sensuously and synchronously from side to side above his back, with the paddle surfaces facing forward, as though tracing little question marks and parentheses in the water. Females show appreciation by rapidly waving their claws or rocking side to side on their walking legs.

But courting gestures are not the principal function of the powerfully muscled and flexible swimming legs. They mainly serve to propel the crab, of course, not only sideways, but also forward or backward, not to mention helicopter-style rotation which permits a crab to hover like a hawk. Most of the time all we see of these actions is a blur. As those who try wading in shallows with a dip net know, a startled blue crab bursts off the bottom in a cloud of mud or sand and darts away with the speed of a fish. Such rapid all-directional movement is of great advantage to swimming crabs. Consider the unfortunate lobster. Its rigid and overlapping abdominal or "tail" segments restrict it to dead ahead or astern. Of the two directions, it seems to prefer swimming backward. Such inclination coupled with dim vision is probably why lobsters are always bumping into things. But again this is probably as it should be. It is to the lobster's advantage to back into corners. Safely positioned in a rocky niche, the lobster is well-nigh invulnerable to frontal attack, thanks to its enormously powerful claws. By contrast, open water speed and burying in soft bottoms are the swimming crabs' main escape tactics.

Less recognized are the blue crab's walking abilities. As befits an arthropod, *Callinectes* has many well-articulated joints. It has no less than seventy, in fact, in its five principal pairs of limbs. Three of these pairs are the walking legs; they permit the crab to scuttle along very nicely both on dry land and on sandy or muddy bottoms. It is true that a blue crab does not like dry land locomotion, yet it does rather well in emergencies. Each year the city of Crisfield, "Seafood Capital of the Nation," sponsors an event known as the National Hard Crab Derby, certainly one of our nation's more bizarre folk celebrations. At the crack of a gun, crabs are unceremoniously dumped from a forty-stall starting gate on to a sixteen-foot board track, very slightly inclined. Thus stimulated, blue crabs that are not stopped by distractions will scurry down the course in eight to twelve seconds. Terrestial species like the nimble ghost crab, for whom running is a principal defense measure, do better, of course. Still, the derby organizers, who have matched many species over the years, consider the blue crab's time entirely respectable. For those who cannot attend the derby, a good way to see crabs moving out of water is to visit a loading dock. Crawling is scarcely the word for what happens when lively individuals escape from a barrel. They streak across the dock in rapid bursts, nine times out of ten in the direction of the water. Handlers have to jump to catch them.

With such advantages do blue crabs go about their life, which is an almost continual hunt for food. They will hunt, in fact, at the least opportunity and with great patience. A good place to observe their patience is at the ferry dock at Tylerton on Smith Island. The watermen here have the habit of dumping their worn-out boat engines right off the dock, asking any who criticize the practice what earthly purpose is served in lugging the heavy things any farther. Although their wives may complain about the impression created on visitors, the local marine fauna love the old engine blocks. Minnows and the fry of larger fish swarm through these rusty castles, swimming in and out of their numerous turrets and vaulted chambers. As might be expected, crabs are attracted. They hold themselves poised in the water, hovering perfectly, with arms rigidly extended. If the tide is not strong, it is another excellent opportunity to appreciate swimming leg flexibility; each leg can easily be seen whirling in medium-speed helicopter rotation, with the paddles serving as the variable pitch rotor blades. When choice minnows present themselves, of course, the crabs dart at them. They usually miss. But being mostly juveniles, they happily try again and again. I have watched this phenomenon at length and often, to the point, I am sure, that the Tylertonians think me strange.

Older crabs are said to be too wise to engage in such shenanigans; they prefer to hunt live prey by burying themselves lightly in sand or mud and seizing by surprise. We cannot say, however, what any blue crab may do in a pinch. Dr. Austin Williams of the National Marine Fisheries Service, an expert who has recently published a definitive reappraisal of the genus *Callinectes*, tells of a singular occurrence which involved three-inch or virtually adult crabs, since at this length blue crabs are but one or two moults away from legal catch size.

"I was working down at the University of North Carolina's Marine Laboratory in Morehead City, and we had just built a series of experimental ponds," Dr. Williams recalls. "The ponds were new, with clay liners, and no established fauna to speak of. Not long after introducing the crabs, I was surprised to see them gathering in numbers near the outlets of the pipes supplying water to each pond. The crabs were highly agitated, stabbing away at nothing that I could see. On further investigation we found that our pumped water was not yet saline enough. We were breeding mosquitos, it seems. The crabs were actually snapping at mosquito larvae with their claws."

It was impossible to see if the crabs gained anything from this exercise. Dr. Williams does not rule out the possibility, since the crabs kept at it tirelessly. "Anyway, we decided we were very bad husbandmen to have our crabs doing this," he says. "They must have been nearly starving." Happily, the ponds soon produced more substantial fare, and the crabs were eventually seen to stop snapping at nothing.

How often crabs hunt and kill each other is a matter of considerable debate. Throughout history, the world has viewed crabs as unpleasant and bellicose animals. "Crab" is synonymous with a nasty or complaining disposition in a great many languages. Both *cancer* and *karkinos*, the Latin and Greek forms respectively, have been borrowed to describe the world's most deadly disease. Thus cancer and carcinogens, much to the annoyance of carcinologists who are forever receiving letters from medical libraries asking what stage of the disease they are investigating. From time to time *Crustaceana*, the International Journal of Crustacean Research, suggests a change to "crustace-ologist," but nothing has come of this.

Most crabbers believe the crab's bad name is not fully warranted. Opinions vary, however. "Who knows?" asks "Chas" Howard of Crisfield's Maryland Crabmeat Company. "Only thing I know is they can crawl, swim and bite like hell."

"Oh, if they're hungry enough, they fight," Grant Corbin has told me. "Get too many crowded together and that's bad, too. You remember the day we went out in June getting pots half full, with maybe ten to twenty crabs? Well, then you remember there weren't neither dead one. More than that, though, and they start beating on each other."

"Undoubtedly, crowding is a big factor, as in the crab floats," says Gordon Wheatley, an experienced crab scraper who is also principal of Tangier Island's combined grade and high school. "But sometimes crabs are just plain belligerent for no reason. Nothing within clawshot is safe."

Beyond fighting, cannibalism per se is certainly not thought to be a favored practice among blue crabs. No one has ever seen one healthy hard blue crab purposely set out to eat another in its entirety. But let a fighting crab get a walking leg or other choice morsel from one of his brothers and he will of course eat it, provided other crabs do not first steal it from him. In nature a crab that has lost a limb has an excellent chance to es-cape. The nearby crab community invariably swarms around the victor, who will be hard put to defend his prize. The loser is thus ignored. He or she is free to wander off and will easily grow another limb by means of a remarkable crustacean attri-bute known as autogeny. (The opposite, autotomy, or dropping off the limb at the socket in the first place, is done even more easily.) This is not the case, however, within the restrictions of a crab float. Quite the contrary, a floated crab with a missing claw or other disadvantage attracts further attacks. Eventually it may be killed and consumed. Thus it happens, a cannibalism of opportunity.

Also arguing against complete cannibalism — necrophagism, I suppose I should say — is the blue crab's aversion to dead of the same species. Crabbers are unanimous in their opinion that a dead crab repels live individuals, as has been repeatedly demonstrated in crab pots. "No doubt about it," says Captain Ernest Kitching of Ewell. "Crabs has got more sense. I wouldn't want to go crawl into a place with dead people, would you?"

Ask the question often enough and you begin to get a guarded and qualified consensus. Persons who know the blue crab best say that it does not normally eat its own kind or go around spoiling for a fight at every opportunity. But given an emergency or crowded artificial conditions, it will. Crowding, in fact, can even touch off wild and indiscriminate fighting under natural conditions. I had an excellent opportunity to observe such combat late one August while driving down a doubtful road on the lonely peninsula in the Dorchester marshes known as Bishop's Head. In spite of difficulties in keeping to the muddy tracks, my attention was drawn to great numbers of *Uca pugnax*, or the mud fiddler crab, scurrying across the road. In an adjoining creek the water continually boiled with sizeable surface explosions. The disturbance, I thought, was nothing less than a school of wayward blues or more probably spawning rockfish. Quickly I began to think of assembling my fishing rod.

But, stopping the car and getting out, I was immediately aware that fish were not the prime cause of the commotion. What had happened was this. An unusually strong spring tide had all but emptied the creek, leaving largely dry its steep five-foot banks, which were riddled with crab burrows. The impression created was of an old-fashioned high-walled bathtub with three quarters of the water let out. Conditions were obviously too extreme for the little mud fiddlers, who even less than their cousin *Uca pugilator*, or the sand fiddler, cannot stand too much drying out. Undoubtedly the fiddlers were marching across the road in search of more water and a calmer venue. But more fascinating than the fiddlers' retreat was the scene in the remaining sluiceway of water, which was very clear and not more than four feet wide and a foot or two deep. Too many large blue crabs had come far up this creek, as they commonly do in marsh creeks in August to mate, and now it offered them too little space. Quite simply, the crabs were getting in each other's way. Courtship practices undoubtedly further aggravated the situation, this being the peak mating period. At courting time male blue crabs show some degree of territoriality, mainly by exhibiting a threat posture, or holding their arms out fully extended in a straight line with the claws slightly open. Between bumping into each other and threat postures that failed to convey their message, therefore, the crabs fought hard and frequently. Being generally excited, they also lunged at anything that moved in the water. Small boils punctuated by a spray of tiny silver minnows broke the surface whenever a partially buried crab jumped at live prey. Larger boils came when crabs met head-on. For the most part they sought to avoid each other, backpedaling and sidestepping, claws at the ready, very much as good boxers bob and weave in the ring. But soon, or at least every ten seconds, little volcanos erupted as one or another crab got cornered and elected to fight. Most often when the mud settled and the water cleared, one of the combatants had the limb of another in its claws. Within seconds came larger eruptions as every crab within sight zeroed in to steal the prize.

Just as insects and a glaring sun began to dictate departure, I saw a female with claws folded into the submissive posture moving carefully to avoid all possible encounters. Sbe was of good size, six inches or better, with the clean shell of grayish cast that is a sign of recent moulting, a sook in buckram condition, in other words. Being unsure of her still weak muscles, she wisely avoided the general fray. At one point, however, her caution went too far. She found herself half out of water behind a mudball cemented with weeds. A rusty looking little male—

two-thirds her size, but hard and fat — suddenly materialized on the other side of the mudball with thoughts other than court-ship obviously on his mind. Both crabs then tested the obstacle with their claws for firmness. Satisfied with its consistency, the male started to crawl up and over it. Immediately the sook climbed backward out of the water a full three feet up the steep bank and settled into a cavity excavated at full tide. There she sat motionless in the broiling sun for a long time, watching me and the little male. I was clearly the lesser of two evils, being close enough to touch her. Only when the male was out of sight did she climb down and re-enter the water. Instantly she buried herself in a quiet corner, until only her eyestalks were visible.

Blue crabs hate direct sunlight and cannot long tolerate it. Loose in a boat, they always run for the shade. The sook's evas-ive action therefore struck me as remarkable. I do not really know how long it lasted. It seemed like five minutes. I received about six mosquito and two green fly bites, in any event, having remained motionless so as not to scare the crab. As I finally left, the creek water continued to boil unabated. The mysteries of autotomy and autogeny would be sorely tested there, I thought to myself.

It takes many moults and a long time before a crab is as smart as that sook in the creek on Bishop's Head. At the beginning of life, in the microscopic larval state, a blue crab is helpless. It cannot truly swim or crawl. The first sign of life shown by larvae emerging from egg casings is heliotropism or an upward drift to sunlit surface waters. These tiny creatures, called zoeal crabs or zoeas, filter up to the surface in great numbers. There they are swept around by wind and tide. Scattering broadly, they be-come part of the Chesapeake's plankton or the topsoil "meadows of the sea" that are the first link in the food chain for all larger organisms. As such, mortality is very high. But, as we have noted before, so is the number of eggs to begin with in each sponge crab, two million being the generally accepted fig-ure. Impressive as this number may seem, it scales down rapidly through various forms of attrition. Many eggs are rendered infertile by fungal attack, improper temperatures, poor oxygenation, and water salinities which can be either too high or too low. Hatched larvae can die for the same reasons or more commonly be eaten by other forms of life. Biologists studying the population dynamics of the blue crab estimate that only one in every million eggs produces an adult crab.

Not much was known about the larval stages of the blue crab and many other crustaceans until recent years. Scientists were not even sure how many moults occurred before metamorphosis or with what frequency. Variable or four to five was the common belief, but it was impossible to test accurately from samplings taken from nature. Zoeal blue crabs look nothing like their adult form. They have enormous eyes, a rather large "head," a shrimplike tail and a single mean-looking dorsal spine. The problem is that so do many other crabs. Larval specialists depending on natural samples have therefore long been plagued by confusion of species.

The controlled conditions of laboratory breeding presented an obvious solution. But blue crab rearing proved easier said than done. Paradoxically, for an animal well known for adaptability and tolerance of environmental insult under natural conditions, the blue crab resists artificial situations to a surprising degree. Once in a laboratory tank, it manifests a stubborn refusal to cooperate in whatever scientists want it to do.

Problems begin with the sponges or brood crabs. Ordinary concrete experimental tanks won't do. The mother crabs do not like the tank bottoms and angrily tear off their developing eggs. An accurate simulation of natural sand or mud bottoms must be made. Even when this condition is satisfied, a certain number of crabs with beautiful caviar-black egg masses — ready to hatch, in other words — will suddenly tear them up for no apparent reason. Perhaps it is not enough to duplicate any old bottom; the exact bottom condition of their favored spawning grounds may be what these fastidious mothers are demanding.

Problems multiply with the hatching of the larvae. Let the tank water lapse into salinities of less than twenty-five parts per thousand and they refuse to grow, eventually dying. The same is true to a lesser degree of water temperature variations. In addition, the tank water must be well oxygenated and constantly circulating, which presents the problem of preventing the microscopic larvae from going down the drain. Getting knocked about in a circulatory pump system is not to be recommended in the care of crab zoeas. They may die from the bruises, as happens by the billions to all microscopic animal plankton that is sucked into the "pass-through" cooling systems of both steam and atomically fueled power plants. In this way more than any other, incidentally, do these plants tragically despoil our estuaries.

"Everything has to be just right, all along the way," says Dr. John D. Costlow of the Duke University Marine Laboratory at Beaufort, North Carolina. An intense man of many talents who has served as mayor of Beaufort and spearheaded the restoration of the town's historic homes, Dr. Costlow knows what he is talking about. In 1959 he and the Laboratory director, Dr. C. G. Bookhout, succeeded in raising the first batch of blue crabs from egg to adult form under laboratory conditions. This was a considerable achievement not only in the study of *Callinectes*, but of crabs in general. Before that time only one other species of crab, a British portunid, had been successfully reared from the egg. Since 1959 Costlow and the Duke University technicians have repeated the experiment many times, thanks to an intricate system of overflow trays, multi-compartmented plastic containers holding a single zoea per compartment and automatic water quality monitors with warning-light panels that would do credit to Cape Canaveral.

From Dr. Costlow's studies it is now known that blue crabs normally go through seven larval stages and sometimes an eighth. At each new stage the odd little creatures, which measure no more than one one-hundredth of an inch in their largest dimension, cast off their delicate shells. Unlike adult crabs who produce mirror images of themselves at each moult, changing only in size, each of the zoeal moults is characterized

by subtle but significant structural changes, mostly in the development of various appendages and the number of setae or tactile bristles they contain. Slight as they may seem to the layman,
these changes are enough to permit biologists to tell which
stage, from first to seventh or eighth, they happen to be working with, As a result all larval studies, theoretical or applied,
now rest on firmer ground.

Costlow's larval findings also have put him on the trail of
important commercial fishery applications. Currently he is pursuing the enormously complex question of wild blue crab
population fluctuations from year to year. In the Chesapeake, at
least, possible answers to this problem were thought to be related to the James River's annual spring runoff. As a hypothesis
this still makes very good sense. The James is a mighty river
with an average flow of over three million gallons per minute
directed squarely at the Bay's most concentrated hatching
grounds. If this water is too cold in late spring, larvae will be
slow to develop. Temperatures in the mid fifties or lower
sixties, in fact, may cause larvae to starve to death. Worse, if the
James runs high in late May or June, it easily reduces lower Bay
salinities to less than twenty parts per thousand, which is
known to cause larvae to hatch prematurely and die. Thus, for
example, when in June of 1972 Tropical Storm Agnes turned
the entire Chesapeake into a chocolate brown and log-strewn
duplicate of the Amazon in flood, both scientists and crabbers
saw pure disaster. Here was water of zero salinity pushing
billions of larvae out to sea at the worst possible time, or at the
height of the spawning season. Scientists thought the new year
class, as they call the crop and the year in which crabs are born,
might be irreparably damaged. Crabbers were sure that the next
summer, during which the year class would become adult,
would tell the tale. But no such disaster ever occurred.

"Larvae are much tougher, it seems, than we ever thought,"
Dr. Costlow says. "More resilient, I suppose I should say," he
adds, punctuating the point with a stab of his pipe.

If, as often happens, larvae are swept out to sea, Costlow believes that they may have heretofore unsuspected survival capability. Certainly this capability is exhibited to an amazing degree at the first of the blue crab's two metamorphic stages. Following the seventh or eighth stage, a larva metamorphoses rather radically into something known as a megalops. Just large enough to see with the naked eye, a megalops has two crude-looking claw arms, three pairs of well-defined walking legs, huge stalked eyes and, still held over from the larval period, a shrimplike tail. It swims in a manner of speaking — in erratic looping patterns like sky writing, Costlow calls it — and can crawl on the bottom. Thus equipped, the megalops are impelled by the mysteries of genetic imprint to travel up estuaries or rivers to the brackish waters that are best for growth. Still, they are unequal to any vigorous currents. Great numbers are frequently carried out to sea. Contrary to prior belief, the experience is not necessarily fatal. Costlow's laboratory experiments have shown that the megalops can put themselves in a holding pattern, so to speak, under such conditions. Faced with too-high salinities, they will prolong the megalops stage, which normally lasts about twelve days, by as much as two or three months. Furthermore, some of Costlow's colleagues at Beaufort who take field samples off the treacherous North Carolina banks have discovered *Callinectes* megalops alive and well as far out as two and three hundred miles offshore. So do these hardy little organisms withstand mighty circulatory currents or gyres, as oceanographers call them, riding them out until they once again find protected and less saline growth water.

This is a remarkable survival asset. We must consider what it means in terms of the animal kingdom. Nestling swifts may go for a week without food when cold rains prevent their mothers from gathering insects on the wing. A young fawn can survive no more than two days without milk. But the blue crab megalops will pass an entire summer in a state of suspended growth.

This asset is of special value to blue crab populations of the Atlantic barrier islands and back bays that stretch south from the Chesapeake. Here the sponge crabs must go very close to the inlets separating the islands to find the requisite salinities for hatching. As experienced yachtsmen know, these inlets are dangerous waterways scoured by strong tides which clash boisterously with onshore winds. They are scarcely what you would think of as nursery grounds. Larvae and megalops must be taken out to sea as a rule rather than an exception. Even in the ample and protected haven of the lower Chesapeake, this happens. Every summer bathers at Virginia Beach, some five miles south of the Bay mouth, complain of strong itches and irritations. The word goes out that the "water fleas" are back and many swimmers stay out of the water. The trouble is not fleas, of course, but our friends the megalops. Their claws may be somewhat rudimentary, but they can bite.

Given the possibility of frequent oceanic exposure, Dr. Costlow suspects that many larvae and megalops may end up in different inlets or estuaries from where they are born. If so, we have one answer to the most puzzling aspect of population fluctuations, or their erratic geographic patterns. It often happens, for example, that a poor crab year in the Chesapeake will be a good one in North Carolina. Or vice versa. The problem is especially acute in Florida. There crabbers and not a few scientists have come to believe that adult crabs may migrate long distances on both Florida coasts. "Oh, yes, crabs left here this year," an old-timer on Pine Island in San Carlos Bay once told me with utter conviction. "They've all gone north to Cedar Key and Apalachicola; that's where they are."

But such a phenomenon seems unlikely or at least biologically unnecessary. The only travel imperatives for an adult blue crab are to go up estuaries for growth and, in the case of impregnated females, back down again for spawning. Those best acquainted with blue crab behavior — with their personality, one wants to say — doubt they would do any more than is required. Free rides in the megalops state are a much better explanation.

"The entire East Coast may be one big larval and megalops mix," Dr. Costlow concludes. "Things begin in one place and end up in another."

Costlow means to find out, since he hopes to establish an off-shore megalops tracking program. It seems a most difficult undertaking, but I am sure he will succeed. Meanwhile, we at least know that the vagaries of blue crab populations are more complex than river runoffs and other purely local phenomena. And that is progress, of a sort.

Surviving gyres, then, and other dangers, the megalops at last moults into what scientists call the "first crab." The term is apposite. Although about the size of a large pinhead, the being that emerges from the second metamorphic moult is in every respect a recognizable blue crab. It has all the senses and organs it will ever have, except reproductory. It can now swim. It can crawl even better, and accordingly exhibits negative heliotropism or a preference for the bottom. Many but not all the perils of larval life are safely past. From here on, good feeding and safe growth are the main concerns of *Callinectes sapidus*. Typically, eggs hatched the first week of June produce first crabs early in August. During this month in the Chesapeake large numbers of these tiny crabs will be crawling or swimming with great determination up either shore of the Bay. Many get confused, however, and ascend the large rivers of the western shore. But there is no harm in this. As mentioned elsewhere, each of these rivers is in effect a sub-estuary with ample salinity gradients and other things the baby crabs need for growth.

By November or some seven or eight moults later, the crabs will have reached a length of one or two inches. Geographically speaking, those sticking to course in the main Bay are close to a line running between the mouth of the Potomac and Smith Island or approximately halfway up their migratory route. But now the water is getting cold. Quietly and quickly they slide into deeper water and bury for the winter just as adults do. So ends the blue crab's infant year.

These same small crabs will be the first to wake the following spring, resuming movement and moulting well before their parents. By late May and June man will be accompanying them in their northward migration, since some will now be moulting to three inches, legal size for peelers, or three and a half inches, the requisite size for softs. Females moult eighteen or twenty times, not counting larval moults, in the course of a lifetime. Males are believed to go through the ordeal twenty-one to twenty-three times. With both sexes the instar or period between moults grows progressively longer, ranging from ten to fifteen days for one-inchers to thirty to fifty days for legal hard-crab catch size and beyond. A long life span for blue crabs is about three years, with males tending to outlive females, but much more study is needed before anything more precise can be said on this subject. One thing is sure. The older a crab grows, the more difficult is the moult, to the point that there may be considerable natural mortality in the process. Considering this and the enormous catches of the crabbers, one expert estimates that a blue crab is lucky to live more than a year in the Chesapeake. Yet many must or the species could not prosper.

Crabs hatched in June reach adult size — four to five inches and better — by August or September of their second summer. There now occurs one more physiological change. It is the last such in the crab's life cycle and brings with it sexual maturity. Only in the female may it be seen externally, or in the change from the V-shaped to circular abdominal apron. The moult producing this change is the female's last, as we have previously emphasized. This coincidental terminal and sexual maturity moult of the females is not found in many other crabs. Among portunids or swimmers, it has only been proved beyond reasonable doubt in the case of *Callinectes*. This may be because no other crab has been fished so intensively and thus observed so much. Among the millions of circular-aproned sooks taken each year from the Chesapeake, only a handful have been recorded with "signs" or evidence of a second soft skin beneath the old. In each case these crabs have proved to be abnormal and have died in their attempt to moult again.

Since the female's period of sexual availability is sadly short, how do males know when to mate? "That Jimmy's smart; he never misses," crabbers will say. By this they mean that in their catches of thousands of doublers, or males holding females in the precopulatory cradle carry, never do they find any females who are not rank or ready to moult. Furthermore, the watermen will tell you, when they watch these females shed out in pails of water or crab floats, they never make an additional moult as immature she-crabs, but invariably turn into sooks. "No, sir, that old Jimmy, he doesn't mess around with the wrong crab," they add. But in laboratory encounters mature males do indulge in a fair amount of indiscriminate selection. They try to cradle carry unready females, brothers of the same sex, and even dead crabs. Biologists therefore believe there may be a certain amount of this trial-and-error activity in nature. If so, I tend to agree with the crabbers that in the end it all somehow works out, with males unfailingly pairing off with nubile females.

Certainly the blue crab has ample mechanism to insure that this is so. There are first of all the courtship rites or visual announcements made by both sexes. Although the first serious studies of sex recognition in the blue crab have only been recently published, Chesapeake watermen have long known about crab courtship. I first heard of it from the old-timers who sit in front of Hugh Haynie's general store on Tangier Island every pleasant summer evening.

"My friend, you never seen crabs making love?"

"Act real horny, they do. Males get way up on their tippy toes."

"Do I think so? I don't think so, I *know* so!"

"That's right, the Jimmies on their toes and the females rocking side to side, contented like."

"They are talking to each other. It's their way of talking."

The description is reasonably accurate. The male first shows himself by raising his body as high as he can on his walking legs. Interestingly, this is the same posture he must adopt later when be makes a guard cage around the female during her final

moult. A forerunner signal, one could say, announcing his protective intentions. Remaining so on "tippy toes," a courting
Jimmy next opens and extends his arms in a straight line, surely
a good attention-claiming device, and then begins the sensuous
waving of his swimming legs, which may be even better. Finally,
to make sure he is not ignored, he snaps his body backward
and kicks up a storm of sand with both swimming and walking
legs. It is a spectacular finish. If all this fails to convince, the
Jimmy will patiently repeat his repertoire, as most courting
animals commonly do.

Soon-to-be mature females get the message very quickly, however. In addition to rocking and waving her claws in and out, "a
highly motivated female will approach a male, then turn around
and try to back under him, waving as she does so," one biologist has put it. Thus reassured, the male next attempts what is
simply called the grab. Hoping for the best, he seizes with his
claws whatever part of the female is handiest and tries to put
her in the proper cradle carry position. It is a critical moment.
In laboratory observations, at least, males that rush in for the
grab too quickly frequently find themselves in violent struggle
with immature or otherwise unwilling females. Again, courtship
signals notwithstanding, there is no reason to believe similar
misunderstandings may not occur to some degree in nature. An
adult and favorably disposed female, on the other hand, will react only to the extent of waving her arms helplessly. This is
sheer coquetry or playing a little hard to get; she does not really
want to escape. The male responds by beating her arms with
his. Soon she quiets down, tucking her claws into the submissive posture, and allows herself to be cradle carried. She is now
right side up, face forward and presumably very comfortable.

The cradle carry lasts at least two days. Some crabbers and
scientists suspect that it may go on for as long as a week prior
to the female's terminal moult. If so, duration may well depend
on how far the pair has to go to find cover. I personally believe
doublers will readily cross the Bay at its widest to this purpose.
While sailing down the mid-Bay channel in September, I have

often seen pairs proceeding from west to east, which means from the relatively impoverished western shore to the rich and abundant eelgrass of the Eastern Shore. It is a touching sight. In calm water the male chugs along close to the surface, his paddles churning tirelessly. The rider female is always quiet and seemingly content. When I explain what is happening to my crew members, they seldom believe me.

But courtship, we must add, is not the only way by which mating crabs are correctly paired. Olfactory stimuli have been tested in the laboratory by introducing water in which preterminal moult females have been resting — just the water, that is, not the crab — into tanks containing mature males. The males usually respond to this scented water by becoming restless, but not with such regularity as to draw comparative conclusions. Scientists have also tried to test the relative importance of the visual stimulation of courtship with seemingly ingenious methods. Technicians have taken the perfect replicas provided by cast crab shells, hardening them with preservatives and delicately wiring the principal limbs to move them in imitation of courtship gestures. Ideal models, one would think, or at least very sophisticated compared, for example, to the crudely painted silhouettes of Niko Tinbergen's famous experiments with the herring gull. But the blue crab runs true to form. It habituates very rapidly, which is the scientist's way of saying it is too smart for their little ruses. A crab may respond briefly on first exposure to the mechanized models, but after that it shows them glacial disdain.

Most probably, crab pairing results from a combination of visual, tactile and olfactory stimuli. The fact that it occurs early or well before copulation is the most important consideration. The long cradle carry is biologically advantageous on two counts. First, it provides excellent protection to the female of the species during her last and nost difficult moult. Secondly and perhaps more importantly, it assures the male's presence during the very brief time when his partner is ready to receive him. Scientists agree that if mating depended on males finding

a terminal moult female by accident during the few hours before her shell started to harden again, the species simply could
not survive.

Protection is afforded the female by the male's urge to find
good cover and, when the female's moult begins, his habit of
standing guard over her by making a cage with his walking legs.
He does this very patiently, since the moult may consume two
or three hours. When at last the female lies exhausted and
glistening in her new skin, he allows her some moments to rest
and swallow the water that is necessary to fill out her weakened
stomach and muscle tissues. This done, the male gently helps
the female turn herself about — she may well have gotten im-
possibly oriented in the final throes of ecdysis — until she is on
her back face-to-face beneath him. It is a most affecting scene.
You cannot possibly mistake these actions for anything other
than lovemaking. To appreciate fully their tender quality, one
must know what other crabs do. After courtship signals,
Gecarcinus or the purple land crab of the tropics, to mention
but one example, indulges in a brusque reversal of roles. A
hard-shelled female will knock the male over on *his* back and
do the necessary without any hesitation or the slightest trace of
foreplay. But perhaps we should not judge these crabs too
harshly. It is not to a female land crab's advantage to go
through the dehydrating effects of moulting on dry land under
a tropical sun. She has therefore evolved out of the necessity of
a debilitating nuptial moult and is thus well qualified to represent women's liberation among crabs. Nor do these land
crabs have such good hiding places as their aquatic brethren.
They have to perform fast, before wild pigs, dogs or other
predators discover and devour them.

When the female blue crab is ready, she opens her newly
shaped abdomen to expose two genital pores. Into these the
male inserts his pleopods or two small appendages underneath
the tip of his elongated abdominal apron. When all is in place,
the female so extends her abdomen that it folds around and
over the male's back, thus effectively preventing any risk of co-

itus interruptus. Truly, blue crabs are locked in love's embrace. They remain so, blissfully, for from five to twelve hours. Daylight or night, it makes no matter.

Following copulation the female, whom we must now call a sook, is again cradle carried by the male for at least forty-eight hours during which her shell hardens and she regains some muscle tone. When finally dropped, she wastes no time. It is now autumn, or nearly so, and she must hurry down to the winter burying grounds. The male sperm packet is not immediately utilized, but banked or held in storage for the following spring. Many sooks do not make it to the lower Bay before being caught by winter's cold. There is no penalty for straggling, however. They may resume their journey in May. If by chance they develop and hatch egg masses before reaching salty enough water, they are still forgiven. Mother crabs can produce a second spawn from the same male sperm packet; it is believed to be just as viable as the first. Here, incidentally, is another possible explanation to the non-disaster of Tropical Storm Agnes. If Agnes was too strong even for the hardiest larvae and megalops, it is possible that the brood crabs of that summer compensated with an extraordinary second hatch when conditions were more normal. Buttressing this belief is the fact that crabbers everywhere in the Bay remarked on the late growth of the Agnes year class crabs in their next or adult summer.

A female crab born in May or June will produce eggs and hatchlings at the same time of year two years later. This statement has a definitive and tidy ring. In fairness to the reader, however, it must be said that sponge crabs bearing eggs ready to hatch are not unknown as late as November. Or that crabs may mate in the first part of the summer instead of the last, giving rise to autumn larvae that may not survive the winter. To think properly about the blue crab, therefore, it is first necessary to assume that the species can and will perform anything in its life cycle at any time, dead of winter excepted. Bearing this in mind, we must then recognize that there are definite *peak periods* during which *most crabs* go through a given stage in the cycle. Everything said about seasons so far in these pages, in fact, is based on these peak periods. The trouble is that a great many crabs do not observe them. The timetable of the great migrations between salty and fresher water, believed to be unique to *Callinectes*, can often go way off schedule. This makes it very difficult for scientists to determine what year — late matriculating class of '74, for example, versus early '75 — they are investigating. Worse, the peak period timetable simply falls apart as one travels south from the Chesapeake. Blue crabs on the Gulf Coast typically have one or two spawns in the spring, but some may do it in December, even though cooler waters in the latter month may make them rather sluggish. Even the range of the blue crab constantly shifts, either naturally or by man's intervention. In 1951, for example, Dr. L. B. Holthius, an outstanding Dutch carcinologist and founding editor of *Crustaceana*, discovered a small female blue crab swimming near a river mouth in Israel. With the help of Israeli scientists he soon found more, including ovigerous females. Dr. Holtbius, who believes the crabs must have been transported as larvae or juveniles in ship ballast, therefore predicted the species might well establish itself in the eastern Mediterranean. His prediction has been amply confirmed; Israel now has a prosperous commercial fishery. (Do not expect to find Crab Imperial Haifa, however, since the crabs are all sold for export, mostly to France, dietary laws being what they are in Israel.) There is no telling where this sort of thing may end. A healthy sook was recently found in the Russian waters of the Black Sea.

Dr. Willard Van Engel of the Virginia Institute of Marine Sciences, a leading authority whose annual crab forecast is widely respected by Chesapeake watermen, well sums up the dilemmas of blue crab research. "It is so difficult," he says. "We don't even have any real age standards, like the otoliths of a fish's skull. Moulting means there are no permanent hard parts. It's a wonderfully tolerant animal, but also so variable, so enigmatic."

To the very end. As the summer of their spawn nears its close, old females go out to sea in great numbers to die. Inexplicably, lesser numbers of these ocean-journeying crabs may return the next year to eke out a purposeless existence for yet a few more summer days. Those that return can be easily recognized. Barnacles stud their shells and sea moss dulls their once-bright colors. They are known as "sea runs" and appear just inside Cape Henry in late July or early August. Often they travel up into the James River, passing through the waters in which most of them were born. It is almost as if these crabs cannot decide. Like other crabs, *Callinectes sapidus* probably evolved from the oceans. But it is now an estuarine organism, having found its best place in life where river and ocean waters blend. What primal drive, then, impels females to die in their evolutionary cradle? Why are they not accompanied by males, who are believed to seek out the deepest Bay channels when their moment comes? And what can we say of the sea runs who return, befouled and spent, to sample briefly once more the estuarine gardens of their youth?

Discussing these questions, a retired Smith Island waterman once looked hard at me and raised his arms in supplication. "Oh, my blessed," he said very slowly. "That old crab is hard to figure out."

So it is, all along the way.

THE WIND BIRDS
by Peter Matthiessen

From his book by the same name. This is a revised version of a monograph Matthiessen wrote for a large-format book titled The Shorebirds of North America, *with many colored plates and detailed descriptions of the seasonal plumages of shorebirds.*

The author grew up on Long Isand and obviously watched shorebirds long before he wrote this book. He is a prolific writer on diverse subjects: At Play in the Fields of the Lord, Far Tortuga, *and* The Cloud Forest, *to name a few.*

⚓

THE WIND BIRDS

> Did you ever chance to hear the midnight flight of birds passing through the air and darkness over-head, in countless armies, changing their early or late summer habitat? It is something not to be for-gotten.... You could hear... "the rush of mighty wings," but oftener a velvety rustle, long drawn out...occasionally from high in the air came the notes of the plover.
>
> —Walt Whitman, Specimen Days

THE WIND BIRDS are strong, marvelous fliers, averaging greater distances in their migrations than any other bird family on earth. Of the several hundred migratory birds of North America, only thirty-five winter as far south as central Chile, and in this group the barn swallow, blackpoll warbler, and Swainson's thrush, the osprey, broad-winged hawk, and per-egrine, with a few gulls, fly that far only irregularly. All the rest of the thirty-five are shorebirds, several of which go all the way to land's end, near Cape Horn. The white rumped-sandpiper, which flies nine thousand miles twice every year in pursuit of summer, is only exceeded in the distance of its north-south migration by the Arctic tern, and the golden plover far exceeds the tern in the distances covered in a single flight; it is thought to travel well over two thousand miles nonstop on both its Atlantic and Pacific migrations. The bristle-thighed curlew, which flies from Alaska to Polynesia and New Zealand, is another distance flier of renown; and so are the ruddy turnstone, wandering tattler, and sanderling, which may be found on the most far-flung strands and atolls throughout their enormous range.

Because of the great distances they must travel, the migrants make preparations to depart again within a few months of their arrival from the north; the flocking and reflocking that is evident on the summer coasts and pampas of the Southern Hemisphere is a symptom of premigratory restlessness. This restlessness is not entirely attributable to activity of the glands, for castrated birds will migrate, borne along, perhaps, by the northward tide of movement. Migration is part of an annual cycle which also includes breeding and molt; what is not yet fully known is the exact pattern of stimuli, physiological and/or external, that puts this cycle into motion.

Temperature, which was long assumed to be the controlling factor, is now thought to have no effect at all, but it is generally agreed that the onset of warm weather, with an increased food supply and a lessened heat loss, gives the bird the excess energy which is expressed in migration and reproduction. Food supply, light intensity, seasonal rains, and many other forces, including internal rhythms of the glands, may help incite the reproductive dance, but the strongest goad of all appears to be reaction to a change in light as the season turns; this reaction, in both plants and animals, is called photoperiodism. The intensity of illumination, however, is probably less important than the longer day in which to remain active. "Daylight probably stimulates gonads not because it is beneficial to general well-being, but because a physiological timing mechanism has been evolved between gonad development and an external factor associated with spring." Thus, birds which winter in the West Indies or the southern states are thought to be stirred in early spring by the lengthening of the days.

But the spotted sandpiper may fly to the region of the equator, where day length is constant throughout the year; and where the white-rumped sandpiper winters in the uttermost part of the earth, the summer days of February, far from lengthening, grow shorter with the advent of the Capricornian autumn. Unless they possess some internal chronometer quite independent of external stimuli, the equatorial migrants must be awakened from the sameness of their days by some such phenomenon as a change in the rains or the northerly drift of the sun, while the species wintering in austral latitudes may be stirred by the *shortening* of days toward such activities as song, mock fighting, and formation of pairs which are the external symptoms of pituitary change.

By February, in Tierra del Fuego, male white-rumped sandpipers are already engaged in mock battles with other males of their own kind. The birds circle like midget roosters, leaping up and down with sexual rage, but never touching. Their mock flights are a sign not of distaste for their own kind but of an impulse to perpetuate it; the time of premigration courtship has begun. On the northern continent, a few woodcock have already begun to nest; the snipe and killdeer, in late February, would be winging northward, crowding the retreat of frozen earth.

Within the body of the sandpiper strange stirrings are taking place. Its gonads quicken and enlarge, though not so grossly as to slow its flight in the great journey to come: fully developed gonads have little or no effect on the migratory impulse, though the impulse is stimulated by partial development of these glands. Deposits of fat — the fuel for the journey — begin to form beneath the skin. The amount of fat is dictated by the rigors of the bird's migration. The Eskimo curlew made long transoceanic flights and its thin skin was stretched so taut with stored-up fat that in the days when it was shot by thousands from the sky, the fat would sometimes burst out of its breast when it struck the ground. In New England, for this reason, it was called the dough-bird.

The gland quickening and fat accumulation which encourage the white-rump's hypertonic belligerence also produce a symptom known as *Zugunruhe*, or migration restlessness, which is confined to migratory birds; many shorebirds travel through the night, and a wild bird held captive in its time of passage will sleep for a short time after sunset, then become more and more fretful until nearly midnight, when the fever of flight begins to taper off. *Zugunruhe*, which is inhibited in spring by a turn of cold weather and in autumn by a spell of warmth, is ordinarily accompanied by compass orientation: if placed outdoors where it can see the stars, the captive will face north in spring and southward in the fall.

The urge to migrate is strongest in birds of the cold climes of the northern continent, where seasonal changes in climate are most pronounced; a few austral species migrate *south* to breed, returning northward to escape Antarctic winter (the lesser seed snipe nests in Tierra del Fuego and winters in central Argentina, while the Magellanic snipe winters north to Uruguay), but the migrations are much shorter, for the range in temperature is less.

Migration routes apply more rigidly to species than to the individual shorebird, which may adjust its heading and even its route and destination from year to year, depending on whim and circumstance. But the piping plover, ruddy turnstone, and sanderling have been known to return to the same nesting ground, in what is known as *Ortstreue* or "place faithfulness," and spotted sandpipers — presumably the same pair — have occupied the identical nest site in consecutive years. A stilt sandpiper banded at Hudson's Bay also returned the next year to the same scrape, and possibly *Ortstreue* occurs in shorebirds generally.

As the time to migrate nears, the shorebirds rise and form huge flocks and veer apart in small ones, accumulating in the air again like bits of mercury, alighting for a quick moment before breaking away anew. They are frantic to be off, yet the last impulse has not come that will whirl them from the shore and send them spinning to the altitudes, perhaps three miles in the air, that are best suited to the spanning of the earth.

A meteorological signal may release them. Electricity in the air affects the migration behavior of curlews, oystercatchers, and others, though these effects are not well understood. And unlike birds of fixed migration dates, such as certain swifts and swallows, shorebirds may be delayed a month or more by high-pressure areas to the north. This indicates that the migration impulse, however strong, is not likely to run away with the bird in the face of adverse conditions.

On the other hand, bad weather encourages the flock instinct in birds by inhibiting spring sexuality and belligerence: "the factors which are associated with increased flocking are those that may be considered unfavorable." Cold or famine or the dangers of migration tend to draw the birds together: as social creatures, they need one another, and in hard times the need triumphs over the seasonal intolerance brought on by awakening hormones. Therefore, the wind birds are flocked and ready to be off when the first pale band of light breaks the horizon.

Most birds of open spaces are gregarious by nature, as if otherwise, in the vastness of a world where all horizons are so distant, they would be little more than wind-blown scraps. The flock, with its cumulative sense of direction, serves as protection for individuals against straying off into infinities; a tired bird can benefit by the experience of the leaders. It is also a defense against the predators; hawks seem daunted by the unity or just plain bulk of a close flock. (This phenomenon has been well described in regard to schools of fish — the "mystical sort of protective anonymity, thought to confound a predator unable to concentrate its hunger on any one of such a host.") Most shorebirds, like ducks and other birds, cluster together in time of peril, and white-rumped sandpipers may rush at a predator in a body and scatter in its face in a "confusion" attack which usually turns it aside.

The ruddy turnstone, though it migrates in small groups, "is not particularly sociable.... I have occasionally observed a marked hierarchy in a party of only two birds, the inferior individual avoiding the superior one." And the Wilson's plover, in company with the snipe and woodcock, the spotted sandpiper, and most of the tattlers (the lesser yellowlegs is an exception), is a casual flocker at best. The solitary sandpiper, even if apprehended in a group, will scatter when it takes flight — entirely unlike the great majority of sandpipers, whose habit of snapping together in the air like magnets was of no small convenience to the gunner in the days when they were shot. Some nonflockers have either a short migration span or inland habitats where flocking would be a nuisance, but the greater yellowlegs may keep its own company all the way from Tierra del Fuego to Alaska.

Then the flocks are gone. On tide flats which at twilight of the evening past had swarmed with shorebirds, dirtied feathers drift across white-spotted mud, and hard shreds of dried algae, and brown spindrift, and the husks of dead crustaceans. The solitary birds that pass look forlorn and indecisive, and in the emptiness their calls receive no answer. These are the sick, weak, injured, and immature, whose impulses were not strong enough to hurl them upward at the northern stars; now they must wait out the southern winter. Greater and lesser yellowlegs are common birds in the Argentine throughout the year, and the Hudsonian godwit was once so widespread on the pampas from April to September that naturalists of eighty years ago called them a population of "Antarctic" breeders.

Most of these nonmigrants are yearling birds. Even in species that are sexually mature in their second year, not all individuals go north to breed; in the surfbird, for one, it appears doubtful that yearlings visit the breeding range at all. And the mature birds make no attempt to breed on winter grounds: there is no nesting record on its winter range for a migratory species from North America. (The jaçana, killdeer, Wilson's plover, American oystercatcher, and black-necked stilt that nest in South America are resident there, and it is conceivable that other species will one day join them; in the Old World, *Tringa hypoleucos*, the common sandpiper, has established a nesting population in its former winter quarters in South Africa.)

The black-necked stilt and the jaçana are all-year residents throughout most of their range, and several other shorebirds — the willet, avocet, oystercatchers, and Wilson's plover — "migrate" largely in a local sense, according to regional weather and conditions, or may even forego migration entirely. The fact that certain populations of the migratory killdeer, snowy plover, and rock sandpiper have become nonmigratory where conditions suit them suggests that migration is not innate behavior, but rather an evolutionary response to external pressures; the glaciers of the Pleistocene, which forced huge populations southward and encouraged a northward surge as they withdrew, must have affected the migration patterns of nearly all shorebirds of the northern continent.

By early March, the flocks have left Tierra del Fuego and Patagonia; moving north, they join those relatives that wintered on the pampas, or along the tropical rivers and savannas, or on white coral shores of the Caribbean. On the moonlike desert beaches of Peru, shrouded by fogs drifted in off the Huniboldt Current, the black-bellied plover runs and watches, runs and watches; already the plumage of its silver breast has taken on a fretting of the bold black that it will carry northward to the Arctic.

Left behind on ocean coasts from Panama to California and New England are those individuals whose energies got them underway but did not drive them to complete their journey. These birds — the ones seen in the northern states on the beaches of late June — may have set out with their fellows out of pure sociability, for birds, like dogs and men, are drawn to movement. On June 26, 1964, there was a flock of thirty-odd black-bellied plover on the ocean beach a few miles from Sagaponack; despite the surprising number, one must assume that all these were nonbreeders, for this plover nests within the Arctic Circle.

Because of the pressures of the breeding cycle, spring migration is performed much more rapidly than migration in the fall. Northbound dunlin, passing a light plane, have been timed at 110 miles per hour, or nearly twice the usual recorded flight speeds of other shorebirds. Birds, when pressed, are capable of a sharp increase in velocity, and in the thin air of high altitudes, migrants probably travel at a rate rarely attained nearer the ground. The bristle-thighed curlew flies the six thousand miles or more from New Zealand to its nesting grounds in western Alaska in about six weeks, while the southward journey may take twice as long. Birds winging northward from the Argentine move with corresponding haste. There appear to be few feeding grounds on the muddy coasts of northern South America and in the almost tideless Caribbean, and the golden plover may sometimes fly from the beaches of Peru all the way to the Gulf Coast without alighting. (The bladder snail *Physa* has been found in both crop and plumage of certain migrant plover, encouraging the startling idea that these birds might deliberately place snails in their plumage before starting on a long voyage in order to provide themselves with at least one meal during the trip.)

By late March and early April, when the wind birds appear in the big skies of the Gulf of Mexico, the killdeer, snipe, and woodcock that wintered on the Gulf Coast may already have flown to southern Canada: the woodcock nests so very early — there are records for December in Louisiana, January in Texas, and February in North Carolina — that sometimes bird and nest together are covered up by snow, and its young may be close to flight by the time other wind birds arrive in the Arctic. A few woodcock, in favorable years, have remained as far north as Long Island, and where warm springs or other special conditions permit, the common snipe will winter north beyond the line of frozen ground; it has been found in Nova Scotia bogs in dead of winter, with the glass near zero. In mid-February of 1965, after a hard January, a lone snipe could be seen each day in a winding cattail "dreen" on the east side of Sagaponack Pond, probing the mud (which proved to be full of tiny worms) along the very edges of the ice cakes.

Shorebirds, being highly mobile, will fly before storm or un-seasonable turn of weather, but sometimes they are caught off guard by sudden freezes. On February 13 of 1899, northbound woodcock, driven back toward the south, appeared near Charleston in the tens of thousands. They were half-starved and bewildered and were killed or died. Yet species of less specialized food habits can endure very low temperatures; at Sagaponack, the sanderlings and greater yellowlegs, which are present until mid-January, will sometimes overwinter, and are usually quite common in March — though Sagaponack in the spring is a lean feeding ground for shorebirds, and even the semipalmated sandpipers, so abundant in summer and fall, mostly forsake the cold Atlantic beaches for an inland journey up the Mississippi Valley.

On the last day of April, a few years ago, there came from the sea a mixed flock of red and northern phalarope, some sixty birds in all. They rode out the two days of an easterly gale on a small pond connected to Sagaponack Pond by the small stream where I saw the winter snipe. Two red phalarope were in full nuptial plumage, bright chestnut and gold, and they led the small band which bobbed on the gray wavelets or ruffled its feathers in the salt grass, awaiting a shifting of the skies that would draw the wind birds onward to the Arctic.

GHOSTLY WATCHERS OF THE DUNES
by Howard J. Shannon

From his book The Book of the Seashore. *Shannon was an artist, the beaches and dunes of Long Island's south shore his studio. As he hiked and sketched he began to notice live things in the water, on the beach, and back in the dunes. He drew and wrote, and* The Book of The Seashore *is the result, published in 1935 but showing almost no age. It's full of pen and inks and color plates, a model of how the naturalist can describe and explain.*

⚓

The Eccentric Behavior Imposed upon a Sea Animal When It Attempts to Live on Land

NEVER will I forget my startling introduction to this ghostly creature. It stood, white as the sand, poised on the crest of a dune; then, swift as a hare, it dashed sidewise away upon its eight flashing feet — for it was a ghost crab. After a time, when again I idly glanced in that direction, *there it was once more*, fixed, immobile, and apparently studying me with a steady, implacable stare. Certainly it is a disturbing creature, so white as hardly to be distinguished from the sand upon which it moves — hence the ghostly name — and the only large crustacean along our north Atlantic shores which has deserted its native water element to live on the precarious land.

In fact, in the eccentricity of its every act, one doubts the wisdom of that hazardous experiment. A fearful caution veils all its elusive goings to and fro, with sudden disappearances from one area to be followed, very soon after, by equally mysterious reappearances in another, and often so close at hand as to seem truly uncanny. These secretive and almost unreal maneuvers seem like confessions of a profound uneasiness experienced by a marine animal while attempting a partial adjustment to that dangerous and foreign realm — the land.

That peering gaze, too, with which it scrutinizes a chance intruder, and that frenzied combative pose which it strikes when apprehended — both seem the result of a confused uncertainty. It also possesses an even more disquieting trait. I refer to its actual advance upon an accidental human visitor. Yet such hidden deviltries seem to inspire that steady approach, such a calculating threat seems to emanate from its prolonged and resentful scrutiny, that one instinctively perceives in this crab an alien being. An emergent apparition from the marine stands before us, foreign and untransmogrified from its elder past when more bestial struggles for existence prevailed in the depths of the sea.

Its curious and ghostly elusiveness had attracted me from the very first. Even now, after twelve years of absence from its habitat, that quality impresses me again, as well as its curious intentness of scrutiny, its sidling advance upon an intruder, and its swifter flight. For again I am on this southern New Jersey shore, near Longport, where *Ocypoda arenaria* lives.

Their burrows are all about me. Some, situated along high-tide line, are almost within reach of the water. But most of them are well above the tidal zone or along the base of the dunes — a congregation of circular openings each accompanied by its mound of cast-up sand. Yet it seems a dead city, a windswept reach of shore punctured with many idle doorways about which small mussel shells or other marine debris are strewn. But they seem bereft of life. Do the crabs often emerge in daylight? Do they feed at night — or when? How did they come to desert their home in the sea for the precarious land? Little is told in the books — and not all of that is reliable.

Let us station ourselves, on this September afternoon, beside a dune slope — and wait. For a long time there is no sign of life.

The settlement of the ghost crabs seems as deserted as Pompeii; a relic, like that tragic city, of a once populous past. My eyes continually glance from one burrow to another seeking *some* sign of stirring life. Still no object moves. Wait! What is that whitish buff object lying low along the edge of a distant burrow? It wasn't there a few moments ago. See! A pair of alert, black-tipped eye-stalks is lifted, periscope-like, above the sand. The creature, crouching low, scrutinizes its surroundings. So persistently does it remain so, motionless, apparently inert, that my eye strays farther up the shore.

Look! There comes a fleet ghost. It's fully exposed — and running! Now it pauses, moves slowly along in a sidling zigzag manner, stops again, lifts itself, with legs atiptoe, watches — and how steadily and persistently! Suddenly alarmed, it crouches low with body close-pressed against the sand. Again it stands erect and cleans a dimmed eye by clasping that stalked organ in its upper, hair-fringed mouth parts, slipping it through the cleansing hairs and then releasing it until the eye once more springs aloft, erect and watchful. Now, sidling along, the crab occasionally hastens its progress by short running starts which bring it farther and farther down the shore. See! It is actually approaching me! Nearer and nearer it comes, until it faces me squarely. More hesitant now, it advances within a dozen feet — then halts as if puzzled by this large dark object reposing within its own domains. Again it moves restlessly about. Quite evidently, the creature is disturbed, uncertain, not at all assured as to what course to pursue. After a moment, it creeps slowly away, crouches for a brief time in a chosen depression for another scrutiny; then rises and slowly disappears far down the shore.

That cautious appraisal and reappraisal of its surroundings interrupts its every activity. Witness, for example, this other crab about to dig out its burrow.

Suddenly two legs emerge along one side of the burrow entrance.Then an eye, supported on its long stalk, appears and studiously scans the neighborhood. This watching phase of the procedure is prolonged sometimes for two minutes, by actual count. But my patience is greater than the crab's. See! Fully reassured at last, the ghostly creature suddenly walks out upon the exposed beach, hugging a mass of damp sand against its left side by means of one claw and two forelegs which are clasped about it. Quickly it throws its burden outward over the terrain with a sharp fillip of these carrying parts, then immediately darts back into the burrow — but only part way. It remains half in and half out, studiously regarding the neighborhood again with the same untiring scrutiny. Finally it becomes fully satisfied and darts out of sight.

Sometimes its cautious study takes on an amusing repetitiousness. For it may start to retreat, then pause, *only to emerge again* part way, and repeat that steady stare, as if some object in the neighborhood had aroused a deeper suspicion. After a final retreat, often a lengthy one, the series of movements is repeated: first, a cautious eyeing of the surroundings; second, the sudden emergence; third, the casting away of the dug material, and then the retreat again.

Its immense trepidation, indeed, is often manifested in other and most curious ways. A fly buzzing overhead will cause its sudden disappearance. So also will a sudden uprushing lip of foam sent far toward its domicile by the incoming tide. Obviously, the crab is beset on every hand by forces not understood and perhaps only dimly seen.

But see! The burrow digger we have been watching now executes a most curious maneuver. It walks slowly out over the lumps of sand so recently cast out, bestrides one, and then, by steadily tamping and pressing it, gradually crumbles it to fragments. We afterward discover that this is not, by any means, a rare procedure. The outer and under surfaces of the claws are employed much as we might use the knuckles and backs of our hands and fingers to pulverize some coherent substance. Meanwhile the animal has been watching me; and now, strange to say, it walks in my direction, slowly, steadily, with an immense deliberation. The creature *is* certainly spookish. It halts, and again moves restlessly about. Evidently the crab is suspicious of the large dark object lying so silently there. Was that breaking up of the sand fragments, then, a procedure designed to clear away the obstructed view?

True, they are occasionally picked over after pulverization, and the creature may be seen daintily carrying small particles to its mouth. So this maneuver may be designed, in part, to uncover small food elements, such as minute crustaceans, which form no inconsiderable part of the crab's food. Often, however, no such feeding transpires. The breaking up and tamping down of the sand lumps seem independent of any such after-act. Perhaps an endeavor to clear the view *is* the true explanation.

Immense trepidation is, undoubtedly, the price this creature has paid for its rash desertion of its native water element. Such an expression seems almost present amid that curious agglomeration of features which is not a face and yet masks an alert and unsleeping intelligence. See! Its suspicions *are* deeply aroused. It retires within the burrow and becomes engaged at some new-found task at the very entrance. (Subsequent observations have shown that the crab first brings up rounded bunches of sand from below and packs them about the immediate entrance, where they form a shelflike support.) Now the crab's right legs reach far out over the beach surface, grasp a generous armful of loose material, and then drag it inward. The crab is sealing the entrance. Now it turns as if on a pivot, to repeat the procedure on the opposite side, and totally disappears. An examination shows that the burrow is completely closed.

Foraging operations, too, are not without interest. Look! Two crabs are now sallying forth to search for desirable food along the tide-swept area. An interruption occurs. A peacock butterfly, fluttering along, flies so low as to pass only a foot above one crab's shell. Instantly, it leaps aloft like a cat, to catch it. The leap falls short; the butterfly sails away. Evidently, the crabs must content themselves with less fancy food today. So a tangled mass of weeds and mussels is found in the tidal zone. One crab grasps this firmly and, by toilfully tugging away, is able to drag it to its burrow. There it is roughly adjusted upon the near-by mound of cast-up sand, when the hungry creature squats upon it, complacently reposes there, and daintily begins to pick apart and carry to its mouth the disengaged fragments. Truly, it's a picture of contentment and sufficiency.

Farther up the beach, a disturbance occurs. Two other foragers have fallen afoul of each other. Rising on tiptoe, they sidle about, looking for an opening; then, clashing their claws, fall to in desperate struggle. However, the encounter is brief. Soon separating, they draw entirely apart and sidle away.

Young crabs, too, little fellows, only an inch wide, that flit like fragments of wind-blown foam over the sand, are also "watchers," although their field of vision is more restricted. Often their burrows are dug only a few feet from those of the adults, thus creating a real community scene. Their movements, too, are possessed of such in instantaneous celerity that the small pepper-and-salt bodies, so closely resembling the sand, can hardly be seen at all. On the open beach, they move by sudden running starts that are interrupted by equally sudden halts, quite in the manner of the beach spiders, which, in fact, they, almost resemble. So, even more than the parents, they are really "ghost crabs," cloaked, as they are, by protective coloration.

Drive a youngster from its burrow or block its return and watch the result. The small creature immediately flattens itself, and, by grasping the loose sand in its outreaching legs, is able to draw it inward and over itself like a garment. Then the legs also sink and bury themselves quite out of sight. Only the rim or forward part of the shell or carapace is now visible — and one alert eye erect on its stalk. Soon, as a reconnoitering measure, the other stalked eye also uprears itself. Now both are shining brightly aloft and surveying the dubious situation. A sudden gesture of my hand — and both eyes snap down into their sockets. Soon, however, the right eye once more lifts itself erect, periscoping to its hidden owner below the sand authentic news of the hazardous conditions above. Again my hand waves. Once more both eye-stalks snap down! After a long interval of quiescence upon my part, however, while I am engaged in sketching, once more both eyes cautiously lift themselves until the little crab is in possession of its full visual capacity. I wave my hand again, and, most amusingly, the left eye alone snaps down. The other, remaining brightly aloft, seems to say, "I am not as frightened as I was." Then, as I move quietly away, the impish creature disengages itself from its blanket of sand and skitters off.

This crab's ancient home in the sea has been forsworn so long that it is adapted for life no longer in that element. So, when danger threatens, it seeks safety in self-burial, as we have seen. Yet, under exceptional circumstances, as when cornered, these "ghosts" will retreat into their former native element, the sea.

One day as I approached the familiar colony from the south side of a breakwater that parallels the ocean, a large ghost crab was seen moving along between wall and sea. Disturbed by my approach, he retreated behind some spiles and remained there. So I quietly seated myself until he should emerge. This soon happened, when he quietly continued his progress up the shore. To test his fleetness, and also to discover what the crab would do when caught between ocean and wall, I suddenly rushed forward and touched him. Immediately, he was off! As quickly, I followed.

Now, fully alarmed, he dashed down into the swirling waters that were rushing, in foam-covered sheets, far up the strand. This ancient home was his no longer, yet he fled to it for immediate protection. As I continued to advance, he retreated farther and farther into the sucking swirl of the onrushing waters, even to the extent of almost completely and irrevocably entering the crashing turmoil of the surf itself. Clutching the wet sand with grasping claws, he held his uncertain foothold. Then, as I mercifully withdrew, he permitted the impulse of the oncoming wave rushes to carry him farther and farther toward his known and habitual home of dry land. At my second approach, he again retreated, and even into greater danger than before. Upon my subsequent withdrawal, however, he slowly and laboriously emerged, with many a setback as the spent waves swept outward over him, and appeared once more upon the sands. Then he moved away toward the farther shore.

Upon second thought, we see there is little mystery in this adoption of land habit by certain crabs. For the oscillating shore levels of prehistoric time might easily have forced certain creatures to a terrestrial mode of life. Even today, some marine species temporarily seek the land of their own volition. Sometimes at sunrises, when a still sea sends hardly a creaming ripple up the strand, blue crabs will emerge and walk along the immediate waterline searching for food. An accidental blocking of a much-used channel may force these crabs to travel over the new-made land in order to reach the sea. Such an occasion has been described by Willard Nye, Jr., who saw a migration of this kind over the blocked entrance of Quick Sands Pond in Rhode Island. Owing to the blocking of their usual autumn channel down to the sea by reason of this drifted bar, many blue crabs, to the number of scores and hundreds, steadily emerged upon the land and "trekked" over into the deeper water beyond rather than endure the winter freezing in the shallows of the pond.

So the transition from a watery habitat to one of a terrestrial nature is not as remarkable and inexplicable as it might appear at first sight. A wholesale elevation of the early continental shores, known to have occurred more than once during our local prehistoric past, might have readily immured many crabs in landlocked bays far removed from the sea. Later, these areas could have become wholly dry. Thus, perhaps, certain adaptive types were persuaded to habituate themselves to an existence on the land and to forget entirely, during the long ages of a gradual habit modification, their former marine home.

Vessels, Afloat and Below

Who will ever forget the teacher who first told you that a body immersed in water is buoyed up by a force equal to the water displaced? Read on to find out what happens when the equation fails.

EACH MAN A HERO
by David Stick

From his book Graveyard of the Atlantic. *Every kid knows that the graveyard of the Atlantic is off Cape Hatteras, North Carolina, where the north-flowing Gulf Stream crashes into coastal waters moving south, creating a series of sandbars and rough water that beckon ships to disaster. Stick catalogues some 600 North Carolina shipwrecks, with stories about brave sea rescues. Divers like such stories, especially if accurate bearings to wrecks are provided — wrecks make for good diving.*

⚓

THE TRAGIC LOSS of the *Huron* in 1877 and of the *Metropolis* in 1878 occurred at a time when the Federal Government was in the process of organizing lifesaving facilities along the North Carolina coast. Actually, the first North Carolina lifesaving stations were put in commission in the winter of 1874-1875, but the early efficiency was greatly hampered by the interference of what the Lifesaving Service termed "petty local politicians, whose aim was to subordinate the service to their personal ends."

The service charged, specifically, that these politicians attempted to "pack the stations with their own creatures, without the slightest respect to use or competency." Apparently they were partly successful, for though a number of the men first employed as lifesavers went on to distinguish themselves, there were so many misfits at the outset that it took four or five yeears to finally weed them out.

By 1879 there were twenty stations already built or planned between Currituck Beach and Cape Fear, and for the most they were manned by efficient, brave, and loyal men. That most of the incompetents had been removed from the service was dramatically illustrated in the record for the next fifteen years; for during the period from 1879 through 1893 some of the most daring resues in the history of lifesaving were accomplished on the North Carolina coast.

M & E HENDERSON

The lifesavers had a comparatively easy time of it at the wreck of the three-masted schooner *M & E Henderson* at New Inlet, November 30, 1879, but the circumstances of the wreck were strange and mysterious from the very outset; so much so, in fact, that the three survivors of the seven-man crew were later imprisoned on suspicion of mutiny and brought to trial in Baltimore.

The 387-ton *Henderson*, an old vessel hailing from Philadelphia, had sailed from Bull River, South Carolina, with a cargo of phosphate rock destined for Baltimore. She had on board in addition to her captain, two mates and a cook (all white men) and three deckhands (all Spanish mulattoes). The evening of November 29 she was seen north of Cape Hatteras, close in to shore but in no danger. There was a stiff breeze and a sizeable surf, but the night was clear, with the entire area illuminated by a bright Carolina moon; no reason there, certainly, for any concern.

At five o'clock the next morning the early morning beach patrolman from Pea Island returned to his station house, started a fire in the galley stove, roused the cook, and mounted the lookout tower for the purpose of inspecting the coast near by. He soon spotted a lone figure on the beach and supposed at first it was a fisherman; but then he noticed that the man was hatless and seemed to be staggering, so he left the tower, awakened the keeper, and took off down the beach to investigate.

His haste was justified, for he soon came upon the man, a haggard and dripping figure, dark-skinned, and able to mutter little more than incoherent sounds. The lifesaver was able to understand that his vessel was aground, the masts already down, and the captain lost.

The castaway was carried back to the station and put under the care of the cook, while the other lifesavers set out in the direction of the wreck. They had gone little more than a mile south of the station when they discovered, near the north bank of New Inlet, great piles of debris in the surf, and offshore, in the breakers, the last solid remnant of the vessel, rising and falling in the eerie false dawn.

Here they met a party of fishermen who said they had discovered one of the survivors and had taken him to their camp on Jack's Shoal, a small island on the sound side of the inlet. The keeper and two lifesavers borrowed a boat from the fishermen and headed for the island, while the remaining Pea Island crewmen began a systematic search of the debris for survivors, a search which proved completely futile.

The keeper had better luck, finding at Jack's Shoal the man the fishermen had saved, now dry, warmed by hot coffee, and swathed in bedclothes. And on his return still a third survivor was discovered, this one crumpled on the sand near the beach. The man was unconscious and hardly breathing, but they hurried with him to the station, stripped him of his wet clothing, rubbed warmth and life into his limbs, administered restoratives, and soon had him sufficiently recovered to be out of danger.

Thus three of the seven aboard the *Henderson* were rescued, but little information could be gained as to the reason for the vessel's loss or the circumstances surrounding the death of the others; for these three were the deckhands, men of foreign birth, unable to speak or understand more than an occasional word of English.

The fact that they were illiterates and of a different race and color seems to have brought suspicion on them in the first place, especially in the eyes of the *Henderson's* owners. Had they been white men, with sufficient knowledge of our language to state their case, no matter how implausible it might have been, the affair probably would have ended there, with nothing more than unspoken questions as to why the vessel had stranded under such circumstances and how it happened that only deckhands survived. But they were dark-skinned foreigners, and on warrants sworn out by the owners they were arrested, transported to Baltimore, and clapped in jail there, to wait in solitude for many months before their case finally came to trial.

That is all there was to it; for the trial produced nothing new in the way of information, and the three men were set free at last for want of evidence, leaving us with nothing but a sketchy and provoking outline of one more shipwreck mystery on the North Carolina coast.

A. B. GOODMAN

Few of the early lifesavers had worldly belongings worth the mention: a shack back in the woods behind the dunes, a horse or cow and a hand-made cart; a gun of some sort; maybe a little boat and a piece of net; and probably a few acres of sandy beachland, theirs through inheritance or the right of the squatter.

It was an unusual sight, therefore, and one probably never since duplicated along the outer banks, to see seven men gathered around a rough table in the Creeds Hill Lifesaving Station before dawn, April 4, 1881, all engaged in preparing simple wills, bequeathing their meager belongings to their loved ones. Most could not write, and the literate ones did double duty, drawing up the plain documents and indicating for the others the spot where they should make their faltering X marks.

Why this sudden concern over the disposition of worldly goods? Why were seven strong and healthy men, each at the same time — and all for the first time — putting their affairs in final order? The reason was that they were soon to put to sea in their light, flat-bottomed rowboat and head out to the very center of treacherous Diamond Shoals at the height of a raging offshore wind against which, if it continued in force, they could have no hope of ever again returning to the safety of land. For a vessel was aground on the shoals, and human beings clung to her rigging; human beings whose names and homes and nationalities were unknown to the seven men, but whose lives were their responsibility.

B. B. Dailey was keeper of the Creeds Hill Station, and the first to make out his will; his crewmen were Thomas J. Fulcher, Damon M. Gray, Erasmus H. Rolinson, Benjamin F. Whidbee, Christopher B. Farrow, and John B. Whidbee. They pulled on heavy clothes and dragged their boat down to the beach, leaving the wills behind. Snow fell as they made ready to launch, large wet flakes that came at them horizontally from the northwest, plastering their clothes and faces on the side to windward.

The sea there on the south side of Cape Hatteras was calm enough to permit the launching; but once offshore beyond the protection of the land the wind struck them from one direction, the strong current from the other, twisting their boat about in crazy fashion, exposing them again and again to the full force of the sea's awesome uprising.

The surprising thing was that they ever reached the vessel out there on Diamond Shoals, but they did; they got close enough to read the name, *A. B. Goodman*, on her stern and to see four men clinging to her rigging (a fifth had been washed overboard and drowned during the night.) The lifesavers realized the futility of trying to rescue the four men with wind and sea at their angry worst, and so they anchored near by, yet kept their oars in constant readiness. An hour they waited, and then another. Their action in writing wills seemed fully justified, for without a change of wind they could neither rescue the castaways, nor themselves survive.

Then, as their hope and strength waned, and the full realization of their plight came to them, as the *Goodman* began to go to pieces and their own frail boat began to fill, the wind slackened, died out almost completely, then shifted around and blew in from the sea.

They pulled up underneath the tangled rigging then; but as the first of the four seamen climbed down almost within reach, close enough to realize the smallness and inadequacy of the would-be rescue craft, he was overcome with a sudden fear and scrambled back once more to his perch high above. Keeper Dailey pleaded then, convinced another that this was his only hope, inveigled the man into coming close, reached out and grasped him as he too held back and pulled him bodily into the lifeboat. Another ventured close, was seized by the keeper and torn from the shrouds; and the other two, perceiving this, followed voluntarily.

The rescued captain was seated in the stern sheets of the little boat, the three crewmen on the thwarts. Oars were manned, the anchor hauled aboard, and at last the eleven of them, almost swamping the lifeboat, began the long pull shoreward. The wind was more favorable, but the sea was as rough as before and the current as strong. Hour after hour they rowed, and finally, late that afternoon they passed inside of the shifting shoals, crossed a gully near the shore, and beached their boat at last on the north side of the cape. The rescued men were taken to the near-by lighthouse where food awaited them; but the lifesavers, not waiting for food, hurried back along the beach the six miles to Creeds Hill, where the would-be beneficiaries of their seven wills were waiting.

DULCIMER

Probably there is no connection between the two, but the fact is that the point east of Hatteras Inlet where the sugar-laden bark *Dulcimer* was lost February 12, 1883, has long been considered by surf fishermen one of the finest spots on the Atlantic coast for catching channel bass.

There was $32,000 worth of sugar in the hold of the *Dulcimer* when she came ashore there, and in those days $32,000 would buy a lot of sugar. But though the eleven crewmen of the 290-ton English vessel were saved, the cargo of sugar, picked up in Brazil and scheduled for use on the tables of greater New York, was left there to sweeten the waters now frequented by great schools of the fighting channel bass.

ANGELA

In these days of large ocean-going steamships equipped with every conceivable device for saving life and preventing disaster, of radar and airplanes and blimps and helicopters, of amphibious ducks and jeeps suitable for rapid beach patrol, the mariner in distress has the odds all in his favor. But in times past, when sailing ships dominated ocean traffic and the lifesaver walked his lonely vigil along trackless sand reefs, before ship-to-shore telephone came into usage, or even wireless for that matter, the odds were strictly on the other side.

During the comparatively short period in which the United States Lifesaving Service was in operation on the North Carolina coast — 1875 to 1915 — hundreds of ships presumed lost off the banks were listed in the annual reports of that agency with the brief notation: "Lost at sea — never heard from." These listings are so numerous, and the information as to time and exact location so sketchy, that they are purposely omitted from this volume. But some idea of the utter helplessness of the crews of these lost vessels, and of the thin threads of chance on which their lives depended, can be gleaned from the accounts of other shipwrecks from which human beings escaped with their lives.

Imagine, for example, the hopeless feeling of the ten Italian crewmen on board the 373-ton barkentine *Angela* when she sprang a leak at sea while en route from Cartagena, Spain, to Baltimore with a cargo of iron ore. The pumps took care of it for a while, then the open seams widened as the vessel wallowed in the sea, until finally it was obvious to all that the *Angela*, heavily laden as she was with the dead weight of the iron ore, could never reach the port for which she had sailed. It was not a situation peculiar to the ten Italians on the *Angela* in the spring of 1883, for the crewmen of many of those "never heard from" ships must have faced the same thing.

Captain Carlo of the *Angela* could have abandoned his craft there, to drift for hours or days or weeks in his frail yawl until it capsized or a passing vessel came in sight, or he and his crewmen died from starvation or thirst or exposure, or the horrible insanity so frequently resulting from any of the three. Instead, he stayed by the ship, headed westward for the coast, hoping that he could beach the *Angela* before she sank completely. Other mariners have chosen the same course and died for it.

At midnight, March 4, with the sky dark and overcast and only the thunderous crashing of the breakers to announce the proximity of land, the *Angela* struck bottom, grated forward momentarily, and then held fast. Still she rolled, as each succeeding breaker struck her, and jagged holes appeared in her hull where only open seams had been before. Having been at sea for weeks without sight of land, and possessing in any event only a limited knowledge of the conformation of this foreign coastline, Captain Carlo was able to do no more than speculate as to the place where they had stranded. It might be the dreaded shoals off Cape Hatteras, or the bar making out from some shallow inlet, or any of a thousand other places on the coast. Land, the dry, hard-packed, above-water kind, might be a hundred yards distant, or fifteen miles. The only thing of which Captain Carlo could be certain was that his vessel was aground, the breakers were fast pounding her to pieces, and now that he had accomplished what he had set out to do the lives of his crewmen were as much in danger as before.

Captain Carlo had his yawl launched there in the dark, hurriedly boarded it with his nine men, shoved off from the *Angela*, and headed seaward. Shortly a light was seen to the west, a brightly burning red light, the international signal that assistance was at hand. Later, shots were heard and at daybreak the Italian captain was able to better undersand the situation.

The *Angela* had drifted within three hundred yards of shore, and a group of men — lifesavers from Paul Gamiels Hill Station — had set up their beach apparatus there and fired a line aboard the vessel.

Captain Carlo headed for shore, intending to beach his yawl opposite the men. But the lifesavers waved him back, displaying a large red flag as a warning. Soon the Italian tried again, was waved back a second time; he moved up the beach and headed in a third time but was still warned away. What he did not know was that the tide was then at its highest and the beach at that particular spot was so steep that it was impossible to successfully guide a boat through the surf. Not understanding this, the captain proceeded out to sea, beyond the farthest line of breakers and headed north. Four miles, five, seven, his crew rowed, until a building came into view and another group of men on the beach opposite. This was Caffeys Inlet Station, and the lifesavers there, having sighted the Italian yawl, had hauled their own lifeboat down to the beach, which sloped much more gradually there than at Paul Gamiels Hill. They launched their lifeboat through the still turbulent surf, shipping a barrel of water or more in the process, but reached the yawl, removed five of the Italians, returned them safely to shore, and then went back for the others.

Thus Captain Carlo and his nine crewmen lived; but the *Angela* and her cargo of iron ore were lost there in the surf a quarter of a mile south of Paul Gamiels Hill Station; and had their luck been different, had Captain Carlo taken to his yawl earlier or a strong gale struck them while heading for shore, or if any one of a dozen different circumstances had arisen, the *Angela* and her crew of ten could easily have been listed with hundreds more, simply as: "Lost at sea — never heard from."

EPHRAIM WILLIAMS

During the first thirty years of operation of the Lifesaving Service on the North Carolina coast a total of twelve Gold Lifesaving Medals, the highest such award made by our government, were presented for exceptional bravery in saving life. Of this number, seven — more than half — were awarded to the lifesavers from Cape Hatteras and Creeds Hill stations who rescued the crew of the barkentine *Ephraim Williams*, December 22, 1884.

The *Ephraim Williams*, a 491-ton vessel loaded with lumber and bound from Savannah, Georgia, to her home port of Providence, Rhode Island, with a crew of nine, ran into a storm off Frying Pan Shoals December 18 and soon became waterlogged and unmanageable.

On December 21 she appeared southwest of Cape Hatteras and was kept under surveillance throughout that day by lifesavers who had assembled near the cape point for service if needed. Late the following morning the vessel, having temporarily disappeared, was discovered north of Diamond Shoals and almost opposite Big Kinnakeet, to which point the lifesavers then proceeded with their boats and apparatus. The sea was described by veteran observers in the area as the roughest they had ever seen, with huge rollers crashing first on the outer reef a half mile or so from shore, and then churning all the way in, across the inner reef, to the beach. Beyond these farthest breakers, wallowing in the huge waves, the *Ephraim Williams* seemed on the verge of sinking, for her decks were awash, and only her masts showed above water.

The lifesavers paused abreast of the vessel, just watching and waiting, for there was no sign of life on board, and even if there had been, it was the opinion of most of them — and of their neighbors who had assembled there with them — that no boat could live in such a sea.

Then suddenly, as they watched, a flag fluttered out on the mast of the stricken ship and was slowly hauled upward as a signal of distress. Someone was yet alive on the derelict vessel!

Keeper Benjamin B. Dailey of Cape Hatteras Station immediately called on his men to launch their boat. With no more hesitation than he himself had shown, they carried out his orders,

Keeper Patrick H. Etheridge (who had recently relieved Dailey as Keeper of Creeds Hill Station) stepping in to take the place of an absent crewman. Cumbersome clothing was removed, each man donned a cork belt, and all loose articles in the boat were carefully lashed down. The boat was hauled to the water's edge. Six men stepped inside, took their seats, each grasping his oar in readiness. Others helped push the craft into the shallow water, while Keeper Dailey jumped in over the stern, stood there, his feet braced, the long steering oar held against his side.

The very first strokes took them into the inner line of breakers, over one wave crashing down in front of them, then over another and another and another. Each wave tossed the surfboat high in the air, then dumped it into the trough beyond, concealing the boat from shore, flipping it up and down, up and down, while the lifesavers pulled with mighty strokes on their heavy oars and Keeper Dailey bent his weight against the sweep.

They passed those first breakers, somehow, moved seaward through the seething, churning turbulent mass of water between the two reefs, paused momentarily as they came to the outer line, waiting for a break in the huge combers before them. At last the break came, Dailey shouted an order, the oars dug in and the little craft fairly leaped forward into the seething foam. Tle first wave capped over, broke before them, pushing the bow of the boat high in the air, until she stood almost vertical so that the anxious watchers on shore could see every one of her crew, and the decking beneath their feet, and the ropes lashed down beside them. Then, as suddenly as that wave had struck, it rolled beneath them, the boat levelled off, and before the next one could come down on top of them the lifesavers had passed through the outer breakers.

They rescued the crew of the barkentine one by one, for even out there beyond the breakers the sea was too rough to come in close to the sinking vessel. Already the castaways had decided to abandon ship, had lashed together improvised rafts, and one, even, had been pushed off from beside the ship. Had they followed that course, had the lifesavers not come to their aid, they would have faced those breakers with slight hope of making shore alive. But Dailey and his men not only reached them, but managed, somehow, to return through those same breakers to the safety of shore.

"I do not believe that a greater act of heroism is recorded than that of Dailey and his crew on this momentous occasion," reported the officer sent down later to investigate. "These poor, plain men, dwellers upon the lonely sands of Hatteras, took their lives in their hands, and, at the most imminent risk, crossed the most tumultuous sea that any boat within the memory of living men had ever attempted on that bleak coast, and all for what? That others might live to see homes and friends. The names of Benjamin B. Dailey and his comrades in this magnificent feat should never be forgotten."

Benjamin B. Dailey, Patrick H. Etheridge, Isaac L. Jennett, Thomas Gray, John H. Midgett, Jabez B. Jennett, and Charles Fulcher. Those are the names; each the recipient of the nation's highest award for saving life.

ARIO PARDEE

By land it is about ninety miles from Perth Amboy, New Jersey, to Chester, Pennsylvania; under normal conditions a sailing vessel can make it down the Jersey coast and then up the Delaware River to Chester in a day or so. But Captain Henry A. Smith of the 198-ton schooner *Ario Pardee*, attempting this trip with his vessel loaded with cement, ran into one gale after another in late December, 1884, and ten days later found himself stranded on the North Carolina outer banks, several hundred miles south of where he wanted to go.

Captain Smith sailed from Perth Amboy at 7 A.M., December 18, with four crewmen. He passed Sandy Hook at 11 A.M., and when off Long Branch early that afternoon ran into a severe snowstorm. By then the wind was blowing strong from the north so Smith decided to ride it out.

That particular northerly gale lasted 56 long hours and was accompanied by continuous high seas which swept everything movable from the *Pardee's* decks.

The wind then shifted to the south and increased again to gale force. Smith rode that one out, too.

The next day the wind went around to the northwest. Once again it reached gale proportions, and for the third time Smith rode it out.

Finally, the wind calming down a bit, the *Pardee* ran for the land, reaching the Five Fathom Bank Lightship, located off the entrance to Delaware Bay, which is just where Smith wanted to go in the first place. It had been six days since the *Pardee* left Perth Amboy but she was still only halfway to Chester; and to make matters worse another gale blew up, this one from the west, so Smith hove to.

Twelve hours later, the wind abating once again, Smith tried to beat his way into Delaware Bay, but the wind hauled around to the north and his jib blew away. Again he hove to, and since by this time the *Pardee's* boat had been stove in and the schooner was shipping a lot of water, he hailed a passing steamer and asked to be taken off. The steamer got a line on board and removed one man, but by then night was coming on, the sea was running very high, so the operation was discontinued.

For the next sixty hours the *Pardee*, with four men on board, rode out the northerly gale. Finally it, too, died out, and Smith set what sails remained and steered a west course for land. At midnight, December 28 — ten days after leaving Perth Amboy — a light was sighted, and Smith let go his anchors. At dawn the next morning he found the *Pardee* almost in the breakers at Wash Woods, North Carolina, with lifesavers standing by on shore.

After that it was a simple matter for the lifesavers to come out in their surfboat and remove the four men, and soon afterwards the *Pardee* slipped her chains and stranded on the shore, both vessel and cargo eventually being totally lost. Wash Woods was a long way from Chester, but even so Captain Smith seemed happy enough to be on dry land once again.

NELLIE WADSWORTH

The little schooner *Nellie Wadsworth* was anchored in Hatteras Inlet the morning of December 5, 1885, her captain intending to wait there until the strong southwest gale then in progress was sufficiently diminished to permit passage through the shallow cut to Pamlico Sound. But the *Wadsworth* never reached the sound, and her remains are probably still there, buried in the shoals on the north side of the inlet, while somewhere near by the body of one of her crewmen lies interred in an unmarked sand grave.

Lifesavers from Durants Station saw the *Wadsworth* soon after she came to anchor and kept her under close watch throughout the day. In fact, when she dragged in over the shoals they proceeded to the scene with their surfboat, but finding her riding smoothly in calm water just beyond the beach, and seeing no signal of distress from the vessel, they made no effort to reach her at that time.

At 9 o'clock that night the beach patrolman found the vessel still firmly held by her anchor, but when his relief reached the scene at 1 A.M. on December 6 he discovered that the 61-ton schooner had dragged her anchors and was lying in the very midst of the breakers, broadside to the beach about 120 yards off. The surfman, W. R. Austin, signalled to the castaways, and then returned to his station with all possible speed. By 3 A.M. the lifesavers were again on the scene, this time with their beach apparatus, and although the night was dark and the schooner had no lights, the first shot fired at the vessel landed within easy reach of the crew.

It was cold that December night, the temperature well below the freezing point. In the main rigging, where they had been forced to take refuge, the five men on board the *Wadsworth* were so numbed by the cold and so cramped in their precarious perch, that they could hardly budge the line.

The procedure in effecting a rescue by breeches buoy from ship to shore is basically simple. First, a shot is fired over the ship with a strong, light line attached; then a block is tied to the shore end of this, with a heavier line (known as a whip line) threaded through the block. The lifesavers hold on to both ends of the whip line and when at last the block is drawn aboard the vessel and tied high on a mast it is possible for the lifesavers to send something out to the vessel (a hawser, or breeches buoy, or life car, or cork jackets) or by hauling on the other end of the whip, to bring men or equipment to shore.

In the case of the *Nellie Wadsworth* the crew managed to get the block and whip line on board, but had just finished tying the former to the mast when the mast gave way, breaking off just above the block and crashing into the water. The lifesavers quickly tied several cork jackets to one end of the whip line and sent them off to the ship, but when within a few yards of their destination they became entangled in floating rigging. One of the crewmen, a man named George Richardson, jumped into the icy water and swam toward the life belts. He reached them at length but was so overcome by the cold that he finally lapsed into unconsciousness before succeeding in untangling them from the debris.

Meanwhile, unable to see what had happened but realizing that the line was rendered useless, the lifesavers tied their end to the lone beach pony they had employed in hauling the apparatus to the scene, and by driving the pony high on the beach succeeded in releasing the line. In this manner the belts and debris, with the unconscious form of George Richardson entangled in them, were dragged back through the surf to shore.

With the line thus clear the lifesavers were then able to rescue three more members of the crew in rapid succession, though the fifth and last man lost his grip on the line and had to be hauled from the surf bodily.

Both Richardson and the fifth crewmen were revived there on the bleak sand spit and a start was made for the station, three miles away. But Richardson, thinly clad and suffering acutely from his exertions and exposure, begged to be left alone, then closed his eyes, and again lapsed into unconsciousness. He died soon after.

Each of the lifesavers then took one of the castaways in charge, and the long trek toward the station was resumed, but long before it was reached the four survivors became so exhausted that they were unable to walk, and pleaded piteously to be left there on the beach to sleep and rest; a course which almost certainly would have resulted in their death. The lifesavers pressed onward, however, sometimes dragging the limp sailors, sometimes carrying them on their backs along the cold and storm-flooded beach, and finally, at seven o'clock that morning, the station was reached, fires were built, stimulants prepared, and the four men were provided with dry clothing and hot food.

They remained there for several weeks, too feeble and ill at first to rise from the beds on which they had been placed, but in time they recovered sufficiently to return to their homes, leaving their shipmate, Richardson, and the little schooner *Nellie Wadsworth* to rest forever in the sands of Hatteras Island.

ACKNOWLEDGMENTS

Grateful acknowledgment is made to the following for permission to include the selections in *The Seaside Reader*:

Henry Beston. From *The Outermost House*. Copyright 1929, 1949, © 1956 by Henry Beston. Reprinted by permission of Henry Holt and Company, Inc.; Wallace Kaufman and Orrin H. Pilkey Jr. From *The Beaches Are Moving*. © 1979 by Wallace Kaufman and Orrin Pilkey. Reprinted by permission. Anchor Press / Doubleday; Willard Bascom. From *Waves and Beaches*. © 1980 by Willard Bascom. Used by permission of Doubleday, a division of Bantam Doubleday Dell Publishing Group, Inc.; Jack Rudloe. From *The Living Dock at Panacea*. ® 1977 by Jack J. Rudloe. Reprinted by permission of Alfred A. Knopf, Inc.; Rachel L. Carson. From *Under the Sea Wind*. Copyright 1941 by Rachel L. Carson. Copyright renewed © 1969 by Roger Christie. A Truman Talley Book. Used by permission of the publisher, Dutton, an imprint of New American Library, a division of Penguin Books USA Inc.; Joseph Mitchell. From *Up at the Old Hotel*. © 1960, 1992 by Joseph Mitchell. Reprinted by permission of Pantheon Books, a division of Randon House Inc.; David K. Bulloch. From *The Underwater Naturalist*. © by David K. Bulloch. Reprinted by permission of Lyons & Burford, Publsihers; John Steinbeck. From *The Log from the Sea of Cortez*. Copyright 1941 by John Steinbeck and Edward F. Ricketts. Copyright renewed © 1969 by John Steinbeck and Edward F. Ricketts, Jr. Used by permission of Viking Penguin, a division of Penguin Books USA Inc.; George Reiger. From *Wanderer on My Native Shore*. © by George Reiger. Reprinted by permission of Lyons & Burford, Publishers; J. Y. Cousteau. From *The Silent World* by Jacques-Yves Cousteau and Frederic Dumas. Copyright 1953 by Harper & Row, Publishers, Inc. Reprinted by Permission of Harper/Collins Publishers; Norman Mailer. From *Miami and the Seige of Chicago*. Used by permission of the author and his agents, Scott Meredith Literary Agency, 845 Third Avenue, New York, New York 10022; Joe McGinniss. From *Going to Extremes*. Reprinted by permission of Sterling Lord Literistic, Inc. © by Joe McGinniss; John Updike. From *Rabbit Is Rich*. © 1981 by John Updike. Reprinted by permission of Alfred A. Knopf, Inc.; William Least Heat Moon. From *Blue Highways: A Journey into America*. © 1982 by William Least Heat Moon. By permission of Little, Brown and Company; Peter Matthiessen. From *Men's Lives*. © 1986 by Peter Matthiessen. Reprinted by permission of Random House, Inc.; from *The Windbirds*. © 1973 by Peter Matthiessen. Reprinted by permission of Donadio & Ashworth, Inc.; John N. Cole. From *Striper*. © 1978 by John N. Cole. Reprinted by permission of Lyons & Burford, Publishers; Van Campen Heilner. From *Salt Water Fishing*. Copyright 1937 by The Penn Publishing Company; Owen Hatteras. From *Fish Stories*. © 1981 by American Littoral Society. An ALS Special Publication in cooperation with the Stephen Sautner Fishing School, a division of Docker, Bunker, Chummer, and Zipf, Inc. A Johnson Words Book; Russell Chatham. Reprinted with permission from *The Anglers' Coast*. © 1976 by Russell Chatham; Joe Upton. Reprinted with permission from *Alaska Blues*. Alaska Northwest Books, © 1992; Izaak Walton. From *The Compleat Angler* by Izaak Walton; John Hay. From *The Run* by John Hay. © 1959, 1965 by John Hay. Reprinted by permission of Doubleday & Company, Inc.; William H. Warner. From *Beautiful Swimmers*. © 1976 by William H. Warner. By permission of Little, Brown and Company; Howard T. Shannon. From *The Book of the Seashore*. © 1935 by Howard T. Shannon. By permission of Doubleday, Doran & Company (Garden City); David Stick. Reprinted by permission of the author and publisher, from *Graveyard of the Atlantic: Shipwrecks of the North Carloina Coast*. © 1952 by the University of North Carolina Press.